Victory ABOVE OWN MEMORY

AT recent years term repressed science" has become commonplace stamp. deprivation freedom opinions right to doubt deliberate inequality competing ideas there is death any science. Totalitarianism repressed physics and biology, philosophy and military history a business and medicine. Actually saying in country
"victorious socialism" did not have a single fundamental or branch scientific discipline, which would not have suffered heavy and irreparable losses. Moreover, expression were subjected not only creators, but and fruit Their intellectual efforts: more than three hundred thousand book titles, more than five hundred and sixty thousand magazines, at least one million newspapers, census population in 1937 year and many other results of the work of scientists, until recently kept in special libraries and secret collections archives [1].

And after all among other historical the science, probably the most affected. Considering the military-strategic meaning medicine, biology, physics, back holding power heart we walked on the product — let and dosed — freedom in them development. This disciplines was in 20s years released some time for creative searches, and them representatives not lost connections With global scientific community. At historys such opportunities not It was. Reply on the question, why exactly historical science has become first hostage totalitarianism, can a simple indication on the then, what, how known history write winners," and there were no historians among the latter. George Orwell wrote about manipulation memory people, when the consignment maybe run hand in past and to tell about volume or otherwise event, what his at all not It was. "Who governs the past that governs future; who manages real, that governs past... All very simply. Need just continuous chain of victories over own Noah memory" [2].

Historical science in Soviet Russia immediately began to develop as semi-official science, with a focus on "the only true" theoretical justification — on the marxism -leninism and party-class taking a look" of the past and real. The establishment of ideological and political unanimity began with the liquidation of the historical science that existed before October 1917. The Bolsheviks proceeded from the notion that social science in Russia was in decline, from which only a Marxist regulation, how the most progressive of all possible methodologies. In accordance, it must be assumed that with it began (and continued for many decades) the class "selection" of scientific directions: "reactionary" historiography, "petty-bourgeois", "Marxist", "progressive", etc. Of course, no one would talk failed to explain why SF Platonov, PN Milyukov, AS Lappo-Danilevsky and other Russian historians, former pride Russian historical science should count reactionary?!

R. Yu. Vipper, in a lecture given in Moscow in 1920, noted: "BUT ." here before our eyes an amazing fact: quantitatively a small group takes possession of a colossal state, becomes the power over an enormous mass and restructures the entire cultural and social life from top to bottom. According to what? — Its ideological system, ... its utopia of an earthly paradise, which until then had lived only in minds few exalted novelists."

Paradoxically, the victory of ideas that have taken possession of the masses, turned his, convinced materialist, idealist This transformation was, in his opinion, the crisis of historical science [3]. There is undoubtedly a fair amount of irony in his remark: a materialist is smarter and more true than an idealist, because Marx was a materialist, whose teaching, in my turn, omnipotent, for right".

Maybe, in first years Soviet authorities historians endured the suffering and hardship associated with the civil war, hunger diseases and terror nothing in this sense not standing out from ranks intellectual elites. AT 1918-1920 years, due to hunger and diseases, died A. FROM. Lappo-Danilevsky, B. BUT. Turaev, BUT. BUT. Chess. AT January 1919 G. "in okay red terror" in answer to Villainous murder in Germany comrades rose Luxembourg and Karla Liebknecht" - shot Honorary Academician Grand Duke Nikolai Mikhailovich. Been under arrest corresponding member BUT. BUT. Kiesewetter, a lot others history professors. FROM. P. Melgunov before his emigration, ensuing in 1922 G., arrested Five times. Diary entries Melgunova, Y.U. AT. Gauthier those years testify not only about difficulties life, unsettled-news, but and uncertainty in the future doubts in need their creative research. 2 December 1917 Melgunov wrote: "Lukin, Bolshevik, spoke Syroechkovsky, what Lenin and company disappointed in WHO- opportunities socialist revolution in Russia and decided that for her acceleration necessary enter cruel monarchism, worse former...»[4]. Gauthier in records from twenty February 1919 when commission from communists decided destiny historians of Moscow University, noted that he still considers himself u n i v e r s i t y professor . "I didn't do anything to So or otherwise declare his attitude to princess peace, and will continue them ignore until bye me or kicked out from university or I I'll get out myself from Councils of Deputies"[5].

By data professors AND. BUT. Kurganova, victims red Terror" during the civil war became 160 thousand students, teachers, artists, writers, professors and academicians. P. N. Milyukov spoke about 6775 dead professors and teachers and suggested that what red terror had goal not at all to exterminate specialists without exception, but only to break the political will of the intelligentsia and subordinate it to its species."[6].

By your opinion P. Sorokina, "most terrible for years... for professorships were 1918-1920 gg. receiving an insignificant reward and then With late on the three month, not having no soldering, professorship literally was dying out from hunger and cold. Mortality her increased in 6 once on compared to pre-war time. Rooms not heated. Not it was neither of bread, neither topic more than others "necessary for existence", blessings. Some eventually died, others were unable to endure all this is — and finished With yourself. So done away with known scientists: geologist foreigners, Professor Tails and more someone. Third carried away typhoid. someone shot"[7].

In the summer of 1922, a high-profile political trial took place in Moscow. process above leaders parties right SRs And at the same time, a large group of Soviet scientists was deported from the territories. Among them were philosophers NA Berdyaev, SL Frank, economist B. Bruckus, historians AA Kizevetter, SP Melgunov and many others. These kinds of signals sent by the power of the better part intelligentsia, perceived her definitely and called escape from countries. By different counting by 1930, approximately 500 scientists were working abroad, including 5 academicians and near 140 professors Russian schools, although, by your opinion L. TO. Shkarenkova, in reality them It was much more than [8].

AT early 20s years life scientific intelligentsia improve only absolutely, but not relatively: professor's salary in university was in a lot of once below salaries janitor or courier [9]. Of course those, who worked in Marxist institutions, had "special privileges" in the form of rations, more high salaries, decent housing conditions, their not "compacted" and t. etc., not speaking already about volume, what in during the in 1924-1929 repeated "purges" of universities quit more precisely, expelled before Total "non-Marxist elements."

Suffocation of "reactionary" historiography [10] was done in two ways. On the one hand, the "old" scientific institutions and were forced out "old" reviewers. On the other hand, the main direction of state policy was the opening of purely communist scientific centers and sharp reduction subsides and other benefits to conduct research not aimed at assimilation of a new worldview. In a short time, the Socialist Academy of Social Sciences (1918), Eastpart (1920), the Institute of K. Marx and F. Engels (1920), the Institute of VI Lenin (1923), the Institute of Red Professors (1921) communist schools (1919-1921), Eastprof (1922) society Marxist historians (1925), Russian association research institutions public science (RANION - 1924) and others All of them got right on the release periodical publications and scientific collections. AT RANION, where more, than in others again created scientific institutions, old ones worked specialists, them offered change theme by making stress on the preferential studying revolutionary movement, socio-economic stories, a for graduate students introduced special exams on Marxist minimum , which were accepted by faculty members parties Bolsheviks.

In chapter these institutions, leading teachers in them were, as a rule, party functions who did not have a special historical education in chapter Eastparta became M. FROM. Olminsky, Institute Lenin headed L. B. Kamenev, Eastprof - YU. TO. Milonov. Many institutions led M. N. Pokrovsky, who occupied then not less 19 posts [11].

Solemnly opened on October 1, 1918, the Socialist Academy consisted of 4 departments: socio-historical, political and legal, financial in economic and technical and economic. Only few members social academy were professors (M. BUT. Reisner), more It was associate professors (N. M. Lukin, AT. P. Volgin) and persons without completed higher education (Bukharin, Lunacharsky, Ryazanov). The task of all departments was to prepare Marxist personnel, coordination all research work in areas Marxism.

Pokrovsky considered the name of the academy to be rather Socialist-Revolutionary than Bolshevik [12], and in 1924 G. she is was renamed to Communist. academy existed eighteen years and was liquidated in 1936 G., when, on In the words of its former graduate AG Avtorkhanov, "two NKVD secret police on the "philosophical front" Mitin and Yudin managed to put the entire Communist Party statement in the basement with just one. academy at CEC USSR, previously considered theoretical laboratory Central Committee VKP(b)" [13]. But in the 1920s, the Komakademiya was considered "the forge of Marxist-cadres", the highest authority in everything related to social science. The charter of 1926 defined its tasks So: "a) development questions Marxism-Leninism; b) struggle against bourgeois and petty-bourgeois distortions of Marxism; c) the struggle for a strict implementation of the point of view of dialectical materialism both in social science and in the natural sciences and the exposure of the survivals of idealism" [14].

Similar goals were set for the Institute of Red Professors. Pokrovsky recalled that the idea of its creation was born at Lenin in november 1920 G., which the said then him Pokrovsky, about plan training high school teachers. To all social science teachers was staged a task: explore in the shortest term basics Marxism and henceforth lead teaching only by Marxist programs" [15]. AT according With this task we walked and selection listeners - more in dependence on their proletarian origin rather than historical training, which led to the graduating of militant but incompetent "red professors", who for the most part brought dogmatic obscurantism and immoral inclination to denunciation.

The basis for writing works that can only be classified as historical with a great stretch were the works of Lenin and the "faithful Leninists" (soon, however, have become "worst enemies of the people"), which were distributed in hitherto unknown circulations. Suffice it to say, what only With november 1917 G. on December 1923 was released more 650 publications Leninist works, in volume numbering approximately 200— in the languages of the peoples of the USSR and foreign languages with a total circulation of more than 6 million copies [16]. The five editions of Lenin's collected works originally published were not complete, they included cropped texts of his works, thereby negating the scientific significance of the very fact of publication [17]. At the same time, the works of Trotsky (21 volumes), Zinoviev (16 volumes), Rykov (4 volumes), Kamenev (12 volumes), books, pamphlets, and Bukharin's articles were published in separate editions and in the form of collected works. It is clear that soon to the fore — how on circulation, So and on meaning — advanced "works comrad Stalin."

All the years of Soviet power, censorship was in effect, a monopoly was established on the use of documents and their publication. four April 1925 G. Central Committee RCP(b) accepted resolution "O ." okay publications letters and documents VI Lenin", according to which all work in this direction should be carried out exclusively through the Institute of VI AND. Lenin. 26 February 1926 G. secretary Central Committee AT. Molotov and the head of the East Party Department of the Central Committee S. Kanatchikov signed indication about termination free access to the archive of the Gendarmerie administration to everyone, except for employees of the Eastparties, the OGPU and the Supreme Court. Soon followed the decree of the Council of People's Commissars of the RSFSR on the procedure for using archive materials.

The Central Committee distributed cadres of historians, established the circulation of historical journals; Eastpart, and then and The Lenin Institute became departments of the Central Committee, that is, they entered into complete subordination nie Secretary General parties. Only in In September 1927, the archive of the October Revolution received the right to receive emigré publications. In January 1928, the Orgburo of the Central Committee declared it wrong to submit the protocols of the Petrograd Military Revolutionary Committee to the Central Archive without their preliminary editing by party authorities. Special Commission (Adoratsky, Bubnov, Pokrovsky, Savelyev, Unshlikht) It was instructed editing protocols and the issue of their publication. IP Tovstukha, Stalin's confidant, was asked to resolve the issue of where the originals should be stored.

In May 1928, the Central Committee adopted a resolution to merge the Institute Lenin With Eastpart, a in March 1929 G. The Institute of History of the Komakademia was created, into which the Institute of History of RANION was "merged". Pokrovsky justified this act by the fact that "there was a problem of creating a change in the field of historical science. When we saw tha t they were starting to cook for us graduate students on prescription 1910 G.,.. way out It was solution move institute stories from RANION in system Comacademies With topics to he, firstly, got into a purely Marxist environment, a purely Marxist atmosphere, a Secondly, to he at this got off from those of its elements that are already absolutely no use in Soviet conditions not subject to" [18].

Organizational innovations could not but affect the system of training historians. Instead of well-established, time-tested historical and philological faculties in schools become be created faculties of social sciences (FONs), teaching program at which was frankly oriented on the propaganda and approval of Marxist methodology. Faculties of history and philology were restored in a number of universities only in the 1930s, when the Stalinist general line triumphed complete and final victory.

In June 1929, the status of the party archives was officially confirmed. The Central Committee changed the composition of the editorial boards of historical journals, approved the topics and lists of speakers at scientific conferences, allowed or prohibited teaching to individuals, etc. Thus, a mechanism was created for purposeful and total control above science, her transformation in ideological and political room service current politicians.

Historians must were understand, what without knowing Central Committee they are nothing. In addition, the secrecy of the archives, the inexplicable atmosphere of secrecy made it possible to manipulate the past - this springboard for battles per future. More precisely, for power [19].

AT early 1923 G. Trotsky complained in Central Committee RCP (b) that the initiative of "referring to the past" belonged entirely to Stalin, then he declared that many of the documents incriminated to him already belonged "entirely to the Eastpart", ie, to history. To which Stalin pointedly replied: "Istpart is not only a repository, but also an interpreter of party documents..." [20].

An important milestone in the history of historical science was the release in the light of four volumes of the "History of the CPSU (b)" (1926-1929) edited by Yaroslavsky. After several remarks by Stalin, this work became the object of sharp criticism. The semi-literate Kaganovich called it "a falsified history painted in the color of Trotskyism", while more erudite reviewers immediately called the authors "a school of Trotskyist smugglers" [21]. Yaroslavsky repented, reworked mine textbook on stories VKP(b), where emphasized role Stalin how leader, standing beside with Lenin, and was most forgiven. (All authors repented, but helped this is not everyone).

In 1931, organizational changes continued: the Institute of K. Marx and F. Engels merged with the Institute of Lenin within the framework of a single Institute of Marx-Engels-Lenin under the Central Committee of the CPSU (b). At the same time, historians were familiar with Stalin's letter to the editors of the Proletarian Revolution magazine. AM Pankratov, having sent this "Letter" to Pokrovsky, declared what it is for historys
"political" and historical milestone, "especially with regard to implementation main slogan - partisanship in historical science. In connection with this "Letter," continued Pankratov, - "at us now put on legs all historical the public" [22].

The history of writing the "Letter" itself has not been studied enough, but the results of its publication are known [23]. In it, Stalin essentially declared himself as the only interpreter of Marxism-Leninism, he expressed condescending disregard for the "archival rats" and the meaning of documents, he demonstrated an example of how to elevate political accusations to the rank of scientific arguments. His letter was taken as a directive to identify "Trotsky- smugglers" and "forgers". The glorification of this "Letter" in the most loyal tone was dedicated their advanced all historical magazines.
The "rotten liberalism" and "conciliationism" of some historians were condemned at a meeting of the institutes of the Com-academy, societies Marxist historians [24].

SA Piontkovsky noted in his diary (November 12, 1931) that "the study of Stalin's letter in practice amounted to the fact that dozens of university professors were dismissed and expelled from the party, people for some mistakes made by five years ago, they threw it out, kicked it out, brought it a little whether not to suicide and insanity. Yaroslavsky himself was brought to such a state that he gave the impression of a man who had received a huge mental Traumatic, almost crazy. Indeed, it's ridiculous and wildly: human, held basic fight with Trotsky, suddenly proclaimed before the whole party the Trotskyite smuggler himself. When I was with him, he was sitting in an empty room in the office of the Central Control Commission, propping his head on his hand, and looking wildly out the window. What hit me the most the fact that he failed to provide a theoretical basis for the entire ongoing elaboration and explained all this by what Stalin not satisfied topics what in four volumes not

Assigned to him the main role, personal motives, not fundamental ones.

In addition to "fatherly suggestions" to those who still insisted on the right to "have one's own opinion," Stalin sent more ominous signals. So, in 1930 G. passed process above "Industrial Party", in 1931 - over the "Labour Peasant Party" and "Union Bureau of the Central Committee of the RSDLP Mensheviks". The inspired nature of these processes was clear to everyone, who not wished be deceived. Except Togo, only for 1931 out of court Special meeting OGPU and his collegium considered affairs "in in relation to 2490 persons, of which: professors - 85, engineering and technical personnel - 1152, economists - 249, agronomists - 310, veterinarians - 22 and other employees (such as accountants, responsible workers for Menshevik affairs) - 666", which amounted to more than 4% of all old professionals working in the country [25].

Finally, the Prosecutor General of the Republic, NV Krylenko, reminded the most obtuse: "In 1926, we shot 26 White Guards, led by the former Prince Pavel Dolgoruky; in 1930 - they shot 48 saboteurs-supplies and by this showed that we were not going to lay down weapon terror we not refuse from him" [26].

The process of nationalization and centralization in management historical science grew up So, resolution
On May 15, 1934, unified school textbooks on history were created, all history teachers had to attend retraining courses, the publication of the journal History in Secondary School, which had a directive character, began at Moscow and Leningrad Universities departments of history reopened. Soon they began to be created in other universities. In 1935, the societies of old Bolsheviks and former political convicts and exiles were liquidated. In 1936, the institute stories Communist academy,
"merging" with the Historical and Archeographic Institute, he served basis for creation Institute NA history USSR.

AT March 1937 G. in "Pravda" under headings type About the idiotic disease — carelessness in the journal "Istorik-Marxist"; "Political Blindness and Carelessness" row articles, where about Friedland, Vanage and others scientists wrote how about "enemies people", a them work were called
"all sorts of rubbish of a clearly counter-revolutionary type." October 31, 1937 among students and teachers branches stories Institute red professors,

where before this years have worked many from arrested, with report Methods and tricks wreck work on the historical front" was made by AV Shestakov. The meaning of his report was the thesis: Pokrovsky should be criticized, and Vanag, Piontkovsky, Dubrovsky, Tomsinsky, accused of terrorism and banditry, should be destroyed. how "enemies people" [27].

Perhaps these articles and their discussion, which chronologically coincided with the "famous" February-March plenum Central Committee VKP(b), came last warning about impending storm 37-38 years. Already prepared for publication "A short course in the history of the CPSU (b)" - this "bible of the era Stalinism", to creation which made hands E. Yaroslavsky, V. Knorin, P. Pospelov. A super-apologetic biography of the "father of peoples" was published (G. Aleksandrov, M. Galaktionov, V. Kruzhkov, M. Mitin, V. Mochalov, P. Pospelov). was born cohort "historians" who are ready to write anything, as long as what is written satisfies the primitive taste of the "bosses", and to curse their recent colleagues sent to the scaffold [28].

Story — in including and story historical science - this is always and before Total people. Perhaps, most representative, demonstrative figure Togo time was an academician M. N. Pokrovsky. Not deprived research talent scientist, he became "mandatory from Bolshevism", supervised development this scientific disciplines in country. Becoming official, he was forced attack aggressively on the their competitors how in areas science, so in sphere administrative control above her. In defending his concept of the historical development of Russia, he had to resort to administrative intrigues, and in defending my bureaucratic job title,- to "scientific" arguments. awesome way he was lifted up at life (we already mentioned about his 19 positions) and defeated after death Perhaps the example of Pokrovsky (discussions about roles whom continue) — most bright certificate to that why scientific study it is forbidden connect with politics, why his statement: story — the greatest tool political wrestling, another meaning history is not has" [29] — deprives lessons history scientific meaning. human the tragedy, not bypassed side and Investigators , forced researchers to pay attention not only on the scientific achievements, but and morality of the scientist. AT Soviet historiography this problem announced yourself only in last thing time, in volume including and at performance evaluation Pokrovsky. AT works foreign history kov these questions were often present. PN Milyukov, a historian and former leader of the Cadet Party, in exile sharply criticized not only scientific work, but also the personal merits of Pokrovsky, whom he had known since his student days. He featured Pokrovsky "informer" and thought his guilty in persecution FROM. F. Platonov and other Russian historians. This point of view was confirmed in the works of individual Soviet researchers . . But it did not suit others and caused them to criticize the monograph on Pokrovsky by the English historian D. Entin, who made an attempt to reconstruct the psychological appearance this scientist and administrator from science, submitting his in book power-hungry and a cowardly personality whose behavior was based on the desire to maintain a leading position in the field of historical science and please the party leadership [31]. However, documents from Pokrovsky's personal fund, kept in former party archive, indicate that Entin is most likely right. Particularly eloquent called secret letters" Pokrovsky.

AT small folder stored letters to Pokrovsky arrested and exiled on "cause" academician Platonov historians: E. AT. Tarle, BUT. AND. Yakovlev, AT. AND. Picheta. They are asked help them, reestablish justice [32]. Letter pechets left without response. On the similar same letter to Tarla Pokrovsky answered, what did you read his testimonies and what his, Tarle, link in Alma-Ata testifies to softness relations to him Soviet authorities. And here same, not without cynicism noticed what study science can and in Solovki, although publish there difficult. "Except that I, how You guess not can to give no categorical answer, not having consulted With by whom follows; a this is the last find it difficult topics circumstance what I sick now lie in bed and this is letter dictate — So how write myself not can. At first capabilities I I'll try to talk With by whom should and then let me know You about result-tah" [33].

On January 28, 1932, the academician considered himself obliged to inform the secret department of the OGPU that he was receiving letters from historians (Tarle, Yakovlev, Picheta) exiled to various regions of the Union. "Since these letters may be of interest to the OGPU, and to me they are completely not needed, forwarding them You" [34].

By all means available to him, Pokrovsky guarded his position as commander-in-chief in science. In a letter to KB Radek (Start 1931 G.) he recommended create Marxist faction of the Great Soviet Encyclopedia and declare the authoritarian ship of this faction over the entire department of social science" [36]. Two years earlier, he approved of the behavior of his colleagues, who conducted his line, which reduced: "1) to the purification of Marxist historical literature of all remnants of bourgeois ideology, of which there are still a lot of remnants in this literature; 2) to a merciless struggle against this very bourgeois ideology, when it It has impudence protrude open, what especially often in recent years. The opposition of this line I met so far only from Trotsky's side and partly of the group of NI Bukharin... I was extremely depressingly affected by the news that some of the historians of the ICP also seem to have a tendency to oppose this lines" [36].

As can be seen, in the late 1920s and early 1930s, when the intra-party struggle entered its final stage, Pokrovsky saw his task not creation new works, a "fight" and "exposure" those, who continued sorry to engage in creative activities. It was then that a series of pogromist works by Pokrovsky and his colleagues [37] appeared, numerous letters Pokrovsky in Secretariat of the Central Committee VKP(b) (1931 G.), very reminiscent of denunciations. AT January letter he wrote about availability factions among reviewers, comparing them With "deviations" in parties and explaining them by the influence of bourgeois and petty-bourgeois ideology [38]. February (1931 G.) letter sheds light on the dull confrontation with Yaroslavsky in the struggle for the right to lead official historical science. AT letter he substantiated my scheme stories Russia, which
"lays as a basis ... the development of capitalism, ... tries to show that capitalism in our country is not a superficial phenomenon that arose either due to the influence of the West, or thanks to ry autocracy, ...a It has deep national roots. Pokrovsky admitted that many doubt this scheme. "So, for a long time I endured as my assistant in the ICP Mintz, whose role is now completely clarified. Losing finally, patience and removing his, I appointed Vanaga in his place,—— sometime, before the XIV Congress, a Trotskyist,— being sure that he had outlived his Trotskyism long ago. it turned out, what I was wrong what Trotskyist connections and acquaintances continue to have an influence on comrade. Vanaga. I had to take off and his... confuses position position comrade Yaroslavsky. In the dispute about Narodnaya Volya, he is at first resolutely became on the side comrad Teodorovich, after began
straighten my line," but before end So and not straighten-

Vil: I did not characterize Teodorovich as a Right deviator. In the discussion about the revolution of 1905, his support was found by concept Elvova-Mintsa, what this revolution was a class peasant revolution, where the main driving force force It was peasantry. How can It was do not recognize in this concept a new edition of Zinovivism, this is the secret of Comrade. Yaroslavsky. But at Elvov-Minz There are better things than this: the impossibility in 1905 of raising the question about outgrowth on the volume basis, what not was where the corresponding level of development of the productive forces has yet been reached... It is quite possible that comrade. Yaroslavsky personally does not share the views of the Mints-Elvov group... A good heart does not belong to the number of Bolshevik virtues. Bolsheviks are "evil" people. They are characterized by an uncompromising struggle against all non-Party and anti-Party deviations. Tov. Yaroslavsky theoretically, of course, is fabulous knows: it is necessary that he connected the theory finally, With practice" [39].

These letters With transparent informing shade in 1931 G., how and article Pokrovsky eighteen December 1927 in Pravda, dedicated to the tenth anniversary of the Cheka-OGPU, in which terror and other extrajudicial actions of this punitive institution were justified and it was argued that from work in Cheka not refused neither one Bolshevik, not did to him honor [40].

AT 1928 G. It was solemnly Noted his 60th birthday, and in 1932 he was buried with honors near the Kremlin wall. Only a few years have passed, and a noisy campaign has begun his criticism. AT her accepted participation Bukharin and Radek (Struggle classes.—1936.— No. 2), survivors students of Pokrovsky, who became the authors of the collections "Against the historical concepts M. N. Pokrovsky" (M., 1939),
"Against the anti-Marxist concept of MN Pokrovsky" (Moscow, 1940), returned from exile by V. Pichet [41] (Historical journal.— 1941.— No. 6). Campaign we walked under motto:
"It is time, finally, for all Soviet historians from the "disciples of Pokrovsky" to become students of Lenin and Comrade Stalin " [42]. Yaroslavsky danced especially famously on the grave of his opponent: "It is necessary to stir up the all inheritance historical "school" of MN Pokrovsky, to reveal the grossest mistakes in works Pokrovsky" [43].

Simultaneously with the nationalization of historical science and the liquidation of democratic societies (former political convicts and exiles, closing museum P. Kropotkin and etc.) we walked process discredit old Bolsheviks physical destruction specialists. Of course all this was directed by the then party leadership of the country, as they also determined the "necessary" topics of historical research. Stalin in closed letter The Central Committee on January 18, 1935 (in connection with the assassination of Kirov) stated: "Knowledge and understanding of the history of our party is the most important means necessary to ensure the fully revolutionary vigilance of party members." It was proposed to study anti-party groups in stories party, methods them liquidation [44].

Drama Destiny Research is currently underway Russian academics science, her renaming into the All-Union in 1925 and functioning in an dependence on the state, the tragedy of the historians who worked in it [45]. The "case" of academician SF Platonov, misadventures of academician EV Tarle, lawlessness, going on With reviewers, working in universities, museums, archives. After all, only in 1929 in different cities It was arrested not less 130 editors [46].

In Soviet and foreign historiography, the 1920s are sometimes characterized as a "golden time" for the development of sciences, literature and art. So, Sheila Fitzpatrick writes about soft and tough lines" in politics parties by relation to intelligentsia, politics tolerance and the policy of repression. Moreover, in her opinion, the latter won in 1928 with the beginning of the "Shakhty process" [47]. It seems that such definitions are rather conditional. Golden time" — on comparison With what? FROM 30s years and their mass repressions? But the arrests of scientists and their deportation also took place in the 1920s. And those who became their victims then are unlikely to agree with the definition time them suffering how "golden".

English editor L. Shapiro noted that already in early 30s gg. freedom discussions came the end. Communist academy was transformed from science center in center training party personnel, in as a result of which its scientific level has sharply decreased. Before 1931 G. publication of works on stories parties It was in the hands scientists, who are still respected data. After letters Stalin in editorial "Proletarian revolution" the situation has changed. "The most important achievement Stalin in establishing control over thoughts According to Shapiro, was the capture of historiography parties" [48].

The process of subordinating historical coverage of the past to the needs of the present, duping the population with a system of orthodox formulas took one and a half ten years. it became result big organizational and ideological and political work of the party leadership. According to A. Avtorkhanova, Lenin "invented." how once that totalitarian mechanism state authorities, using which his heirs immortalized and spiritual terror and nearly on the whole century turned off Russia from families civilized and prosperous states...". Absolute primacy state authorities above human became basic feature this supertotalitarian states, differentiating from other similar modes absence private property and the slightest independence of people. Heart of the matter turned out not in criticism Stalinism a in overcoming totalitarianism, how more and moral disease societies 49.

Trotsky in preface to book Stalin falsification school" (cm. in reissue: M., 1990.— FROM. 8-9) three turn official historiography October in 20s years: in 1923–26 years, when story parties reworked on the need days main way Zinoviev, in 1926–29 gg. appears new opposition" and history again being revised especially Bukharin and Yaroslavsky; With 1929 G., after gap Stalinists With right, theory and story are being reviewed in third times [50].

There are several judgments about the reasons for the drastic changes in party policy, about the place and role of historical science. in end 20—beginning 30s gg. Alone (M. Geller, A. Nekrich, V. Solovey) see the root cause in the then change in the ideological situation from the expectation of a world revolution to the strengthening of socialism in one, separately taken country. Now there was no need for vicious criticism of imperial traditions, but, on the contrary, it was important to strengthen the empire. If even at the beginning of 1931 Stalin spoke about the fact that old Russia was constantly beating for backwardness (T. 13. - P. 38), then the May In 1934, the resolution of the Central Committee and the government "On the teaching of civil history in the schools of the USSR" indicated a change in course. Now it was necessary to educate patriotism and pride in the state, arguing: Russia beat everyone and won. According to Pokrovsky, the revolution happened because the people wanted freedom, now, according to Stalin, because they wanted strong power. Remarks by Stalin, Zhdanov and Kirov on the prospectuses of history textbooks The USSR and modern history meant that memory was subjected to nationalization. Marxist-Leninist history was declared the only scientific true about the past and its functions were proclaimed the legitimization of Stalin's power and upbringing Soviet person [51].

Other (D. Volkogonov, M. Reiman), also highlighting changes are primarily political motives, note in them Stalin's desire to use history for personal purposes, for fortifications personal authorities [52]. it so. But everything was much more difficult. The idea of a world revolution was not abandoned. However, there was a change of priorities: the focus on complete subordination to the emerging totalitarian regime.

Nowadays, the conclusions of foreign historians are more and more readily recognized. about close interconnections historical science in the USSR with the opportunistic policy of the authorities [53]. Confirmed conclusion former professors stories ancient and middle ages (after 1945 — emigrant) Konstantin Shteppa that "Russian historiography during the period of Soviet power most clearly reflected each stage of the internal development Soviet building. Each nuance in the politics of the ruling party found its expression in this or that event on the "historical front". In that sense, historiography in the Soviet state was a microcosm in macrocosm" [54].

Of course, there is a great temptation to shift all the troubles onto politicians and the "terrible time". Yes, Stalin was an experienced political "spider", skillfully dragging victims into his nets. Was a master of intrigue, inciting and exploiting some to destroy others, so that soon those who supported him would be turned into victims. This technique was clearly seen not only in relation to politicians, but also to historians. Karl Radek joked about the impossibility of an academic discussion with him: "You are a footnote to him, and he - link" [55]. And among historians, the first to suffer old expert - business academician FROM. F. Platonov, military historys BUT. E. Snesareva and AA Svechina (1930) [56], then on a far-fetched pro- cess "Mensheviks" was convicted politician and Editing N. N. Sukhanov [57]. Then began the "showdown" between Marxist historians. Probably the first time it's in such a bright form appeared at talk letters Stalin in magazine "Proletarian" revolution" (1931 G.).

At first glance, Stalin's letter was directed against individual historians. But among them was EM Yaroslavsky, together with a group of his colleagues, who at that time disputed the leadership in historical science with MN Pokrovsky and his students. Stalin's letter supported the latter. First began mass repentance for the "mistakes" of the authors of the 4th volume - nickname "History of the CPSU (b)", published under the editorship of Yaroslavsky, those whom Stalin accused in many political "sin" BUT. Slutsky and AT. Volosevich [58]. Those who until recently came out with insulting labels, unsubstantiated and scandalous speeches and articles against representatives "bourgeois historiography." FROM them then cost "softer" how With arrested in the "case of academician Platonov". The latter were kept under arrest in solitary confinement, exiled, left in powerless position. "Marxist Historians" sent to link in Sverdlovsk or Kazan (P. FROM. Drozdov, N. N. Elvov and others) with permits of the Central Committee of the All-Union Communist Party of Bolsheviks. They were offered chairs, they did not lose no right correspondence, neither rights to travel on country.

Stalin's letter went through many provincial historians like a hard roller, everywhere they began to look for "Trotskyist smugglers" and thunder them. It seemed would, then Letter publish Yaroslavsky and supporters, and Pokrovsky and his students could triumph... But after the death of Pokrovsky (1932), a critical campaign began, aiming to debunk them and his students [59].

It was not about consolidating Stalinist influence in the historical science (TO. Radek, R. Medvedev), not about change in the emphasis of education of the population (class feelings on patriotism — K. Simonov) [60], a about nationalization of historical science, turning it into an obedient ideological tool service totalitarian mode. As conceived by the creators of this "eternal regime", historians had to adhere to a universal theory that explains everything and everyone. — Marxism-Leninism. Naturally, in the interpretation of those in power. They had to explain everything that was happening as a blessing for the future, to cut off, keep silent, falsify everything that did not fit into the proposed scheme. Historians were supposed to contribute to the transformation of man into "Pavlov's dog." But even publicly declared loyalty was no guarantee of their safety. Since the regime created in the country could not exist without violence and terror, artificial maintaining environment civil war.

To maintain tension among historians, the authorities used various methods: study, self-exposure, unsound elite formations in state (referring on the Bukharin, a tomorrow he — "enemy of the people"), countless purges and executive orders, and finally arrests, exiles and physical destruction. Historians accused in political "crimes" preparing "terrorist ." acts" against party leadership and other absurd, never perfect actions [61].

In early 1935, the director of the library was arrested. Lenin VI Nevsky and his students, employees of the group on stories proletariat Institute stories PA Anatolyev, PP Paradisov, VS Zeltser; Dean of the Faculty of History of Leningrad State University GS Seidel and many others. AT 1936 G. arrested professors N. N. Vanag, Yu. M. Bocharov, MA Rubach, Dean of the Faculty of History of Moscow State University GS Fridlyand [62], director historical and archeographic Institute USSR Academy of Sciences SG Tomsinsky, Director of the Leningrad Historical and Philosophical Institute AG Prigozhin, Director of the Institute stories parties Leningrad OK VKP(b) OA Lidak, Dean of the Faculty of History of the Azerbaijan University and BN Tikhomirov, deputy. Director of the International Leninist school 3. L. Serebryansky, historys BUT. AND. Malyshev, B. M. freedlin, 3. B. Lozinsky, AND. P. Tokin, AT. M. Da-ling BUT. AND. Lomakin, T. M. Dubynya and other.

AT 1937 year were arrested dean history faculty LSU S.M. Dubrovsky, Director of the Institute of History of the Leningrad Branch of the Komacademy SS Bantke, Director of the Institute of Red Professors, historian VI Zeimal, Director of the Historical and Party Institute of Red Professors V. G. Knorin, his deputies P. Ya. Viksne and FA Anderson, Deputy Director of the Institute of History of the Academy of Sciences of the USSR AG Ionnisyan, Head. Department of History of the USSR, Moscow State University PO Gorin, Head departments stories peoples USSR and universal stories IKP P. FROM. Drozdov, F. F. Kozlov, historys B. B. Grave, AND. AT. Frolov, M. BUT. Lurie, L. G. Raisky, EI Rivlin, IM Trotsky, AG Slutsky, NM Voitinsky, AI Urazov, D. Ya. Kin, E. P. Krivosheina, and others. Many of them died. At the same time, hundreds of historians were arrested in many cities of the country. It is known that two-thirds of the 200 historians graduating from the Institute of Red Professors in Moscow died at that time. On March 31, 1937, NM Lukin, director of the Institute of History of the USSR Academy of Sciences, announced at a party meeting that the institute had taken first place in the system of the Academy of Sciences in terms of the number of identified " enemies of the people." Only in the Leningrad branch of the Institute of History from twenty employees arrested fourteen.

On May 5, 1937, representatives of the journals Historian-Marxist, Krasny Arkhiv, Historical Zhurnal spoke at an open party meeting of historians of the IKP in order to respond repentantly to criticism addressed to them. co pages newspapers "Truth". Editor magazine

"Historian-Marxist" academician N. M. Lukin acknowledged Cree-

tick correct and Noted what from eight members three editorial boards turned out to be "enemies of the people" (Fridlyand, Dalin, Frolov). The most odious was the speech of the representative. editor magazine Red archive" professors AT. AT. Maksakov. He spoke about publications in 1935 year in document journal about 9 January 1905 G. and interrogation Emelyan Pugachev. Foreword to him wrote FROM. BUT. Piontkovsky (to time meetings arrested and shot). "Again here t h e r e was no doubt political carelessness, not probed, what gave here Piontkovsky. Us seemed to be weak thing, hacky thing. But, comrades, this is was not hacky thing, she is had certain political installation, hostile us - and we overlooked it. So what and among authors, which we attracted who penetrated us, we had two exposed enemies people" [63].

Soon was arrested Lukin, representative directors IMEL VG Sorin and others. Criticism of Pokrovsky and the arrested historians assumed a frenzied, scale. She is reduced to ridiculous extravagant political and not scientific accusations. AT end 30s years Pokrovsky and his students were called "a gang of spies and saboteurs, agents and scouts of world imperialism, conspirators" boxes and killers." That epithets applied then to Bukharin and his students who died in concentration camps. similar "accusations" become then the norm.

Doom many historys — part universal, national tragedy. Know how it happened a little.

One of the still little-known sources that reveal methods for eliminating just the slightest, and often dissent, are investigative and rehabilitation cases kept in the archives of the former KGB of the USSR. On their basis, first of all, and written Essays on the historians killed in the mid-1930s and their distorted fates. These essays form the basis of this book.

A special edition of the book was carried out by a candidate of historical science L. M. Ovrutsky.

* * *

[1] jimbins FROM. Epitaph spetskhranu?..//New world.—1990.— No. 5. S. 244; tolz M. Repressed census // Rodina.- 1989. No. 11.- S. 58-60 .
[2] Orwell J. 1984.//New world.—1989.—No. 2.—S. 145.
[3] wipper R. Y.U. A crisis historical sciences.—Kazan, 1921.—S. 12.

[4] Melgunov FROM. P. Memory and diaries.— Paris, 1964. — Issue. IC 239.
[5] Gauthier Y.U. AT. My notes//Questions stories.- 1992. — No. one. — FROM. 127.
[6] Milyukov P. N. Russia on the fracture. - Paris, 1927.- T.I. - S. 174, 194; Russian-Jewish dialogue. - New York, 1971.- S. 131.
[7] Sorokin P. Moral and mental condition contemporary Russia // Will Russia. — 1922.- No. 5. - S. 26.
[8] Shkarenkov L. TO. Agony white emigration.— M., 1987.— FROM. 94.
[9] cm.: Pravda.—1924.—16 May.
[10] To her belonged and social democratic. Note what Marxist historiography, born more in pre-revolutionary Russia, never not was single. AT her clearly stood out co creation time 'parties new type", on extreme least two directions: Bolshevik and social democratic. First It was represented by works AT. AND. Lenin, N. AND. Bukharin, G. E. Zinoviev, L. B. Kameneva, to him adjoined research professional editors N. M. Lukina, M. N. Pokrovsky and others. To this direction, with a little adjustment, should be attributed works L. D. Trotsky, to his varieties, gaining With 20s years force, Stalinist historiography. social democratic direction, presented by the works of GV Plekhanov, Yu. O. Martova, F. AND. Dana, by the works of historians N. BUT. Rozhkova, D. B. Ryazanov and others after no revolution received development in country, a her publications move per frontier.
[11] Ivanova L. AT. At origins Soviet historical science (personnel training Marxist historians in 1917-1929 gg.).—M., 1968.—S. 181.
[12] Herald Socialist Academy.—1922.— No. one.- FROM. 41.
[13] Avtorkhanov A.G. Technology authorities//Questions of history.- 1992.- No. 1.—S. 74.
[14] cm.: Organization Soviet science in 1926-1932 // Sat. Doc.—L., 1974.—S. 233.
[15] Pokrovsky MN Decade of the Institute of Red Professors // Pravda.— 1931.—11 February.
[16] Fokeev AT. BUT. From stories study and dissemination works of VI Lenin in the first years of Soviet power (1917-1923) // Knigovedenie.— 1970.—No. 2.—S. 7.
[17] Edition essays Lenin in twenty volumes (26 books) — 1920-1926 years, 2nd and 3rd publications in 30 volumes—1925-1932 years; 4th - in 45 volumes 1941-1957 years; 5th edition - in 55 volumes - 1958-1965 gg.
[18] fifty years Soviet historical science. Chronicle scientific life. 1917-1967.—M., 1971.—S. 83, 94, 102. Center for the Study and Storage of Documents of Recent History (hereinafter - RTSKhIDNI), formerly TsPA IML. - F. 71.—Op. 3.—D. 9.—L. 13, fifteen, 24; F. 147.—Op. 1.- D. 33.—L. 27; Historian-Marxist.—1929.—T. 14.—S. 6.
[19] So many works have been written about how the past mistakes of political leaders (real or imaginary) were used by Stalin in settling scores with his opponents that we do not need to stop on the this any in detail.
[20] cm.: Questions stories CPSU.—1990.— No. 5.- FROM. 53.
[21] Kaganovich LM For the Bolshevik study of the history of the party.- M., 1932.- S. 24; Struggle classes.—1932.—No. 2-3.—S. 5.
[22] RTSKHIDNI.—F. 147.—Op. 1.—D. 73.—L. 7.
[23] Dunayevsky AT. BUT. O Stalin's letter in editorial magazine «Proletarian revolution» and its impact on science and destinies of people//History and Stalinism. - M., 1991; and others Bye more No answers to the questions: did Stalin himself write this "Letter"? Why were the articles of Slutsky and Volosevich the main object of his criticism? In Stalin's archive there is corrected them typescript "Letters" (not manuscript)

AT her his hand inscribed gain formulations. So, phrase sounded: "Let's turn to some facts from history." Corrected by Stalin's hand: "Let's turn to the most famous facts from history", etc. // RTSKHIDNI.—F. 558.—Op. one.- D. 2983.—L. 5.

[24] Herald Communist academy.— 1932.- No. 1-2; Archive Academy of Sciences of Russia. - F. 377.— Op. 1.- D. 262.

[25] Mode personal Stalin's power. To stories formations. - M., 1989. — S. 71-72.

[26] Krylenko N. conclusions and lessons from process "Industrial Party". — M.- L., 1931.-S. 42.

[27] CGAOR— F. 5143.—Op. 1.— D. 613.—L. 1-7, 27-43. Shestakova supported MV Nechkin and especially party bureau member Institute Pugovkin, who declared that all the convicts "followed a certain order of fascism - to harm in our historical science." The only one who managed in his speech to confine himself to his own repentance and in no way mentioned names their colleagues was B. D. Greeks.

[28] Maybe, in downgrading "moral slats" historical science played my role and circumstances natural character. To the middle 30s years gone from life most featured pupils AT. O. Klyuchevsky. M. TO. Lyubavsky died in 1936 G., N. BUT. Rozhkov — in 1927, M. M. Theological — in 1929 BUT. BUT. Kiesewetter — in 1933 Remained truth, returned from links Y.U. AT. Gauthier, AT. AND. Picheta, E. AT. Tarle, but this is were already broken people. From historys old, pre-revolutionary school more worked FROM. B. Veselovsky, M. H. Tikhomirov, BD Grekov and some other. Some were frightened by repression more, other — less, but fear felt everyone.

[29] cm.: Story USSR.—1991.—No. one.- FROM. 106.

[thirty] Milyukov PN Two Russian historians (SF Platonov and AA Kizevetter) // Modern notes. — Paris, 1933.- No. 51.- S. 312; Brachev VS A dangerous profession is a historian. Pages of life of an academician FROM. F. Platonova//Bulletin AN USSR.—1991.—No. 9.—S. 65 71

[31] Enteen G. The the Soviet Union Scholar-Bureaucrat: M. BY. Pokrovsky and the Society self Marxist Historians.— L., 1978; История CCCP.—1988.— No 4.— C. 210.

[32] The letters have not been published in full.— Bulletin of the Russian Academy of Sciences.—1992.— No. 6.— S. 104-112. So, from letters pechets Pokrovsky fell out ending: Michael Nikolaevich! You me few know and never to yourself close not let me down but I I know You. Understand my fate and save me from death. Give any job under your control and I am her I will do it. I can ask only you more me not to who to apply for help and per true" // RTSKHIDNI. - F. 147.—Op. 2.—D. 11.- L. 16. AT actually there is one more letter Picheta from solitary cameras No. 73 at home preliminary conclusions dated October 22, 1930, in which he reported that he graduated from Moscow University in 1901, worked as a teacher and in archives, was an expert of the Soviet delegation at the Riga Conference in 1920, in 1921 — 1929 — Rector of the Belarusian University. Picheta's teacher was Lyubavsky, significant, what exactly his teachers Lyubavsky

Pichet vinyl in all their troubles. (FROM. 17-25).

[33] RTSKHIDNI.—F. 147.—Op. 2.—D. 11.- L. 5. E. AT. Tarle was arrest-van at the end of January 1931 and was one of the main figures in the "academic business". Investigative imagination then concocted a "deed", As if historians were preparing for the restoration of the monarchy in the country, the creation of a Provisional Government headed by Platonov and Foreign Minister Tarle. Tarle appeared in the same capacity at the trial "Industrial Party" (November December 1930 of the year). About this cm.: Process

"Industrial Party". Transcript. - M., 1931. - S. 13; Fedorov L. How they came up with party // Rodina.— 1990.— No. 5.

[34] RTSKHIDNI.—F. 147.—Op. 2.—D. 11.- L. one.

[35] There same.— D. 46.— L. 5.

[36] There the same.- D. 35.— L. 40.

[37] Pokrovsky M. H. How and by whom Russian was written story before Marxists, Moscow, 1931; Zaidel G., Zvibak M. The class enemy on the historical front. - M. - L., 1931; and others

[38] РЦХИДНИ. — Ф. 147.—Оп. 1.—D. 42.—L. 5- 13.

[39] There the same.- D. 33.— L. 42- 46.

[40] Justice needs to be seen what and his opponent E. M. Yaroslavsky differed little in this respect from Pokrovsky. To match Pokrovsky were many of his students, who later became victims of repression themselves. PO Gorin was one of them. 21 April 1931 Mr. he wrote in secretariat Central Committee, copy Pokrovsky: Recent two years are characterized by a stubborn struggle in the field of historical sciences. This, of course, is not accidental, since the intensification of the struggle among Marxist historians located in close connections With exacerbation class struggle in our country. In the field of historical sciences ... we are also seeing vivid cases of ideological wrecking (Yavorsky) and open counter-revolution (Tarle, Platonov and others), attempts to revise the Leninist scheme of the historical development of Russia are becoming more frequent (Teodorovich, Dubrovsky and others), the desire to use historical science for substantiation of modern various reactionary views (Trotsky, Sukhanov, etc.). And following the denunciatory information, he assured what "society ." Marxist historians, led MH Pokrovsky, subordinated his work to the tasks of the party and, working under the direct leadership cultural prop Central Committee VKP(b), velo active fight against enemies and revisionists Leninism" (RTSKHIDNI. - F. 147.- Op. one.- D. 30.— L. 10). Considering these and other similar documents, it is difficult to agree with the statement that the repressions against historians began simultaneously with the criticism of Pokrovsky.— Artizov AN Criticism of MN Pokrovsky and his school (on the history of the issue) // History of the USSR.—1991.— No. 1.— P. 107. Repressions against historians began long ago before this and not without help most Pokrovsky.

[41] In 1934 all the surviving excluded historians were returned to scientific work. Muscovites Lyubavsky and Yegorov, Leningraders Platonov died in exile and Christmas.

[42] Historian-Marxist.— 1936.—Kn. 1.—S. 22.

[43] Yaroslavsky Em. Anti-Marxist perversions and vulgarism So called "schools" Pokrovsky // Historical magazine.— 1939.— No. 2. - S. 54.

[44] News Central Committee CPSU—1989.—No. 8.—S. 100.

[45] cm.: Repressed science. - L., 1991; pepper F. F. Academy of Sciences on the great fracture" // Links. Historical almanac. - M., 1991.-Issue. 1.— S. 163-235; Zankevich E. Kh. On the history of Sovietization of the Russian Academy of Sciences.— Munich, 1957; Graham L. The Soviet Academy of Scinces and the Communist Party. 1927-1932. —Princeton, 1967; and others

[46] See: Brachev VS "The Case" of Academician SF Platonov // Questions of History.—1989.— No. 5; Goryainov AN Once again about the "academic history" // Questions of History.—1990.— No. 1; Chapkevich EI Evgeny Viktorovich Tarle.— M., 1977; He same. Pages biographies Academic E. AT. Tarle//New and recent history.—1990.— no. four; Antsiferov N. P. From memories//Star. —1989.— No. four; Wheat AP Repression archivists in 1930s years//Soviet archives.— 1988.— No. 6; Prostvolosov L. N., Stanislavsky BUT. L. "We teach Soviet

of people, a not ancient Greeks" (from stories university historical science end 30-40s years) // History USSR.—1989.—No. 6; Historical the science in 20-30s years // Story and reviewers. - M., 1990.- P. 83.

[47] Fitzpatrick Sh. The «Soft» Line on culture and its Enemiest: Soviet Cultural Policy 1922-1927 ///Slavic Review — 1974.—
№ 2.— P. 267-287 .

[48] Shapiro L. The Communist Party of the Soviet Union. - Edizioni Aurora, 1975. - S. 656-657. A similar view was expressed by the old Bolshevik AS Snegov: "If Stalin had not succeeded in curbing, distorting party history could to appear today in such a vulgar wording—"Stalin is Lenin today!"//All-Union Conference on measures to improve the training of scientific and pedagogical personnel in historical science 18-21 December 1962 years. - M., 1964.— FROM. 266.

[49] Avtorkhanov BUT. Lenin in destinies Russia//New world.—1991.— No. 1.- S. 179; a also cm.: Shubkin AT. sad true//New world . - 1991.- No.6.— FROM. 187; Concepts "totalitarian" state" and "totalitarian mode" enough full explored Anglo-American political scientists. F. Hayek emphasized genetic connection totalitarianism With socialist exercises (Path to slavery//New world.— 1991.—
No. 7, 8), Hannah Arendt noted two authentic forms of totalitarian rule: the dictatorship of National Socialism after 1938 and the dictatorship Bolshevism after 1930 and gave their structural analysis (The origins of Totalitarianism.—N. Y., 1973.—P. 149 etc). About other views, see: Yu. Following the discussions, Soviet philosophers published a collection of articles "Totalitarianism as a Historical Phenomenon" (M., 1989), in which they identified the features this mode: absolute power states above society and man; the dominance of a single ideology; immorality and complete contempt to man (FROM. ten). BUT. N. Sakharov named feature of the regime in the country is "revolutionary totalitarianism", the main thing in which rum — egalitarian attitude to property (Communist.—1991.—
№ 5.— S. 71).

[fifty] But and this is was not last revision. He we walked before 1938 G., before the appearance of a short course in the history of the party, in 1956 a new revision began and So on this day... Indeed, at countries unpredictable past!

[51] Geller M., Nekrich BUT. Utopia at authorities.—London, 1982.- T. 1.- S. 283, 309, 313.

[52] Volkogonov D. Stalinism, essence, genesis, evolution // Questions of History.—1990.— No. 3.— S. 12; Reiman M. Perestroika and the study of the Soviet stories//There same.—1989.—No. 12.—S. 146.

[53] See: V.D. Solovey, The Process of Formation of Soviet Historical Science (1917—mid-1930s) in the Coverage of American and English historiography//History USSR.—1988.— No. 4. - S. 200-215; she: Historical science and politics in the USSR, 20-30s // Historical _ meaning NEP.— M., 1990.—S. 149-168.

[54] Shteppa K. Russian Historians and the Soviet State.— New Brunswick, 1962.—P. 380; Heer N. Politics and history in the Soviet Union.— Cambridge, 1971. Also written about this: Daniels R. Soviet Thought in the Nineteen - Thirties. An Interpretive Sketch//Indiana Slavic Studies.— 1956.— Vol. one.- P. 100, 107; Alekseeva GD Party management of historical science in the transition period. 1917-1936 (Organization and research planning). Diss. ... Doctor of Historical Sciences.— M., 1984. It is curious that even "hated tsarism" encourage the creation historical institutions in case if they eliminated from socio-political questions (cm.: Chesnokov AT. AND.

Government politics and historical the science Russia 60-70s_ _ XIX century. Research essays.— Voronezh, 1989.- FROM. 184).

[55] links, expulsions and arrests historys practiced and Lenin. Known for his correspondence With editor N. BUT. Rozhkov. Rozhkov became Bolshevik in 1905 in time funeral Nicholas Bauman in Moscow carried red flag, in 1906 G. lived With Lenin in Finland, on the V congress RSDLP became member Central Committee. Later them way dispersed. AT January 1919 G. Rozhkov wrote Lenin about economic catastrophe in country and advocated per free trade. He recommended to him install one-man dictatorship Considering complexity situations. Lenin objected, assuming that in conditions gigantic bureaucratic apparatus "sol dictatorship" unthinkable. AT March 1921 G. Rozhkov was arrested in hostage in connections With speech sailors in Kronstadt. Then there was a release solution about expulsion per border replaced link to Pskov. — RTSKHIDNI.—F. 2.—Op. 1.—D 8492. —L. 1-2; Novikov AT. AND. "I must was to finish before end..." (from correspondence N. BUT. Rozhkova With AT. AND. Lenin) // Soviet archives.— 1990.— No. 5; Volobuev O., Simonov N. Become dictator Vladimir Ilyich! // Motherland.— 1991.— No. 11-12.

[56] By falsified "justifications" special departments in late 1930 of the year were condemned more 3rd thousand military. — Souvenirs O. F. People's Commissariat of Defense and NKVD in pre-war years //Questions history.— 1991.— No. 6.— FROM. 26. Investigative a business No. 1657 stored in archive of the former KGB USSR, testifies what former Major General of the General Staff royal armies, division chief Red armies Professor Alexander Andreevich Svechin arrested twice. In time arrest in March

1931 Svechin told the investigator that he hoped for a softening of the class fight in country. "Soviet power I met hostile and never completely did not perceive her. We, the former officers of the old General Staff, who lost those privileges, that position and those prospects that the past promised us, found ourselves in the conditions of Soviet power, throughout the entire period of its existence intertwined our hostile attitude towards it with the hope of the degeneration of Soviet power in a democratic republic that would open up for us great scope and great freedom." In business — characteristic of Svechin, given on May 22, 1924, which emphasized his fruitful Work in chapter departments stories military art. And Further about German: Comprehensively educated military specialist. It has huge an experience two wars (Japanese and imperialist), in a variety of positions (from work at Headquarters to regiment commander). A very talented person, witty, Svechin is the most valuable professor in Military Academy". Svechina accused of participating in a monarchist conspiracy and, despite his denial of guilt, on July 18, 1931, he was ruling to a 5-year stay in camps. February 7 1932 he was released. December 26, 1937 Svechin was again arrested and on the basis falsified slander July 29, 1938 shot. During the investigation and trial, AA Svechin courageously, accusations denied; rehabilitated 8 September 1956 During his arrest, 1780 books were taken from him. IV Svechina, his wife, paid compensation on the basis of: for a hardcover book —3 R., in soft -2 ruble.

[57] Of the 58 volumes of investigative files on the "Union Bureau of the Central Committee of the RSDLP" Nikolai Nikolaevich Sukhanov (1882-1940) is dedicated to the 9th (Archive of the former KGB USSR). He was arrested on July 20 1930 G. on the charge of that he "was a member of the k/r Menshevik Party, which set the goal, together with other k/r organizations (TKP and the Industrial Party) with the help of and under leadership foreign Central Committee Menshevik party,

the overthrow of Soviet power by organizing sabotage activities aimed at preparing for intervention." Search warrant signed G. Berry. interrogated Sukhanov I. Agranov, Chertok and Dmitriev. These were the department's leading investigators, known for their penchant for falsification and extortion of testimony. Sukhanov gave them written answers to the questions posed—because many protocols written ink, his hand.

In the case of the "Union Bureau" 14 people were arrested - all former Mensheviks, and by the time of the arrest - loyal employees of the State Planning Commission, the State Bank, the People's Commissariat of Justice. They were charged with an attempt to prepare an intervention in order to restore capitalism in the country. Investigators wanted show, what all "contra" acted together, and therefore sought affirmative answers to the connections of the "Mensheviks" With "industrial party" "peasant labor party" and others

Sukhanov was participant revolutionary movements in Russia With 1904 of the year. visited in prisons links and emigration, went through a period hobbies programs SRs and social democrats, was familiar co everyone pre-revolutionary leaders these currents. After February 1917 G. Sukhanov - member presidium Petrograd Soviet. Exactly about this period his life he left the most interesting from their works - "Notes on the Revolution" (Pb., 1922-1923.- Book. 1-7). There is various versions reasons arrest Sukhanov in 1930 G., in including and Trotsky: Sukhanov declared in "Notes", what Stalin produced on him impression "grey spots, sometimes looming dimly and without a trace", a because and paid the price life. - Trotsky L. D. Stalin. - M., 1990.—T. 1.—S. 267; a also cm.: Kornikov BUT. BUT. N. N. Sukhanov and his "Notes on the Revolution" // Sukhanov N. N. Notes on the Revolution. - M., 1991.—T. 1.—S. thirty.

During the August interrogations in 1930, Sukhanov noted that he was familiar with professor-economist ND that "by the spring of 1929, he finally lost faith in the possibility of a reverse turn to the NEP by the forces of the existing party leadership"; that his "gloomy moods" about the possibility of the country's transition to fascism and Bonapartism reached apogee by February 1930; that the course of party economic policy since 1927 has been wrong. He convinced Chertok December 1, 1930 G., what always was against interventions.

In January 1931, Sukhanov's testimony under the influence of torture methods have changed he became "in everyone confess", in volume including and quite sincerely that "by the beginning of 1929 G... came to the conclusion that the policy of the CPSU(b) is disastrous, and itself dictatorship Com. party is the greatest evil from the point of view of the interests of the country and the world socialist movement ... I came to the conclusion that the replacement of the dictatorship of Kom. party by the democratic regime is the task, for the implementation which must and can fight everyone means."

In the case of Sukhanov, there is an autobiography written by him, in which he confirmed his rejection of the "Jacobin dictatorship of the Bolsheviks", starting with the policy of war communism. At the beginning of 1920, he was with Trotsky in the Urals and proved to him the importance of the immediate abolition of requisitions. Trotsky disputed my provisions,—wrote Sukhanov, and summed up this kind of conversation in what sense, that the party is not going to change its food policy. Subsequently, it turned out that it was exactly at this time that Trotsky by telegraph from the Urals came up with a project to introduce NEP, and during the campaign Against him, in one of the party meetings, demonstrated the corresponding telegraph tape.

Sukhanov was convicted, was in prison, was in exile in Tobolsk, then in Omsk prison, there same was and shot. Investigative a business

Sukhanov for 1930–1931. may be evidence of the editing of his testimony, their distortion during the publication of the transcript of the "Process of counter-revolutionary" organizations Mensheviks" (M., 1931).

Many people knew Sukhanov. Arrest and conviction of him, like many others were to obey the regime. Otherwise... massacre.

[58] Yaroslavsky wrote to Stalin on October 28, 1931. "It is especially hard for me to realize that due to an oversight I omitted in Volume IV such a characterization of your views in the spring of 1917 upon my return from exile, which really pours water on the mill of the Slutskys and Voloseviches... Tov. Stalin indicate me the one "a series of errors fundamental and historical character", which you mention at the end Your his letters"//RTSKHIDNI.—F 89.— Op. 1.—D. 72.—L. 1-2. At a meeting of the Society of Marxist Historians on November 11, 1931, with a report "Lessons from the article of comrade. Stalin and tasks on the historical front" was made by VG Knorin. On the one hand, he noted that Stalin's letter not should consider how new in our literature, and how clear, bright exposition major provisions Leninism", on the other — called the provisions of the letter indisputable and called for criticism of Slutsky, Friedland and other historians. He had one justification: "We ... are against the right to freely propagate anti-Marxist, anti-Bolshevik theories, ... we must declare to them the most resolute fight." On the meeting With sharp condemnations their
"mistakes" spoke slutsky, kin, piontkovsky, mints, Vanag. Against them With accusations in "insufficient" self-disclosure — Shestakov, Radek, Lurie, Bayevsky. AT result meeting decided exclude Slutsky from "ranks societies Marxist historians". Volosevich was fired from numbers employees Leningrad branch Comacademy.— RTSKHIDNI.— F. 147.—Op. 1.—D. 30.- L. 16, 25, 46, 106 169; Herald Communist academics — 1932.
№ 1-2. — C. 40- 66.

[59] More about this cm.: Artizov BUT. N. Criticism M. N. Pokrovsky and his school (to stories question) //Story USSR. -1991.-No. 1. - S. 102-120.

[60] Medvedev R. O Stalin and Stalinism.— M., 1990.— FROM. 273; Simonov K. Through the eyes human my generations.— M., 1989.- S. 183-184.

[61] AT end December 1934 of the year were arrested 19 human, in volume including GE Zinoviev, LB Kamenev. The case of the so-called "Moscow center" was created. Among those arrested was the historian AI Anishev, Investigation a business No. 3257 (archive former KGB USSR) reports on the tragic fate of the author of "Essays on the history of the civil war. 1917-1920 years." (L., 1925). Anatolia Isaevich Anisheva (present surname - Shapiro) then condemned on the 6 years jail, accusing his, like many others, in preparation Kirov's assassination. He was then 35 years. Per his shoulders It was participation in civil war, underground work in the rear of the Kolchak troops, before his arrest, he worked as deputy director of the Institute of Physics and Agronomy in Leningrad and was a member of the CPSU (b) since 1919. In September 1936, he was brought from Verkhneudinsk to Moscow, again accused of participating in the assassination attempt on Kirov. Investigator Mikhail Yakhontov excelled in torturing and humiliating Anishev, but none confessions not achieved. Anishev any my guilt denied. Court under Assignment Ulrich swear his
3 October 1936 G. to execution. four October sentence was given in execution. Yakhontov survived my sacrifice, his shot 22 February 1939 g. for violation in time consequences of "socialist legality". But So how Anishev accused in connections With Zinoviev,

Kamenev and others politicians, then and was rehabilitated together with them only 13 June 1988 of the year.

[62] A. Avtorkhanov, graduate of the Moscow Institute of red professions sura, made a mistake in his memoirs, indicating that Vanag and Friedland were arrested on New Year's Eve 1937 (Avtorkhanov A. Memoirs // October.— 1992. — No. 8 - S. 143). They were arrested in 1936, both were shot on March 8, 1937. Before being shot, they underwent a test of torture. A. Orlov, an NKVD officer who fled the country, later recalled the following. One of the employees heard screams from investigator Kedrov's office. "He went in and saw: Kedrov was beside himself. Enraged, he accused the prisoner — it was Friedland, professor, ... — in trying swallow inkwell, standing at him on the table.

"I dumbfounded - told employee, seeing this inkwell - massive from faceted glass, size in two male fist."—

"What you such speak," uttered Friedland, clearly intimidated by the investigator. Here to me came in head, continued employee - that Kedrov crazy"//Orlov BUT. Secret story Stalinist crimes. — M., 1991. — S. 91.

[63] Patriotic history.—1992.—No. 2.—S. 135.

TWO PERSONS VLADIMIR ADORATSKY

Considerable literature has been devoted to the life and work of the Bolshevik since 1904, Academician Adoratsky (1878-1945): documents, excerpts from the diary, memoirs about him, biographical essays, articles on the philosophical heritage and contribution in organization archives in the country, studied individual periods of his revolutionary work [1]. He was not repressed, and his life, as it were, illustrates the fate of that part of the Russian intelligentsia that courageously spoke against autocracy, but fell prostrate before Stalinist mode.

Lenin endowed Adoratsky with flattering characteristics: 'personally known", "deserves complete trust",
"knowledgeable Marxist", etc. [2] Adoratsky can be called a representative of Lenin's guard, about whose role in the country's history there are polar opinions [3]. Adoratsky, being scientists organizer science, systems archives, did not hold key state and party posts. Is it his fault what happened? If there is, what does it consist of? Indiscriminate accusation of everyone and everything denied yet group M. N. ryutina, when noted in the "Platform of the Union of Marxist-Leninists" (1932), that "the main cohort of Lenin's associates was removed from leadership positions, and one part of it sits in prisons and exiles, the other, capitulated, demoralized and spat upon, - drags out miserable existence in the ranks of the party, third, final but decomposed, turned in faithful servants "leader-" dictator's uncle" [4.] It may seem that Adoratsky belonged to the "third" group according to outward signs. Is not it this is?

Adoratskiy was born in Kazan, here finished gymnasium,
Faculty of Law of the University (1903), here he began to study the theory and history of Marxism. In his autobiography (1921) he wrote: "I began to be interested in questions of the theory of scientific socialism long ago. In 1900 I came across a French translation of the Manifesto. "Manifesto" completely captivated me - I irrevocably became a supporter and student of Marx. Education and knowledge at me It was few. Not It was habits to systematic

scientific labor and absolutely not It was leader. I had to before Total reach on one's own. spring 1903 g. i graduated well legal faculty, a winter Togo the same year first left per border. AT Berlin I pounded on social democratic literature. Then move to Geneva, tried to re-read as much Russian as possible illegal..." [5]. AT others texts autobiographies (1922/1923 .) gg.) Adoratskiy reported what in 1900 G. he became member Kazan social democratic organizations in 1901 G. was subjected to search, a in december 1903 Mr.. went abroad , provided with letters and appearances. AT Geneva met With materials II congress RSDLP and firmly decided how Bolshevik [6]. Returning Adoratskiy became member Kazansky committee RSDLP.

First meeting Adoratsky With Lenin happened in Geneva in the spring of 1905. Finding out that they studied at the same faculty, Lenin began to question Adoratsky about the university professors, recalling his conversation with the arresting his bailiff in time student unrest of 1887 G. Well what you rebel young man—it's a wall!" — the bailiff said. Lenin replied: "The wall, but rotten ,— poke and fall apart!" [7]. FROM light arms Adoratskogo this episode . became textbook.

On the night of December 12, 1905, Adoratsky and other members of the Kazan committee RSDLP were arrested. AT March 1906 Adoratsky was deported to the Astrakhan province, but summer link was replaced travel abroad, without the right to enter Russia for two years. Arriving in Cherny Yar, the place of settlement, Adoratsky, comprehending what had happened to him, wrote to his wife: "In the end, tsov, obviously, to me expensive Total my mind, his development, growth and sophistication. Knowledge is important to me, sometimes I feel how to develop this passion, to make it independent valuable and valuable for humanity, my mind obscures in me all, I ready to be cruel bring what kind sacrifice, if only in this way to become useful and necessary people. to me not necessary for this glory, because what if I became famous by chance and myself If I knew that my fame was not due to merit, then I would be unhappy. AND, vice versa - I was would happy, if would remain completely unknown to anyone, but only he himself would know what he did a business, which is needed and important for humanity" [8]. This combination of scientific ambition with cruelty the bone and at the same time the sacrifice of the revolutionary was very characteristic, reflecting in many spirit era.

mother, daughter rich Kazan merchant not embarrassed

son in means. AT September 1906 G. Adoratskiy With family left in Switzerland. lived in Geneva and Zurich, repeatedly met With Lenin a lot of was reading, was engaged self-education. On their last meeting in Geneva (1908 G.) they spoke about future revolution in Russia, which how they were sure, "inevitably will give power in arms our parties." Got up question, how to be co servants of the old mode. Other words "what will be Vladimir Ilyich in roles Robespierre". Vladimir Ilyich outlined such plan actions: "We will to ask: You per whom? Per revolution or against? If a against — to wall if yes, go to us and Work". Adoratskiy remembered that Krupskaya , who was present during the conversation, doubted correctness such approach. Myself same Adoratskiy supported Lenina [9].

Autumn 1908 of the year Adorati returned to Kazan _ data Kazansky local gendarmerie management, per him straightaway same was installed vowel police supervision [10], but any active participation Adoratsky in revolutionary movement discover not managed. Apparently he plunged in creative job: wrote a book "State With materialistic points vision", corresponded with the Social Democrats living beyond border: Krupskaya, M. M. Litvinov. Manuscript books and review on the work philosopher P. AND. Novgorod- tseva "A crisis contemporary sense of justice" (M., 1909) Adoratsky showed Lenin in time another meetings with him in paris in April 1911 d. [11]. By the way, then or Lenin asked him to inform K. Kautsky (in Berlin) that the Bolsheviks have had right claim on the money bequeathed to Russian social democrats N. P. Schmitt, owner furniture factories, dead in royal prison [12]. _ Adoratskiy prudently evaded from instructions, citing poor knowledge of German, although the address of the Stuttgart lawyer, finished participate in this In fact, sent to Lenin . Another order from Lenin — hold off Kazan provinces working on the elections in IV State thought - too left unfulfilled.

War caught Adoratsky in Germany, where he together was interned with his family. In August 1918, Adoratsky already in Moscow and straightaway starts work in Narkompros and at the same time - Head of the so-called Novo-Romanovsky archive, where he sorted out the papers of the dynastic archive of the Romanovs and the former Ministry of Foreign Affairs. In November 1918, he was elected "competitor member" Socialist academics public

nyh science, a With spring 1919 G. proceeds to reading lectures
"on the history of the scientific worldview" at Moscow University and pedagogical Academy.

AT early July 1919 G. Adoratskiy With family moved to Kazan. Before leaving, on June 27, he talked with Lenin, which the recommended to him gather materials and prepare feature article on stories October revolution. Lenin believe writing such essay deed important and necessary, Adoratsky receives a mandate signed by him: "The giver of this, comrade. Adoratsky, I personally know how scientist and writer. I beg render anything to him assistance on extradition books from any libraries, in volume including and on the house under mine personal guarantee" [13]. It wasn't just a courtesy. Ahead of the train that was taking away Adoratsky in Kazan, flew Leninist telegram in Kazan urban and university libraries: Telegraph you have whether kits Izvestia and "Pravda" With October 1917 of the year. If a No at you, No whether in another Kazan library. to me needed for hasty work, entrusted me Kazan" [14]. AT flow 1919 - beginning 1920 gg. Lenin repeatedly requested Adoratsky about the progress work, but that nothing not could please his mighty correspondent and in letter from 6 January 1920 must was to explain. Dear Vladimir Ilyich! Highly already a lot of account for overcome all sorts of rubbish. That's why how this is neither unpleasant, account for not is- fulfill the promise. AT Kazan to me had to for a long time wander - give, before how managed take paid place, necessary for food. Business trips to me not allowed, big I not I can. left from Moscow "So". AT Kazan I had to lecture, I for a long time not spoke and necessary was strenuous get ready. So, in different affairs passed time before november. BUT here fell ill... FROM promised work things are going So: I view newspapers With April before eleven August 1918 and from October to the end of 1918. This is all that is available here. per 1918 G. Material, available in view me newspapers, I extracted and he at me under hand. When there will be a little lighter and warmer I I will bring in order and send... Kazan — bad hole, a in Moscow impossible to live - none forces not enough work out on the family maintenance. Here same all cheaper and there is some trash, co- second sold out. I tired and weakened health. Takova life". AT answer on the this is letter Presovnarkom asked the Kazan authorities to help the Adoratsky family with rations, firewood and other [15].

In Kazan, Adoratsky lectured on historical materialism to students of the provincial party school, students of the workers' faculty of the university - on the history of socialist doctrines and world history; gave reviews of literature on social and politi cal sciences to students of the Higher Institute of Public Education. The course "Scientific Communism of Karl Marx" was offered to students of all educational institutions of the city, where Adoratsky taught at that time. In his autobiography, written in October 1919 when he entered the university as a teacher at the workers' faculty of the university, Adoratsky substantiated his right to read lectures and lead lessons co students: "Theory" history socialism I studied in flow more fifteen years, both theoretically and practically. Familiar with the history of Russia and West. I own languages german, English and read in French, Italian, Spanish ... Ref- ki both to me may to give knowing me and mine activity B. AND. Ulyanov (Lenin) and M. N. Pokrovsky"[16].

The programs of lectures on the history of socialism given by Adoratsky have been preserved. 18 topics: three dedicated to French utopian socialists, one — German classical philosophy, five — Marxism rest — Russian revolutionary democracy, social democrats, history of three Internationals.

On April 22, 1920, Adoratsky spoke in the assembly hall of the university with a speech "VI Ulyanov (Lenin). Doer- ness and personality." It gave a periodization of the history of the party, inseparable, according to Adoratsky, with the activities Lenin: 1. 1895-1903. Struggle against "legal Marxism" and "economism"; 2. 1903-1908. Fight against Menshevism; 3. 1908–1914. The fight against liquidationism; 4. World War and the fight against the traitors of socialism - social patriots. 1914-1917; 5. Struggle for the dictatorship of the proletariat. March-October 1917; 6. Dictatorship the proletariat. 8th-9th Party Congresses[17]. Lectures and reports by Adoratsky delivered by them in various training establishments Kazan, lay down in basis row his scientific works[18].

During the formation of Marxism as a state definition, Adoratsky acted as its apologist, believing that that what is happening can be explained only from a materialistic point of view. The materialist historian needs to know, he wrote, "where did this consciousness come from, why some leaders recommend cooperatives and cheap credit in then most time, when other name is to strike or even to armed speech, why one mile "founder", a other stand per power Soviets etc. But, being interested in the origin of ideas, the materialist historian does not stop at this. He tries understand the whole public process in in general and answer question, how that or other idea, expressing interest of one class or another, is carried out in life, or, in other words, how and why does this or that class win in the class struggle, and how does its "idea", its interest, get its embodiment in life. The materialist considers human society primarily as a phenomenon of objective reality that independent. from subjective consciousness" [19].

While promoting a class approach in assessing historical events, Adoratsky opposed ideology as such, seeing in it something idealistic. "Ideology can define,- wrote he,- how a consciousness detached from reality, having lost its conscious connection with this reality and reflecting the latter incorrectly, upside down form. Marxism - enemy of ideology" [20.] At the same time, Adoratsky relied on the statement of K. Marx and F. Engels about the illusory nature of ideology, visissitudes Images in her reality, that the materialistic worldview is the end any ideologies [21].

AT august 1920 of the year Adoratskiy move in Moscow at the invitation of MN Pokrovsky. Biochronicle of Lenin captures the meeting of old acquaintances. This time, Lenin instructed to prepare Marx's letters for publication in Russian. and Engels [22].

In September 1920, the Politburo of the Central Committee of the RCP(b) approved the composition of the Istpart commission, where Adoratsky joined as secretary. Together with Pokrovsky he supervised creation of the first chronicle October revolution [23].

In the 1920s, Adoratsky stood out among many party members with pre-revolutionary experience who were engaged in similar work, great professionalism, education, and extremely careful and precise implementation of directives. prescriptions.

Along with many other social scientists, he took part in the condemnation intra-party opposition; his excursions into the history of the Bolshevik Party confirmed the correctness of Stalin's political line [24]. The largest of this series of opportunistic works was a study on the history of Bolshevism during the years of reaction [25]. By your opinion Adoratsky, exactly then, t. e. still before start first world wars (in Bolshevik-skoy parties before, than in all others parties II International), there was a "cleansing ... of opportunist elements, and it was thus prepared to fulfill its role of leader and organizer of the proletarian dictatorship and the approaching revolution" [26]. The conclusion suggested itself: without the elimination of any opportunism (read: dissent in the party), it is impossible to carry out role leader construction socialism in one separately taken, country.

AT early 20s for Adoratsky, his work in Istpart and Glavarkhiv, where he was Pokrovsky's deputy, meetings with Lenin were determining. The materials of Lenin's biochronicle, Adoratsky's memoirs "For 18 Years" speak about this in sufficient detail. Lenin contributed to the publication his books "TO. Marx and F. Engels. Letters. Theory and Politics in the Correspondence of Marx and Engels" (Moscow, 1922), where Adoratsky acted as a compiler and commentator "Programs on the Fundamental Questions of Marxism", in which Adoratsky, without going beyond the official doctrine, based on the division into historical epochs on such a criterion as the level of development of the productive forces. In April-May 1922, Adoratsky, on behalf of Lenin prepared benevolent review of NI Bukharin's forthcoming book "The Theory of Historical Materialism", where he noted that it contains more correct than controversial, and suggested that in the textbook more space be devoted to the essence of Marx's dialectics, as well as to explain So, "to none doubt not it remained that one a business material reality, another thing ideas, expression about her" [27].

After of death Lenin Leniniana became one from major topics of scientific activity of Adoratsky. He wrote memoirs, was one of the editors of the third edition of Lenin's works, his selected works in one, three and six volumes, Leninist collections. Such it would seem that academic work could dull the "revolutionary vigilance", but Adoratsky, having made caution his second nature, "set himself up" only once. So, in reviews on the fifth Leninist In the collection in which materials from the time of the first Russian revolution were published, Adoratsky remarked among other things that "it is absurd to try to apply the thoughts of Vladimir Ilyich, expressed by him in relation to the situation of that time, to the present" [28]. This methodological important conclusion on the background inner-party wrestling, which often turned into a quotation war, from the point of view of deliberate orthodoxy sounded on lesser measure ambiguously.

Proximity to Lenin (albeit relative) for many became a well-known obstacle in the transition to the camp of Stalin's apologists. The evolution of Adoratsky took place imperceptibly and, apparently, painlessly. Be that as it may, in the late 1920s he entered the close ranks of the builders of the Stalin cult. December 21, 1929 on the day of the 50th anniversary of the "leader of peoples" editorial article "Pravda" named his "outstanding theorist Leninism". Adoratskiy in Izvestiya (Togo same days) echoed: "Role t. Stalin like a leader the proletariat generally accepted even our enemies. But much less known and rated his meaning as a theorist Leninism". And Further followed conclusion, stamped: "Tov. Stalin is the leader proletariat and simultaneously most outstanding theorist Leninism". AT preface to the six -volume collected works of Lenin (1931 d.) Adoratsky, editor publications, advised Lenin's works study together co Stalinist and claimed what most concentrated exposition Leninist ideas implement in Basics Leninism" Stalin [29]. Of course Stalin passionately dreaming become "outstanding-Xi theorist"; new stage "fight per construction socialism in one separately taken, country" gave to reason for that. read them well lectures About fundamentals Leninism, wide published and advertised, brought Stalin desired recognition [30]. The latter should have been secured by the authority of scientists, among whom was Adoratsky . To him It was given away preference quicker just because what he was known how publisher works Lenin, as reporter, having an experience canonization leader, and man from environment Lenin. His certificate: in parties there were two leader - Lenin and Stalin sounded would earnestly. D. BUT. Volkogonov mentions about correspondence between Stalin and Adoratsky, which, How many can judge, was fairly trustworthy. Thus, the latter suggested publish performance Stalin in time celebrations 50th anniversary Lenin, where, Besides other things talked about mistakes Vladimir Ilyich, on the what Stalin modestly replied: "Speech recorded on merits right, although and needs in editions. But I would not wanted her print: unpleasant talk about mistakes Ilyich [31]. Later, already in 30s years, Adoratskiy asked Stalin write for the forthcoming Comacademy "Philosophical encyclopedia" article about strategies and tactics of Leninism. Truth, and on the this time Stalin answer refusal, citing on the employment practical affairs, and advised apply to Molotov [32].

Emerging in progress fight With opposition theory two leaders in parties and revolution demanded although would quasi scientific justification. Apparently this is circumstance was one from grounds ☐ critics four volume history VKP(b) under editorial Eat. Yaroslavsky, see light in 1926-1929 years, where role Stalin in party history and countries, how considered apologists, was not reflective enough. Anniversary praise Stalin in December 1929 of the year revealed trend to establishing cult his personality in social science, With one hand, a lawsuits over Creative, technical, military intelligentsia, religious figures (the end 20 - start 30s years), mass expressions in relation to a significant part peasantry and So called nepmen, With another, testified about various methods achievements one goal - the destruction of pluralism of opinions, the establishment of unanimity. This process was difficult and multifaceted, but obviously, what creation canonical stories countries and VKP(b) occupied in it important place. Sadly known letter Stalin in magazine "Proletarian" revolution" (1931, No. 6) played in transformation historical-party science in apologetics cult personalities "leader all times and peoples" decisive role [33].

AT end 20 - early 30s gg. administrative career Adoratsky developed on increase: With May 1928 G. he is a representative directors Institute Lenin, then director institute; With March 1930 G. — director of the Historical and Party Institute of the Red Professors [34]; With november 1931 G. - director Institute Marx-Engels-Lenin (IMEL) at Central Committee VKP(b) [35]. AT March 1932 G. general meeting academics science USSR . Adorati valid member academics on specialties story and the theory of scientific communism. He spoke with reports at the international conference and congress (1928, Berlin, Oslo), went out in Paris for collection handwritten materials and personal of things, stored at relatives of Marx [36]. All this is testified about trust to him with sides Stalin and his associates. Adoratskiy promoted to leadership positions in social science at the time of the pogroms of dissidents or those suspected of dissent. Purpose his director IMEL halo on the him a responsibility per propaganda truths "in last authorities." And can It was would definitely assess the role Adoratsky in time pogroms philosophers and history kov, the closure of the Institute of K. Marx and F. Engels at The All-Russian Central Executive Committee, the arrest of its director DB Ryazanov, the curtailment of historical party research ... if not for one circumstance.

As you know, there was no noticeable force that resisted Stalinism in the country. At the time of planting denunciations and threats of real physical violence, proclaiming violence the main method of achieving the set goal, it was difficult to maintain human dignity and scientific honesty. honest man then, on definition one from characters AT. Grossman, forced was commit meanness, but he did it reluctantly. Perhaps this kind of "decent man" was and Adoratsky.

At a philosophical discussion at the Communist Academy (end of 1930), "Deborin's group, Kareva, stan, t. e. those, who not wanted to see in the philosophy of Marxism the theoretical justification of the policy pursued by Stalin [37]. Against the backdrop of fierce controversy and insulting elaboration full of labels, Adoratsky's speech sounded quite restrained. Moreover, he even tried to take Deborin under his protection. Since the latter was accused of underestimating the role of Lenin as a philosopher, of exaggerating the importance works of Hegel and Plekhanov, in isolation of theoretical developments from the political struggle in the country, Adoratsky recalled the respectful attitude of Lenin towards Plekhanov and dwelled in detail on Deborin's introduction to Lenin's collection IX. He noted that although the Lenin Institute edited this introduction, the wording in it was not clear enough, but "on the whole, the editorial melts away that this article is fundamentally correct. Of course, it can be assumed that Adoratsky, defending Deborin, also defended the "honor of the uniform" (after all, the Lenin Institute headed by him was responsible for publishing the Lenin collections), can reproach his in volume, what per Deborina he interceded, a per D. B. Ryazanov No, but after all can and suppose what Adoratsky did then, what to him it seemed possible.

Then, in 1930, there was a discussion about the "Narodnaya Volya". During it, the issue of continuity between the "Jacobins" of the 60s of the 19th century was vigorously discussed. and the Bolsheviks [39]. Adoratsky did not take part in this discussion, but in first rooms magazine "Proletarian" revolution" for 1930, he made a rationale for the need to create scientific biography Lenin "strictly on facts" [40].

39

He considered it important to find out what influence the people of Kazan and Sama ra had on Lenin. "That "Narodnaya Volya training", which NK Krup- skye, not could to be acquiring nowhere once in Kazan and maybe later in Samara" [41] he wrote. This point of view was rejected by the official historiography [42] although she do not refuse depth. Adoratsky failed to write a scientific biography of Lenin (in fact, there is none to this day). In the mid-30s, Lenin's biography could only see the light of day on the condition that cooperation was shown. Lenin and Stalin. It is characteristic that in plan theses, developed IMEL to 10th anniversary of the death of Lenin, the sixth section briefly but expressively called "Stalin".

Adoratsky became part of the administrative system established in the 1930s. Since 1931, having headed the largest social science research institute — IMEL, he had to constantly demonstrate his approval of Stalin's policies and, moreover, to promote her implementation.

On February 12, 1932, at a meeting of IMEL staff, Adoratsky in his speech emphasizing the importance of merging the institutions of Marx, Engels and Lenin into a single institution, because "to study Marx and Engels without Lenin is now, of course, Completely impossible, and, conversely, Lenin cannot be studied. without Marx and Engels". it It was prelude to harsh criticism of the repressed Ryazanov, whom he personally know a lot of years [43]. Adoratskiy stood at the origins of the 4th Collected Works of Lenin, the worst in terms of the selection of documents, he was a member of the editorial board of the 4th and 5th editions of the CPSU (b) in resolutions and decisions of congresses, conferences and Plenums of the Central Committee, the Paris Commune series in documents" and others, he was also among the initiators of the of Stalin's writings. By 1940, the begun in 1928 G. first edition Compositions Marx and Engels (the last two volumes were published due to the outbreak of war in 1946-1947). Of the 28 volumes of the publication -15 were edited by Adoratsky. According to the then existing rule, Stalin decided what to publish from Lenin and what no. Thus, he did not authorize the publication of volume XXXI (3rd edition) of Lenin's Works. Adoratsky's letters to him have been preserved in the Stalin fund. On July 27, 1931, Adoratsky informed Stalin that the Lenin Institute was preparations for the publication of Lenin's collection XIX. Among the documents there are Lenin's statements about concessions. Adoratsky asked permissions on the them publication. Stalin once-

I decided to do it, but with the appropriate comments. There are several similar letters of Adoratsky, and not on all stood Stalin's permissive resolution. They dealt not only with the documents of Lenin, but also of Marx and Engels [44].

After severe criticism of the four-volume "History of the CPSU (b)" under editorial Yaroslavsky, in 1932 The Central Committee of the All-Union Communist Party of Bolsheviks created a group to compile a multi-volume history parties in 3—7 volumes. Member this groups became Adoratsky. On January 16, 1932, the first meeting editorial team, It was decided create
"an extended history of the party, fully covering all periods and problems and designed for party tiv» [45]. To participation in work at first was NI Bukharin was also involved. In June 1933, he reported: "I know all the periods from the preparatory steps abroad to the Fourth Congress inclusive. But I afraid To you promise an article, because the deadlines are short, but there are many things to do, and I won't be able to - almost certainly - fulfill promise" [46].

In March 1935, M. Orakhelashvili, Adoratsky's deputy in the IML and responsible for the publication, informed the members of the editorial board of the "History of the All-Union Communist Party of Bolsheviks" (Stalin, Kaganovich, Molotov, Postyshev, Stetsky , Adoratsky, Pyatnitsko- th) and Secretary of the Central Committee Zhdanov that the development of a draft plan for a four-volume book on the history of the party is being prepared, Xi articles - sections and bibliography. Discovered myself and specific problems. So, AP Kuchkin, one of the authors, Noted what to him difficult write chapter about time before Lenin's arrival in Russia in April 1917, for it is necessary to show by examples (which did not exist in nature) de) that "Comrade Stalin has brought the Party close to a new orientation" and that "the main provisions of Stalin's articles are completely match With main provisions first
Letters from far away" Lenin, in which Noted what
47 "in some local organizations, the beks were part of a united organization with the meks" and this "difficulty educating the masses and bringing them under the Bolshevik banner" [47].
Commissar during the Civil War, a Bolshevik since 1912, Kuchkin probably understood that a true description of the positions of Lenin and Stalin in relation to the Provisional Government or the prospects for the further development of the revolution after February 1917 G. impossible and even dangerous, a because wanted get precise instructions.

In the mid 30s. the idea of a multi-volume edition was absorbed aspiration create textbook on history of the CPSU (b)

— obviously, per thrust to brevity wings fear

to say too much, to talk. Adoratsky received an offer from the commission of the Central Committee to take part in writing this textbook, but considered per the best dodge from this honor. AT letter Stalin (1936 .) G.) he requested not turn on him among the authors of the textbook, motivating this by the fact that busy with the work of publishing the works of Marx and Engel- sa. Adoratsky's refusal was accepted [48] but was not forgotten. Textbook same under editorial personally Stalin came out in light in the second half of 1938 and received the title "History of the All-Union Communist Party (Bolsheviks). Brief well".

Soon Adoratsky completely departed from studies of historical and party topics. Not in the diary entries that Adoratskiy in that time led (although and irregular) or he did not touch on these issues in his letters, so what about the motives failure account for only guess.

In 1933, as the director of IMEL, Adoratsky had to approve a "purge" among the staff of the institute, the expulsion of Rubin, Nikolaevsky, Ter-Vaganyan and others from the institute, the publication of the "hidden" Ryazanov documents of Marx and Engels directed against Kautsky [49] _ . AT then same time he high and, probably, sincerely appreciated the work of MN Pokrovsky, whose memory he dedicated the article. Most of all in the work of Pokrovsky, Adoratsky was impressed by the desire to elucidate the entire history of Russia in a Marxist way, reverence towards Lenin, the desire to put historical science at the service of the proletarian revolution [50].

AM Larina, in her memoirs of NI Bukharin, recalled a trip to Paris at the end of February 1936 by a commission (VV Adoratsky, A. Ya. Arosev and NI Bukharin) to acquire the archive of K. Marx and F. Engels. Stalin expressed a wish get not only those the documents Marx and Engels, who were not in Russia, but also those who were in copies, naming the price for which it was necessary to acquire archive. "Arosev no doubt to bargain Maybe, but I doubt Adoratsky's knowledge, he can slip anything instead of Marx. Only you can check the manuscripts,"— said Stalin [51].

Adoratsky traveled abroad in the 1920s and had experience in acquisition edits Marx and Engels, he rightfully considered one of the best experts and translators of the texts of Marx and Engels, he was the publisher of their first collected works in the country, and all of a sudden this is a comment. One must think that his aim was to flatter Bukharin as soon as possible. than humiliate Adoratsky.

In 1938, the responsibilities were distributed among the members of the IMEL Directorate as follows: Adoratsky — general management of the institute; VG Sorin — management of the work of the Lenin sector; M. BUT. Saveliev - management sector Marx and Engels. The general leadership also included the collection of valuable materials for the party archive. With the start of political processes middle 30s many personal archives began to settle in the NKVD. In many cases, their safety was questionable. February 22, 1935 Adoratsky reminded then boss NKVD G. G. Berry:

"We agreed that upon the arrival of Agranov from Leningrad, You discuss the issue of transferring Zinoviev's libraries and Kamenev IMEL. Adoratskiy then beat alarm: row valuable books from these libraries were discovered in bookstores. At the beginning of 1936, he rejoiced- to the fact that the German Social Democrats are selling IMEL important documents [52].

At that time, there was no place for the materials of convicts even in archives. AT 1939 G. commission Central Committee VKP(b) — MB Mitin, VA Shelomovich, PF Sakharova, VV Adoratsky — found "crime" in the party archive: "Especially necessary Mark, what archive clogged papers of enemies of the people - Trotsky, Zinoviev, Kamenev, Tomsky, Shlyapnikov, Ryazanov, Antonov-Ovseenko and a number of others ... These papers need to be developed in order to reveal the ties of the enemies of the people. Of course, there can be no place for them in the archives of the Party." Measures were taken: "disgraced" documents turned out to be in Sealed safe [53].

To to that time Adoratskiy already not was director of IMEL. twenty January 1939 G. he was released from this position and put in charge editor institute. Stalin spared his, maybe, remembering loyal behavior and old merit. Other fate intended his substitute, Vladimir Gordeevich Sorin the head of the sector Lenin. Sorin was arrested announced "enemy of the people" and died in camps [54]. Director IMEL was appointed M. B. Mitin, . then same academician. AT years wars Adoratskiy was evacuated in Alma-Ata, in October 1943 he returned to Moscow. The last thing he worked on was Marx 's Life and Works .

5 June 1945 G. Adoratskiy died in Kremlin hospital from hypernephroma of the right kidney and was buried at the 4th site cemeteries at Moscow crematoriums [55].

M. N. Pokrovsky, speaking in April 1924 G. on the collect-

Institute of the Communist Academy, said: "... Lenin had his own historical concept, was mine method study of social phenomena, and this was not only with Lenin alone, it left its mark on the entire group that followed [Lenin]. This group was undoubtedly but, and Adoratsky.

* * *

[one] VV Adoratsky about October // Questions of History.—1967.—No. eleven; Maksakov VV Adoratsky VV and his role in the organization of archives in USSR // Proceedings MGIAI.—1962.—T. fifteen; and others

[2] Lenin AT. AND. Full coll. op.— T. 54.— FROM. 233-234.

[3] Alone consider, that the Lininists changed their moral principles and helped Stalin establish a regime of personal power; others - that Stalin was not qualitatively different from the representatives of the Leninist Guards dii and all of them "have the same face, are sewn with one bast, are smeared with one world."— See: Klyamkin I. Why is it difficult to tell the truth // New World.— 1989.— No. 2; Tsipko A. If Trotsky had won... // Daugava. - 1990. - No. 7.

[four] News Central Committee CPSU—1990.—No. 8.—S. 203. [5] RTSKHIDNI.—F. 559.—Op. 1.—D. 2.—L. 2. [6] There same . - F. 124.—Op. 1.—D. 18.—L. 3, four.

[7] Lenin AT. AND. Biographical chronicle.— M., 1971.— T. 2.— FROM. 53.

[eight] RTSKHIDNI.—F. 559.—Op. 1.—D. 184.—L. 68-69.

[9] Adoratskiy AT. AT. Memory of Lenin // Memory about Lenin. - M., 1984.— T. 1.—S. 66-67.

[ten] CGA RT.— F. 199.—Op. 2.—D. 926.—L. 157.

[11] Lenin collection.—M., 1970.— XXXVII.— pp. 15-16. Book of Adoratsky a lot has been published about the state later, see: Adoratsky V. O state. (TO question about method research).— M., 1923.

[12] These money — near 258 thousand rubles - become subject famous litigation between Bolsheviks and the Mensheviks. Bolsheviks handed them over to Kautsky, F. Mehring and K. Zetkin for safekeeping, believing that, having prevailed in party, will receive them entirely. However, because the split in RSDLP reinforced they prudently decided spend them for purely Bolshevik needs. Alas, the "holders" of the money refused.

[13] Leninsky collection. — T. XXIV.— P. 291.

[14] B. I. Lenin and Tatarstan. Sat. dock.— Kazan, 1970.— S. 88.

[fifteen] RTSKHIDNI.—F. 5.—Op. 1.—D. 878.—L. 3; Lenin AT. AND. Full coll. op.-T. 51.—S. 176.

[16] CGA RT. - F. 4882.—Оп. 1.—D. 8.—L. 6.

[17] There ж.— Д. 1.—L. 45- 46.

[eighteen] Adoratskiy AT. Scientific communism Karla Marx. - M., 1923; He same. O theories and practice Leninism. - M. - L., 1924; and others

[19] Adorative B. Scientific communism Carla Marx.— M., 1923.— Ch. 1. - S. 82.

[twenty] Adoratskiy AT. About ideologies // Under banner Marxism.— 1922.— No. 11-12.—S. 201-202.

[21] Marx K. and Engels F. Op.— T. 39.— P. 83. In Soviet social science, p. since Marxism-Leninism adopted a fully ideologized view, these statements traditionally hushed up.

[22] AT. AND. Lenin. Biographical chronicle. - M., 1978.- T. 9.- FROM. 216.

[23] AT parts personal archive Adoratsky, stored in GARF, content-

copies of several documents relating to the history of the creation of the chronicle of history in 1917 are condensed: reports of the meetings of the Eastpart commissions, a note compiled by Adoratsky about the collection of articles devoted to the October revolution, in which he myself was going to participate in as the author of an article on Soviet legislation on church and religion. See: GARF.—F. 332 — Op. 1.—D. ten, 12, fourteen, fifteen. First chronicles
revolution 1917 G. were published in 1923 year. Them the authors N. Avdeev and V. Vladimirov thanked for the advice and practical help before Total Adoratsky.

[24] Adoratsky VV Bolshevism in the struggle for the party in the era of reaction // Communist revolution. - 1926. - No. 23; He is. Lenin in the fight with the opposition // communist revolution.— 1927.— No. 21-22; He is. The October Revolution and the dictatorship of the proletariat in the Menshevik lighting // Revolution rights.- 1927.- No. four. and others

[25] Adoratsky VV Bolshevism during the years of reaction (in the fight against liquidationism, otzovism and Trotskyism. 1908-1914 - M. - L., 1927.

[26] communist revolution.—1926.— No. 23.— FROM. twenty.

[27] RTSKHIDNI.—F. 2.—Op. 1.—D. 23130.—L. one, four.

[28] Seal and revolution.—1926.—Kn. 7.—S. 123.

[29] The six-volume collection of selected works by VI Lenin was translated into Ukrainian, Georgian, Jewish, Tatar, Armenian, Chuvash, Tajik and other languages.

[thirty] cm.: Volkogonov D. BUT. Triumph and tragedy. Political portrait I. AT. Stalin.—M., 1989.-Kn. one.- Ch. 1.—S. 213-216; Tucker R. Stalin. Path to authorities. - M., 1990.- S. 434.

[31] Volkogonov D. BUT. Decree. cit.—Kn. one.- Ch. 2.—S. ten.

[32] There same.— FROM. 154.

[33] See: Mankovskaya IL, Sharapov Yu. P. The cult of personality and historical and party science//Questions stories CPSU.—1988.—No. 5.- FROM. 60-61 .

[34] RTSKHIDNI.—F. 347.—Op. 1.—D. 6.—L. one, 54, 57. For Admission to the institute required at least 10 years of party experience and five years of practical party work. Admission of students to the first course was determined at 200 people. Among them were party worker IG Solts, the future academician BN Ponomarev, and others. The term of study was 3 years. Institute functioned before 1938 of the year.

[35] Adoratskiy wrote in 1931 G., what works on the 17 positions member of many editorial boards of journals and publications, lecturer at universities Moscow and etc.

[36] RTSKHIDNI.—F. 347.—Op. 1.—D. 190.—L. one.

[37] Its results were summed up by Stalin himself, who noted that "in the person of the Deborin group, we have an ideological agency of Menshevism deeply hostile to Marxism — most harmful anti-Marxist group, which must to be exposed before end." it It was Both a political accusation and a sentence. See: Vestnik Kommu- Nistic Academy.—1930.—Kn. 40-41.—S. 13, 17, 19; Mitin B. Combat questions of material dialectics.— M. 1936.— FROM. VI-VII.

[38] Herald Communist Academy.—1930.—Kn. 42.—S. 20-23.

[39] And again, its results turned out to be political rather than scientific assessments. Thus, in the theses of the Department of Culture and Propaganda of the Central Committee of the All-Union Communist Party of Bolsheviks, the interpretation of populism as the ancestor of the Bolsheviks was condemned. ma. cm.: Truth.- 1930 - 9 April.

[40] Adoratskiy AT. To question about scientific biographies Lenin // Proletarskaya revolution.—1930.—No. 1.—S. 3-17; No. 2-3.—S. 3-28. He same. To question about scientific biographies Lenin. - M., 1933.

[41] Proletarian revolution.—1930.— No. one.- FROM. 5.

[42] cm.: AT. AND. Lenin. Biography.- M., 1987.—T. 1.—S. fifteen.
[43] "At the head of the old institute stood Ryazanov," said Adoratsky, "who allowed to in institution, wearer the names of the great leaders of the proletariat, people with an ideology hostile to the proletariat have accumulated, who have distorted and emasculated Marxism... The emasculation of Marxism has become in general the profession of Social Democracy, the Menshevism of the Second International, of which Ryazanov turned out to be an agent." Adoratsky assured, what institute will be work "in light installation Stalin in a letter to the "Proletarian Revolution".— See: RTSKHIDNI.— F. 71.— Op. one.- D. 24.—L. 2, 3, ten.
[44] RTSKHIDNI.—F. 558.—Op. 1.—D. 2974.—L. one; D. 2998.—L. one; D. 2996.—L. one; D. 3040.—L. one.; and others
[45] There же.— Ф. 71.—Оп. 2.—D. 120.—Л. 3-5, 10.
[46] There ж.—Оп. 3.— Д. 189.—Л. 1.
[47] There ж.—Оп. 2.—D. 138.—L. 1; D. 140.—Л. 1- 2.
[48] There же.— Ф. 559.—Оп. 1.—D. 122.—Л. 4.
[49] There же.— Ф. 71— Op. 3.—D. 53.—Л. 2.
[50] Adorative B. B. M. N. Pokrovsky as revolutionary party member, scientist // Archive case. — 1933.— Vyp. 3-4.— S. 10, 12.
[51] Banner. — 1988. — No. 12. - S. 109.
[52] Soon attitude to Soviet organizations in connections With terror turned negative, the International Institute for Social stories, and admission documents due to frontier on the a number of years practically stopped.
[53] cm.: Yakushev FROM. AT. Central party archive in 30s years // Questions of History.—1991.—No. 4-5.—S. 29, 31; He is. From the history of the creation of party archives in USSR//Questions stories CPSU.— 1990.— No. 5.- FROM. 62.
[54] See: AP Kuchkin, Vladimir Gordeevich Sorin//Questions of the history of the CPSU.—1965.—No. 1.—S. 97.
[55] RTSKHIDNI.—F. 559.—Op. 1.—D. 184.—L. 90; D. 155.—L. one.
[56] Herald Communist Academy.—1924.— Book. eight.- FROM. 389.

HOW NIKOLAI VANAG "ATTEMPTED" ON THE STALIN

From his autobiography: "I was born in 1899 in Riga. Latvian. Father is an accountant. He died in 1900. In the years following the death of his father, his mother was a seamstress. I was partly brought up on the funds brother and sisters (old member of the CPSU (b)). cumshot gymnasium, was engaged teaching. To revolutionary movement joined in 1917 G., joining the Bolshevik youth organization (Wolmar, Latvia). AT VKP(b) entered in 1918 G. in Moscow, where ... joined the People's Commissariat of Justice of the RSFSR as a secretary of the publishing house. At the end of 1918 I was sent to Soviet Latvia, where I was appointed a member of the board of the People's Commissariat revisions and control, but actually working as a pro-Darmey in the front line. With the fall of Riga, I remain on the territory of the Owls. Latvia as a member of the revolutionary committee and member county committee parties in front-line Motsinsky county. AT 1919 G., autumn, I am sent to short-term courses in Moscow (the future "Sverdlovka"), which I do not finish due to a shell shock received during an explosion MK in Leontief per., where, along with With some other "Sverdlovites", was present as one of the agitators-propagandists. After being enrolled in the Sverdlovka group, however, I was sent to the Azov-Black Sea region, to Krasnodar (Ekaterinodar) for party work. In Krasnodar I work as a manager. propaganda department district committee RCP(b), a then and secretary one from urban district committees parties.

AT 1921 G. returning in Moscow leaving I volunteered for the Kronstadt front, where I take part as an ordinary soldier in operations on the southern combat sector. In 1922 I entered the institute of the red profession surah, cum his in 1924 G. on historical department. Since my stay at the IKP, I have been teaching at a number of educational institutions in Moscow (Sverdlovka, KUTV, in t them. Liebknecht) and party work in quality propagandist in Krasnopresnensky, Baumansky and Khamovnichesky (now Frunzensky) areas.

Upon completion of the ICP, I remain a teacher of the preparatory branches IKP and scientific employee East-desk Central Committee VKP(b). To this time relate my first scientific work, published in first two volumes of the anniversary publications 1905 year". AT 1925 G. sent to Ukraine (Kharkiv), where working in quality owner departments on stories Russia and Ukraine in communist university them. Artem. AT end 1926 G. from - business trip on the teaching work in IKP (Moscow) and appointed member Presidium RANION, and . and representative owner. AT RANION worked before moment his liquidation (1930 G.). FROM 1926 G. on the present time working continually in IKP in as a professor a also owner departments on history of the USSR. One time (in 1930 G.) was in charge historical branch IKP. hosted active participation in work... on the historical site theoretical front (member Presidium societies Marxist historians, report on the 1st All-Russian conferences Marxist historians). AT 1930 valid member Communist academy. FROM 1932 G. I pass on the work in institute stories Com. academy in quality representative directors institute. AT flow all recent years lead scientific and teaching work (IKP, COUPON, history faculty). AT his area specialties I have row scientific works.

FROM 1927 G. my party work in Moscow flowed in as a speaker, in 1927-29 he was a member of the bureau of the RANION cell, candidate, then and member two compositions Frunzensky district committee VKP(b), in 1930 G. member the Bureau cells of historical branches IKP. AT institute stories before 1934 G. member the Bureau cells. Per time my stay in parties had deviations from general lines parties, expressed in the presence of vacillations of a Trotskyist character in 1924 and 1927 years." [1]

So, we have an autobiography of a relatively young long scientist-historian, who died at the age of 38, ie, in the prime of his creative powers. Biography typical for that time: Bolshevik, participant in the Civil War, studies, teaching and scientific Job. His single out A quick service career, scientific works that became fundamental in the study of the economic history of Russia at the beginning of the 20th century. He was independent of thought, talent researcher [2].

Vanag was a student of Pokrovsky, "a native" of his seminar, but soon became a critic of his teacher. First major Work 26 years old Vanaga - 'Financial capital from Russia on the eve of the World War. Experience of historical and economic research systems financial capital in

Russia" (M., 1925). At that time there were disputes around the Leninist interpretation of imperialism. Lenin spoke of finance capital, seeing in this the merging or merging of banks with industry. There were other definitions: banks dominated industry (R. Hilferding); between capitalism generally" and There is no essential difference between imperialism (MN Pokrovsky). Vanag, Studying the processes of financial capital in Russia, he emphasized the role of foreign capital in its creation and the country's transition to imperialism. In this way, he appeared author hard (and, how it turned out, not universally accepted) conclusion that Russian imperialism was mainly formed by foreign banks, it followed that Russia in the system of powers occupied a semi-colonial position.

This conclusion acquired not so much scientific as political significance, since it was associated with the elucidation of the nature October and prospects socialism in country. Vanag and his supporters (M. Golman, L. Kritzman, S. Ronin) with their developments, they supported the point of view that Russia was not ready to carry out socialist transformations. Even Pokrovsky - what is not less important — announced the concept of "denationalization" of Russian capitalism as the last word science [3].

Then same came to light and other position. Works BUT. Sidorov, E. Granovsky, AND. Ginina proceeded from thesis about availability in Russia national capital, having provided shego R u s s i a n independence . These two directions in studying Russian imperialism — "European" and national — lay down in basis acute political and scientific discussions end 20 - start 30s gg. Of course these directions not were monolithic supporters everyone of them diverged in particulars and between yourself. But essence was exactly in respect to degrees economic development and independence Russia before 1917 year.

Disputes on the All-Union conferences Marxist historians (December 1928-January 1929) were preceded by articles Vanaga and his critics [4]. To this time political situation changed: victory Stalinists ended internal party struggle, on the armament were taken orthodox dogma, rethought historical sources. Under influence conjuncture Vanaga's position evolved. And although on the conferences Vanag stated, what 'refuse from something significant from what has been said we not see grounds", row former its provisions he revised. So, now he not thought Rosthis very semi-colony European powers. Approve, that Russia became colony French financial capital, it was said in his report, It was would so it's ridiculous how much ridiculous is negation other forms dependencies, beside colonial. Russia was in dependencies from foreign financial capital in the form of one from those various forms, which conceivable in era financial capital." Vanag acknowledged also, what in years first world wars National financial capital crepe, appeared own financial entrepreneurs in Russia type Ryabushinsky, Guchkov and others. Vanag saw solution Problems in studying not only statistical and economic material, but and "all aggregate economic and social conditions, in which evolved system financial capital in Russia". Criticism of the Vanaga report was mainly political and labeled. character. AND. Mintz: "I I think what's the circuit t. Vanaga... is only working hypothesis; She's not enough more savvy Leninist material and sweat-mu causes a lot of doubt."

P. Gorin: "I not want to tell, what t. Vanag belongs to Trotskyist breed of people, but all same some warnings and conclusions he could would do and myself". The nature of the criticism was set off by a witty remark M. Golman: "I have to turn to Lenin — Not only to topics quotes, which led t. mints, but also and to those quotes that he did not give either due to ignorance or for strategic reasons (laugh in hall)" [5].

The course of the discussion led the participants of the conference to the need to continue its discussion of the problems of development tiya capitalism in Russia. FROM main report "Problem two ways development capitalism in Russia in works of Lenin" in the section of the history of imperialism of the Society of Marxist Historians, Vanag spokes. He proceeded from the position that "the whole history of Russia since 1861 Until 1917, there is a history of the struggle between two ways of developing capitalism in Russia", that "there is not a single major factor in the social and party life of Russia, starting with the reform 1861 until 1917, which, according to Lenin, would stand aside from the main axis of the struggle of classes and parties for one path or another ("American" or "Prussian") of the bourgeois transformation of Russia" [6]. For Vanaga, Russian capitalism is still was backward and primitive.

This time, the criticism against him was especially harsh. Point in her set Stalin in his letter in magazine

"Proletarian" revolution". Vanag must was put up with and write an open letter to the editors of the Marxist Historian (1932.-№4-5 .— _ pp. 355-359), in which he acknowledged the fallacy of his theory and the fact of "smuggling Trotskyist ideas". He blamed the fact that in his last report and brochure Obviously distorted Leninist decision- Like the question that the proletariat, in its struggle for socialism, is exhausting the revolutionary energy of the struggle of the peasantry against serfdom in order to immediately pass, after the victory over tsarism, together with the poorest peasantry, to the socialist revolution. Miraculously, the semi-colonial position of Russia was transformed into an average level of development of capitalism. The era of the world revolution departed in past, now in price were proof "patterns" victory of socialism in one country. Vanag understood this and refocused. Scientific evidence has given way to political expediency .

For the last four years of his life, Vanag worked actively. Wrote. Learned. In the published textbook for the system of party education, he interpreted serfdom as the strengthening of feudalism, the annexation of new lands from the 16th century, as the creation of a colonial empire. In this regard, he and Tomsinsky were picked up the documents for anthologies [8]. AT works Vanaga end 20 - start 30s gg. already there was no reverence for "commercial capitalism" that was characteristic of his teacher — M.N. Pokrovsky. In 1934, his article was published on his understanding of the military-feudal character of Russian imperialism [9]. He saw in Lenin skoy interpretation this term peculiarity imperialism in Russia, its difference from development in other countries. It was more complete formula, different from those, who under military-feudalism was inclined to understand the policy of tsarism or the specifics of Russian monopolies (BUT. L. Sidorov).

Vanag taught history at Moscow State University, the Pedagogical Institute, and the Institute of Red Professors. He had many students, some of them became professional historians. Among them was Abdurakhman Genazovich Avtorkhanov, Chechen With difficult destiny famous now books
"Technology of power" (Munich, 1959); "The Origin of Partocracy" (Frankfurt am Main, 1973) and others. In his personal file of a student of the Institute of Red Professors, Vanaga's review (June 11, 1934) of his publications, submitted upon admission to the IKP, has been preserved. Wa- naked wrote: 'Works t. Avtorkhanov popular character

and cannot be classified as works of scientific importance, despite the fact that sometimes the author attracts all archival material. The main method of compiling brochures — quotes from the literature of the issue, archival documents, fastened with text author... It seems to me that comrade Avtorkhanov, having received systematic scientific training at the ICP, could become a genuine scientific worker in the field of history. His pamphlets show the author's interest in the subject, familiarity with the archives and a known theoretical background. I do not note individual historical errors found in Avtorkhanov's brochures " [10]. Vanag, in fact, gave Avtorkhanov the opportunity to teach Xi and saw in German future reporter.

Much later, Tarnovsky drew attention to the inconsistency of Stalin's statements [11]. So, in the late 20's. Stalin, following Lenin, Russia attributed to the imperialist countries with medium-developed capitalist relationships. AT this spirit Vanag and wrote and in 1932 he published the textbook "A Brief Essay on the History of the Peoples of the USSR" for students of the middle levels of party education, and with a group of employees prepared a summary of a textbook on the history of the USSR for schools. In 1934, comments followed on the this abstract, signed AND. Stalin, A. Zhdanov, S. Kirov: "The Vanaga group did not complete the task and did not even understand the task itself. She made a summary of Russian history, not the history of the USSR... In the summary... not taken into account dependent role how Russian tsarism, and Russian capitalism from Western European capital, which is why the significance of the October Revolution, as the liberator of Russia from its semi-colonial position, remains unmotivated" [12]. One can only guess what impression these remarks made on Vanaga. - after all, he was required to return to positions that he had recently defended and from which only under pressure refused.

After comments leaders followed decree Central Committee of the CPSU (b) and the Council of People's Commissars of the USSR, which noted: "Especially the textbook on the history of the USSR, presented by the group of Professor Vanaga, was compiled unsatisfactorily, and the same textbook on the elementary course of the history of the USSR for elementary school, presented by the groups of Mints and Lozinsky. The fact that the authors of these textbooks continue to insist on historical definitions and attitudes that have already been repeatedly revealed by the Party and are clearly untenable and based on well-known errors Pokrovsky, Council of People's Commissars and Central Committee not may not disnivate how certificate Togo, what among some parts of our reviewers, especially historys USSR, rooted anti-Marxist, anti-Leninist on essence affairs liquidator, anti-scientific views on the historical science" [13] Decree It was published in "Pravda" 27 Janry 1936 G. BUT one June 1936 G. NKVD began "a business" Vanaga, No. 3257. The thesis about the semi-colonial nature of Russian imperialism (however, without reference to its author) has varied in the historical literature for decades, we walked in Brief well", in then time how Vanag was announced "enemy people."

AT questionnaire arrested Vanaga underlined: professor since 1926, representative. Director of the Institute of History. Family status - wife, Antonina Erastovna Salnikova, daughter Irma - 13 years old, son Valery - 3 years old. During a search of the Moscow apartment, personal documents, writings by Trotsky and Zinoviev, Browning, and notebooks were confiscated. Three weeks after the arrest, on June 21, 1936, the Party Control Commission, in the presence of the NKVD representative Molchanov, ruled out Vanaga from VKP(b). On the next On the next day he was transferred to Leningrad, where arrests were taking place and face-to-face confrontations were being prepared.

Through month active elaboration (already in Moscow, at Lubyanka) he signed all, what to him recommended tracevate major Luzhin. reservations myself, loved ones, simply acquaintances. Two volumes investigative affairs testify about transformation brilliant scientist polemist, personalities in unconditionally consonant on the all dummy. doom, fatigue from ongoing nonsense a wish end - here how blows from written triumphant hand convict protocols.

The scheme was simple: the investigator interrogated the detainee about where he worked, about his acquaintances, and then he united all those named into another "counter-revolutionary organization".

28 July 1936 of the year Vanag "confessed" in volume, what adjoined to Trotskyists With 1923 G., a together With him and The historians Fridlyand, M. Lurie, Tatarov, Piontkovsky, Mints and Elvov. Then signed "indication" about volume, what supposedly Trotsky-Kist-Zinoviev groups functioned in Academy of Sciences, IKP, Moscow State University institute stories, international farm institute, institute Soviet rights, t. e. in all institutions, With which was somehow tied Vanag.

The investigator demanded "evidence" and new names. Those named were immediately immediately arrested, so it was created dossier on the the following victims.

AT flow august from Vanaga knocked out testimony about volume, what somehow at meeting With Tomsinsky that told him about terror and transition to active methods wrestling, that Friedland, in preparing his book on Marat, collaborated With disgraced L. B. Kamenev and "I was amazed at his extensive knowledge in the field of the history of the development of social thoughts". AT September Vanag "remembered" that he "also supported the counter-revolutionary group of Nevsky, which included Nevsky, Anatolyev, Paradisov and Seltzer. Connection With this group established through Pankratova and suggested that the members of the group be published on the pages of the journal "History proletariat", of which he was one of the editors. A few days later, he confirmed: "Dubrovsky, in his work "The Stolypin Reform" and in his essays on the history of agrarian relations, acted as a typical ideologue of the kulaks."

Vanaga's "confessions" are striking in their absurdity. At first, Vanag recalled that once, in 1932, "Volgin told to me about their relatives relations With Teodorovich than, indicated on the importance and need attract him to work in institute stories Comacademy". And here same, from as if would held then same conversation With Volgin:
"We were talking about Stalin's letter to the editors of the Proletarian Revolution magazine. In a conversation with me, Volgin condemned Stalin's letter, talked about the suppression of theoretical thoughts and With outrage responses about repressions against Trotskyists and other counter-revolutionary elements in VKP(b)".

AND, finally, to full delight convict Vanag makes an extremely important statement: "By order Friedland I must was personally kill Stalin." it happened October 14 1936 Vanag explained that he had to make terrorist Act in 1934 year in time discussions on the Politburo question about textbooks stories. AT signed Vanag protocol confession looked So:
Chaired on the meeting Molotov. AT as speaker on question about teaching stories in high school spoke People's Commissariat for Education Bubnov. From acquaintances to me persons in hall meetings saw piontkovsky, Trachtenberg and Focht (teacher middle schools). Hall meetings I left in that moment, when discussed question teaching geography in middle school. At outlet from hall meetings to to me came up Yenukidze. He tried to return me back in Hall. However I, disappointed in failure his intentions kill Stalin hastily retired from building and

came back home." The protocol explained that Vanag did not carry out his terrorist intention, because that there were many people at the meeting; he was late and was far away, he was afraid of not hitting the target, although the browning carried in pocket. Except Togo, Vanag supposedly was sure that at him will be personal conversation co Stalin and then he can shoot him. In the autumn of 1934 he was again in the Kremlin. He and NM Lukin were received by Zhdanov, who conveyed to them Stalin's proposal to rework prospectuses of textbooks and introduce them on the consideration secretaries of the Central Committee. And, of course, in accordance with the cliches of the accusation that existed at that time, Vanag admitted that Friedland offered him to kill Stalin not on his own initiative, a on instructions Trotsky...

AT this protocol truth interspersed With monstrous fabrications. Vanag attended on the meeting but to him, certainly, and in head not came thought neither about what assassination attempt and nobody With him on the this topic not spoke and could not talk, Yes and browning, Considering density Stalin's guards carry in pocket It was absolutely impossible. Here how described this is meeting Piontkovsky in his diary. meeting took place twenty Martha 1934 G., record in diary dated 23 Martha.

"On March 20, unexpectedly in the morning, on behalf of People's Commissar of Education Bubnov, I was summoned to a meeting of the Politburo. They said that they were calling 12 people, without specifying whom. They said the address — Kremlin, Trinity Gates. At 2 o'clock he came to Troitsky gate, but in the Bureau passes it turned out, what nothing about this don't know Yes and passes in building They don't give the Council of People's Commissars from the Trinity Gates, but they give them at Nikolsky gate. I waited for about 10 minutes, Vikhrev drove up, someone else came up, again they went to demand passes. We found out for sure that you can get passes only at the Nikolsky Gate. got there before Nikolsky gate, people added. When we got to the window for issuing passes, they started dictating lists over the telephone in front of us, indicating 12 people. Finally issued passes.

At the meeting of the Politburo got - I, Vanag, Kozlov, Vikhrev — four communist rest non-party — Vasyutinskiy, Gukovsky, Trakhtenberg, Efimov, the author of a textbook for secondary school, Focht... There must have been Lukin and Pankratova, but them on the face not it turned out...

We entered the meeting room in single file. This is a large room, bright, carpeted, no footsteps can be heard. There is a table in the middle of the room, and perpendicular to it are three long table, per which on sides

those present are seated. In total, there were 100 people in the room. Molotov presid ed, Bubnov made a report on textbooks. Stalin sat at a perpendicular table in the In the middle of the middle, Voroshilov was sitting opposite him, and Kaganovich was behind Stalin. Spinning around Kaganovich Rabichev, apparently my, pointed out to him, who has entered in room and gave brief biographical information about us. Stalin got up all the time, smoked handset and walked around between tables serving then and a business replicas on the report Bubnov. Bubnov did disgusting report. clenched time, he focused the entire focus of his report on Nikolsky's textbook. In the end, Stalin interrupted him and asked if he supported whether he his sentence, which It was on hands at members Politburo in written form. Bubnov I said - I support and that it comes from what Stalin said on the past meetings.

Krupskaya came to the aid of Bubnov and began to report that by the end of the second five-year plan, the difference between physical and mental labor would disappear in our country. While Bubnov and Krupskaya were, there was noise in the room, those present were talking among themselves, exchanging impressions and looking at us, as if at an exhibition brought from zoological garden animals.

After Krupskaya, Stalin immediately took the floor. Once began talk Stalin seated in end hall got up and came closer, so a semicircle formed around Stalin, only those closest to the table sat, the rest stood semicircle and With tense attention listened. On the persons It was deepest Attention and complete reference. Stalin spoke very quietly. In his hands he held all the textbooks for high school, spoke with a small accent hitting hand on textbook, stated:
textbooks these nowhere not fit"... What, He speaks, this is such "epoch feudalism, "epoch industrial capitalism",
"age of formations" - all eras and no facts, no events, no people, no specific information, no names, no titles, no content itself. It's no good. That textbooks fit nowhere Stalin repeated repeatedly. We, Stalin said, need textbooks with facts, events and names. History must be history. We need textbooks from the ancient world, the Middle Ages, modern times, the history of the USSR, the history of colonial and oppressed peoples. Bubnov said, maybe not the USSR, but the history of the peoples of Russia. Stalin says — no, the history of the USSR, the Russian people in the past collected other peoples, to the same gathering he started and now. farther, between

by the way, he said, what's the circuit Pokrovsky not Marxist scheme and all trouble went from times influence Pokrovsky ...
". So this is looks in diary records Piontkovsky. AT her, of course No nothing, what testified about some scandalous incidents during the meeting. On the contrary, respectful attention to Stalin's speech, coming ongoing restructuring of historical education, where there should be events, names carefully censored and given in necessary party ideologists interpretation...

Vanag, during interrogation, "suddenly remembered" that Piontkovsky was connected with the Lepeshinskys and knew from them about the impending assassination attempt on Kirov, about which he informed him, Wanagu.

In January 1937, the indictment was signed. In it, Vanag was charged with: "1. Exceptional emphasis on the backwardness of the capitalist development of Russia, denial of the relative progressiveness of such factors how reform 1861 G. Target... was to push through the idea of the impossibility of building socialism in the USSR - the absence of material and subjective prerequisites; ...2. Denial of the Leninist theory of the development of bourgeois-democratic revolutions into the proletarian one. Target — deliberately pushing through the idea of the non-socialist character of the October Revolution. Especially sharply this view smuggling on the face in brochure Vanaga
"Leninskaya concept two ways development capitalism in Russia"; 3. After letters Stalin in editorial journal- "Proletarian revolution" Vanag could not openly deny the theory of the development of the bourgeois-democratic revolution into a socialist one and switched to the position of a veiled denial of the proletarian character of the October Revolution. In fact, this was a direct denial socialist character this revolution; four. Co-deliberately ignored the historically transitory significance of the bourgeois democracy and parliament his the crisis and the opposition of bourgeois democracy to the Soviet, proletarian democracy as its highest form; ... 5. In his writings, Vanag emphasize the organization, expediency and strength of the peasant movement and individual peasant revolts ... This idea was to accurately ... justify the inability of the proletariat to lead the multimillion masses of the working peasantry in USSR, ... 7. AT project and in textbook on stories USSR for middle school and in his teaching Vanag consciously idealized populist fight against tsarism emphasized and stuck out meaning terror

how method revolutionary struggle; ... eight. Vanag deliberately ignored history individual peoples USSR; ....ten. Wa-
naked ignored successes socialist construction in the USSR. ".

And here is a quote from his "confession" "The idea of terror matured in me during 1932-1933". gg. since the publication of Stalin's letter to the editors of the journal Proletarian Revolution. AT early 1934 G. this the idea received quite specific content "I decided to kill Stalin ."

On February 3, 1937, the indictment was approved by Vyshinsky. The main point was the preparation of a terrorist act against the leadership of the party, and therefore Vanag was subject to the application of the law of December 1, 1934 to it. On March 6, he signed that he had read the final version of the indictment .

Almost all the accusation was "based" on the "confessions" knocked out of Vanag and on similar "witnesses" stva" arrested historians SG Tomsinsky, AI Malyshev and others. Stencil and absurdity charges and testimonies written by the investigator's hand were obvious. So, in order to prove the "guilt" of Vanag and the "exposing" of his "criminal activity", the investigation file contains "indication", given 2 June 1936 G. professor S. G. Tomsinsky: From conversations With Vanag I found out his hostility to ... Stalin's letter. Although in an official speech Vanag confessed to his Trotskyist mistakes, in a conversation with me he expressed the exact opposite, saying that he, Vanag, was entirely right. Piontkovsky was of the same opinion and boasted that no Trotskyist mistakes had been exposed in him, although in fact he books abound Trotskyist smuggling." A.I. Malyshev, during interrogation on June 17, 1936, testified: "I tried to hide that I was one of the leaders of the counterrevolutionary Trotskyist-Zinoviev organization LOKA (before his arrest in 1935, Malyshev was deputy director of the Leningrad). branch of the communist academy.— BUT. L.) and what our organization in the fight against the leadership of the CPSU (b) recognized the only possible means individual terror".

"Judged" Vanaga 7 Martha 1937 G. on the closed meetings. Military Collegium of the Supreme Court of the USSR chaired by AT. AT. Ulrich met half an hour: With 18.40 until 19.10.

On the question owner court, recognizes whether he myself in and-new, Vanag answer affirmatively. AT last word he said what mercy at court not asks, on the condescension none hopes not It has. Also not wants make excuses to court and talk about softening circumstances of his guilt. Vanag said what any sentence court he accept how quite deserved.

Sentence read: shooting With confiscation property, in deed stored reference about bringing sentencing in action eight Martha 1937 G.

Through nearly two class 21 May 1956 of the year, Antonina Erastovna Salnikova, widow Vanaga [14], applied in military prosecutor's office USSR With request about destiny husband. According to existing then instructions her reported what Vanag was convicted on the ten years camps and there died.

Tim not less "a business" Vanaga became be checked. Feedback about him, on request convict gave FROM. M. Dubrovsky. He reported what know Vanaga in 1921-1936 gg. "On the Vanag investigation slandered myself and others— wrote former convict and Professor Dubrovsky, - due to this died. I sure, what when revising affairs will be proven what none counterrevolutionary crimes he not did."

fourteen July 1956 G. military collegium Supreme Court of the USSR issued a conclusion: "Checking the case showed that the materials of the investigation of 1936-1937. cannot serve as proof of Vanag's accusation." Soon Vanag was rehabilitated.

* * *

[one] Archive AN Russia. F. three hundred fifty.- Op. 3.— D. 194.— L. 1-4 .

[2] cm.: Tarnovsky TO. N. Soviet historiography Russian imperialism. — M., 1964.

[3] Pokrovsky M. N. October revolution. Sat. Art.— M., 1929.- S. 62.

[four] Vanag N. Toward a Methodology for Studying Financial Capital in Russia, Gindin AND. F. Some controversial questions stories financial capital in Russia//Historian-Marxist. -1929.- No. 12; Vanag N. On the nature of financial capital in Russia.— M., 1930; He is. Leninist concept two ways development capitalism in Russia.-M.-L., 1931.

[5] Proceedings of the First All-Union Conference of Marxist Historians.— M., 1930.—T. 1.—S. 318, 332-335, 353, 359. For more on the discussion, see: Sokolov AT. Y.U. Story and politics. - Tomsk, 1990.- S. 132-147.

[6] Historian-Marxist.—1931.—No. 22; Vanag N. Lenin's concept of two paths development capitalism in Russia.

[7] Historian-Marxist.—1932.— No. 4-5.— FROM. 356.

[8] economic development Russia/Comp. N. Vanag and FROM. Tomsinsky.- M.- L., 1928-1929.—Iss. 1-2.

[9] Vanag N. Lenin about military-feudal imperialism royal Russia // Historian-Marxist. - 1934. - No. 1.

[10] GARF. F. 5143.—Op. one.- D. 255.—L. 12. Avtorkhanov worked in seminar FROM. BUT. piontkovsky, which the featured his So:
"Alive and active. Maybe and wants work. To work apply conscientiously. Undoubtedly growing" (L. fourteen).

[11] Tarnovsky K. N. Decree. So. 56- 57.

[12] To studying history. - M., 1937.- S. 22-23. Thesis about semi-colonial dependence of Russia on the Western European powers was canonized in Brief course stories VKP(b)".

[13] To studying stories.- FROM. 21.

[14] BUT. E. Salnikova fifteen May 1937 G. was expelled from Moscow in Bugu Ruslan, there arrested how wife "enemy people" Vanaga and stayed 8 years in camps.

PER Lack of COMPOSITION CRIMES...»

Before me are two series of investigative cases of Evgenia Solomonovna Ginzburg (1904-1977). On the first of them—1937— neck "keep forever", on the second - 1949 — "secret". in business records of interrogations of Evgenia Solomonovna Ginzburg in Kazan and Magadan, indictments, verdicts of the visiting session of the Military Collegium of the Supreme Court of the USSR and the Special Meeting under the Ministry of State Security USSR, letters and statements of the convict, decision of the Military Collegium of the Supreme Court of the USSR dated June 25, 1955 on the complete rehabilitation of ES Ginzburg "due to the lack of crimes."

The book "Steep route. Chronicle of the Cult of Personality, written by Evgenia Ginzburg, immediately brought her international fame. So much so that sometimes, imagining famous writer Vasily Aksenova, assert that son Evgeniya Ginzburg...

18 years of Evgenia Ginzburg, so cruelly and artlessly described by her in The Steep Route— An unheard-of tragedy for generations of the Soviet people who fell victim to lawlessness and arbitrariness. This is the life of a talented person who has gone through all the circles of hell, who has proven that physically a person can live in incredibly difficult conditions, but not everyone can preserve their spirituality in them. evge- research institutes Ginzburg this is managed.

I confess began read protocols interrogations Ginzburg with prejudice: how much can they be trusted? Do they correspond to what wrote Ginzburg many years later, leaning in mostly on the my memory?

Of course, there are no descriptions of camp and prison life in the protocols, no characteristics of Ginzburg's meetings with fellow camp members and guards, Togo huge peace, what lived in those years behind barbed wire and depicted with merciless accuracy in her book. But they help to reconstruct the past, reveal the psychological, moral confrontation between the two worlds: normal, human, reasonable, wanting to understand why they were arrested? what is the accusation? And a soullessly implacable machine, with devilish tenacity and ingenuity, dragging her victims to the scaffold and per lattice.

O method falsifications and tricks consequences and judicial investigations Ginzburg wrote in letters on the the name of the Chairman Presidium Supreme Council USSR Voroshilov (9 May 1953 G.) and military prosecutor Chief Military Prosecutor's Office , Colonel of Justice Vasiliev (12 February 1954 G.). Wrote from Magadan, asked about rehabilitation (both original letters stored in affairs). From protocol closed judicial meetings away session Military colleges Supreme court USSR in Moscow one august 1937 G.:

"Ginzburg Yevgenia Solomonovna shall be imprisoned for a period of ten years, with the defeat of political rights for a period of five years, with the confiscation of all property belonging to her personally. Term of serving the sentence With offset preliminary conclusions count from February 16, 1937. The verdict is final and subject to appeal. not subject to."

In The Steep Route, Ginzburg admitted that the main her goal in flow eighteen years conclusions and links was to remember to after describe. AT In a letter to her sister, she was more skeptical about the power of her memory. "It's hard for me now, after almost 18 years, to write about all this terrible network that I got into, - Evgenia Solomonovna emphasized, - to try to unravel this network. I don't remember some of the details, The scales of accusations and interrogations have already been erased in the mind, traumatized by the whole subsequent course of events - 18 years of varied and varied suffering, physical sical and moral." She admitted that she could not remember everything, "after all, they did not let me read the whole" case ", with testimonies "witnesses" I know was in excerpts. May be, So and more something there is".

The first volume (No. 2792, 137 numbered sheets) opens with a decree on February 10, 1937 on Ginzburg's arrest. The junior lieutenant of state security Tsarevsky, who drafted this resolution, decided: "Ginzburg Evge- Niya Solomonovna, born in 1904, Jewish, c. USSR, an employee of the newspaper Krasnaya Tatariya, expelled from the CPSU (b) in 1937 for Ph.D. Trotskyist activity living on st. Komleva, house No. 6 sq. 3, - arrest, with production at her search on place her residence, bringing her to criminal liability under Art. 58-10 hours one UK, about how her announce under receipt. Content under guards elect — interior insulator UNKVD by TR. Ginzburg's hand: "The present decision has been announced to me."

Then comes the protocol of the search, as a result of which the 9 general notebooks With edits and 2 convolution Various correspondence, profile of the arrested person. And further — protocols of interrogations. The first one in the case —February 15, 1937 G. Vel his captain Wevers.

— You are accused of participating in the counter-revolutionary Trotskyist organizations and in active Trotskyist struggle With party. Recognize whether You myself in this guilty?
— I do not admit. No Trotskyist struggle with the party led. AT Trotskyist counter-revolutionary organizations not was.

>**Reference.** Tsarevsky Sergey Vyacheslavovich, born in 1898 birth, Russian. Was born in Kazan, member party since 1918, participant in the civil war, higher education. On December 31, 1937, Tsarevsky was arrested in Kazan for "defending the counterrevolutionary enemy position people Bukharin. During consequences got sick. Died in prison hospital 2 May 1938 G.
>
>Vevers Jan Yanovich, born in 1899, Latvian, member of the TASSR troika since 1935. In the post-war period, the minister State Security Latvia. fired from bodies
>12 Martha 1963 G. Died and buried in Riga.

On February 16, Lieutenant of State Security Livanov began interrogating Ginzburg. In the questionnaire arrested instead of "Daughter of a pharmacist" appeared "daughter merchant."

— The evidence you gave to the investigation on February 15 is false," Livanov began. The investigation knows that you are a member of a Trotskyist counter-revolutionary organization and a participant in the active Trotskyist struggle against the party. Recognize whether You myself in this guilty?
— I am my testimony given by me to the investigation on February 15 for 1937, I confirm and do not plead guilty, categorically I deny.
— What do you know about the existence in Kazan of a counter-revolutionary Trotskyist organization under the leadership of Elvova?
I did not know about the existence of a counter-revolutionary Trotskyist organization in Kazan under the leadership of Elvov, found out about this after arrest Elvo...

Hours of daily interrogation Ginzburg, reflected nye in protocols With 16 on twenty February 1937 of the year, concerned her dating With Elvo, Korbut, Ischenko and other already arrested employees of the republican newspaper, the university, the pedagogical institute, the Writers' Union, ie those institutions where Yevgenia Ginzburg worked before her arrest .

Dialog Ginzburg With lieutenant Livanov look- cases So:

— You continue to deny your involvement in activities news counter-revolutionary Trotskyist organizations?

— Categorically I deny.

— You continue to occupy the line of denial. Consequence more once To you recalls, what in there is irrefutable proof of your participation in a counter-revolutionary Trotskyist organization. The investigation once again invites you to think over the line of your behavior and to give investigation sincere indications.

— In the counterrevolutionary organizations are not was. O existence such organizations to me not It was known. Then appeared "proof of": this is were evidence-slanders arrested and face-to-face rates With co-worker tsami.

Elvov, interrogated on April 28, 1935: "Among the editorial staff, the Evgenia Ginzburg, with whom I have been connected at work and personally since autumn 1932 and literally until the moment of his arrest... Ginzburg is the type of a pronounced political gossip who does not know any restraint from philistine-domestic questions to large-scale political ones.

Ishchenko, interrogated on June 10, 1936: "Of the participants in the counter-revolutionary Trotskyist organization, I know the following persons: Elvov NN ... Evgenia Ginzburg was in great friendship with Elvov — worked in the editorial office of Krasnaya Tatariya, a member of the CPSU(b). The task of the organization was to master the leadership of culture in Kazan. In Kazan, the Trotskyist organization was headed by Elvo.

Reference. Elvov Nikolai Naumovich, born in 1901, Jew, party member since November 1918. At the end of the civil war, regimental commissar. Graduated from the Communist University. Ya. Sverdlov in Moscow and the Institute of Red Professors. History professor. One of the authors of the four-volume history of the CPSU(b), published in 1926-1930 gg. under general editorial EM Yaroslavsky. Last job — Head of the Department of History of the Kazan Pedagogical Institute and Professor Kazansky university.

Arrested ten February 1935 G. shot fifteen September 1937 G. Rehabilitated 28 February 1958 G.

Ishchenko Timofei Semyonovich, born in 1903, Russian, member of the party since 1920. Graduated from the Communist University. Ya. Sverdlov in Moscow and graduate school. In 1935, head of the philosophy department of Kazan University, professor. In 1935 he was expelled from the party, before his arrest he worked as a controller East Siberian offices zagotzerno. Arrested 20 May 1936 G. and transported in Kazan. convicted 21 September 1936 to 5 years of ITL. He died in prison on December 1, 1938. Rehabilitated posthumously.

Mikhail Korbut, born in 1899, Pole, party member since 1919. Graduated from Kazan University, historian. Professor of Kazan University and the Institute of Soviet Law and Soviet Construction. convicted twenty February 1933 of the year. shot one august 1937 G. Rehabilitated 28 July 1956 d. Previously consequence led Jr lieutenant Bikchentaev. it he arranged Ginzburg face-to-face rates and firmly lingered in her memory how personification ignorant rudeness and martinetism.

Reference. Bikchentaev gareisha Davletshievich, Born in 1902, Tatar, party member since 1924. Graduated from the Kazan Pedagogical College and the regional Soviet party school. AT Tatar-Bashkir military school in Kazan taught social science. Since 1931, in the organs of the OGPU-NKVD. In 1937, junior lieutenant of state security. On November 26, 1937, he was arrested, "convicted of belonging to a counter-revolutionary right-wing Trotskyite nationalist organization." According to the verdict of the Military Tribunal of the Volga military districts swear to shooting in August 1938 On appeal, the sentence was changed to 10 years in prison, with a loss of political rights for 5 years and confiscation of property. On February 22, 1940, the Military Collegium of the Supreme Court of the USSR ruled that Bikchentaev was convicted on falsified materials. In May 1940, Bikchentaev was released from the Solovetsky prison and returned to Kazan. Further fate Bikchentaeva not clarified.

Witnesses named in Cool route", editorial staff N. Kozlova, AT. Dyakonov, BUT. Azov, BUT. Crinkin, confirmed your opinion consequences about volume, what in edition existed Trotskyist Group and in her included Ginzburg. Later in letter Voroshilov she is wrote how "So called "witness" Dyakonov, signing trembling hand slanderous testimony, formulated investigator, hurt bitter tears here same, at investigator body, pleading forgive his, So how he "not maybe now perish, because what at him only what was born child".

So, Ginzburg was a member of this mythical Trotskyist organization. But what was this organization doing? What did you achieve? What is was in her role Ginzburg?

For Clarification this attracted testimony Safa Vafovich Burgan, deputy editor of the Krasnaya Tatariya newspaper. From testimony Burgana 19 April 1937 G.: "At us in editions Red Tataria" between Trotskyists... there were talks about volume, what Central Committee parties installed incredibly heavy mode, which the absolutely does not allow no criticism superior party body, leaders and them solutions. We were resolutely against such mode B volume including have had in mind and central organ parties
Pravda, which enjoys an unlimited right to criticize and which others criticize not allowed". AT including Trotskyists was listed and Ginzburg...

> **Reference.** Burgan Safa Vafovich, 1899 of the year birth, Tatar, member parties With 1920 G. Graduated Communist university peoples East, journalist and literary editor. Arrested and shot in 1937 G. Rehabilitated posthumously.

21 October 1949 G. Evgeny Ginzburg arrested again. AT then time she is lived on the settlements in Magadan on address: Old sangorodok, frame 2, sq. 21 together With who came to her son future writer Vasily Aksenov. AT this apartment With search came lieutenants play and Chentsov, taken away Photo, personal correspondence, notebooks, certificate, replacing the passport. "Property left son Aksenov AT. P.," she wrote. Ginzburg on protocol search.

In the second volume of the case Ginzburg 43 pages. Their main content is protocols interrogation ginzburg, conducted by the lieutenant Gaidukov. Second my arrest last only month,- wrote Ginzburg in letter Voroshilov.— None new accusations to me not presented, only re-wrote old protocols 37th of the year, specifying row actual data". Really, passed years, much changed. Her father Solomon Natanovich died in Kazan 1938 mother — Rebekah Markovna, pensioner, now lived in Yaroslavl areas, husband - Aksenov Paul Vasilevich — was arrested and was in conclusion, eldest son — Alexei — died in 1942 G. at defense Leningrad, and Jr lived With her in Magadan and studied in ten class. Gaidukov clarified her social origin: merchant's daughter or pharmacist? per what expelled from parties? place work before arrest? asked about volume, what she knows about practical Trotskyist activities persons convicted together With her in 1937 G. And received clear answer:

— On the Trotskyist activities of the persons named by you to me nothing not known.

— You were reading the testimonies of the arrested Trotskyist Safa Burgan, with which you are exposed in the Trotskyist accessories. You confirm them?

— Safa Burgan's assertion that our acquaintance with him was in the nature of Trotskyist relations is false.

— You plead guilty on the merits of the To you accusations?

— I plead not guilty to the charges brought against me. because i never in a Trotskyist organization not was.

AT end affairs — protocol about graduation consequences

On November 15, 1949, the Investigator recorded that Ginzburg, having familiarized himself with the materials of the investigation file, "does not want to add anything to the investigation, he has no complaints, claims and petitions." Here is the medical certificate what Ginzburg suffering vice hearts, a because fit for lung physical labor.

In 1953-1954. Ginzburg addresses the Presidium of the Supreme Council, the Minister of the Interior, and the Federal Prosecutor's Office with a request to review the case. As a result, the investigation of her case was entrusted to the military prosecutor's office of the Volga Military District, at the place of her residence at the time of the first arrest. On October 12 and 13, 1954, on behalf of the military prosecutor of the district, Captain of Justice Kolesnikov met with Ginzburg's former colleagues, who in 1937 accused her of "Trotskyist activities." Protocols interrogations these colleagues preserved.

Dyakonov: "Their testimony from 9 and 19 April 1937 about the participation of Ginzburg in the counter-revolutionary group ... I do not confirm, since I did not know anything about this. AT then time such situation, what Ginzburg, along with others, was arrested and it was announced to all of us that what she is arrested how Trotskyite and enemy people, and because I thought what she is in reality was in counter-revolutionary organizations, a on merits me, except good relationships Ginzburg With Elvo in the service nothing not It was known and unknown and in the present time".

Krinkin stated that he "knows nothing about the existence of any counter-revolutionary Trotskyist group in the editorial office. In this part, my testimony of April 14, 1937 is incorrect... Investigator Bikchentaev, who interrogated me, behaved biased. These testimony, which there are in protocol from 14.4.37 g., I signed because, what at that time formed the situation was very difficult and the contemplative claimed that all this was proved by the material." Other former witnesses tested the same. accusations.

Kolesnikov, having then familiarized himself with the cases of those arrested and their testimonies in a relationship Ginzburg found that they not are basis for her condemnation

On May 31, 1955, the military prosecutor of the Main Military Prosecutor's Office, Captain of Justice Gerasimov, having reviewed the archival and investigative case on charges of Ginzburg ES and the materials of the additional investigation carried out in this case in connection with the complaint of the convicted found that "an additional investigation established new data that confirms Ginzburg's statement that she was convicted on the basis of materials falsified by the investigating authorities. Under these circumstances, he concluded, verdict of the Military Collegium Supreme court USSR on cause Ginzburg E. FROM. cannot remain in force due to newly discovered circumstances subject to cancel."

June 25 1955 Military Collegium of the Supreme Court of the USSR decided a business Ginzburg E. FROM. stop, her out special settlements release.

A receipt from Evgenia Solomonovna stating that she With this decision 3 august 1955 G.

Evgenia Ginzburg told about her "going through the torments" in Cool route". Can to tell, she is suffered right tell reader about volume, what It happened With her and millions of fellow citizens, about those who have passed the martyr's way. On her own fate, Ginzburg showed how, by the force of circumstances, she turned from an atheist and a Bolshevik in believing and anti-communist.

There is almost nothing in the book about the lost specialty, the collapse of professional plans and hopes, about the disqualification professional editor — because they were not repressed only of people, but and future science, those, which more had to work actively. Evgenia Solomonovna, of course belonged to such.

The family of the pharmacist Ginzburg moved from Moscow to Kazan in 1909. Evgenia Solomonovna studied at a private women's gymnasium, graduated from Soviet school No. 3, as they said then, the 2nd stage. In the autumn of 1920 she — Student of the Faculty of Social Sciences of Kazan University. However, two years later, the FON at the university was closed, and Ginzburg was transferred to the 3rd year of the public department (with a specialization in history) of the Kazan East Pedagogical Institute, from which she graduated in June 1924. For some time she taught social science students of the Turko-Tatar workers' faculty, students of the experimental school at the Pedagogical Institute, worked as an assistant at the Department of the History of the West Noah Europe in Tatar communist university.

In 1925-1930. Ginzburg — Assistant at the Department of Methods of Teaching History at the Kazan East Pedagogical Institute. She worked under the guidance of Professor Sergei Platonovich Singalevich [1]. She wrote a lot, enthusiastically dealt with the problems of teaching in schools in France and Germany, local history. The journal Social Science in a Labor School (1928-No. 1; 1930-No. 5-6) saw the publication of her articles Teaching History in the Secondary School of Modern France and On the Question of Teaching research institutes public disciplines in middle school Germany (on the methodological platform of the "Union of Resolute Reformers"). The tone of her articles is quite critical: in French programs omitted fact revolutions 1905 G. and 1917, in German — "above-class phraseology" dominates; but, notices she is, in Germany and France "Even in the conditions of a bureaucratic-centralized school apparatus, teachers pave new paths, fight per new staging teaching history" (1928.—No. 1.—S. 57).

The list of publications by Evgenia Ginzburg includes methodological developments for teachers: "Studying the October Revolution in school II steps" (Kazan, 1927-20 With);
"Noble Kazan. Excursion-methodical essay" (Kazan, 1927,-23 p.) ; Modern Village in School Study. The experience of social science study" (Kazan, 1927. - 15 p.) ; "Social Science Program for the 2nd Concentre of the School of the 2nd Stage" (Kazan, 1927.—18 pp. Jointly With BUT. D. Shaniro).

Soon Ginzburg With her alive enterpricing mind

it began t o seem that, outside of practical work, her studies in methodology were futile. In an autobiography written with admission on the work in Kazansky university, she pointed out that, being a teacher-historian by education, "from the end 1929 retired from work in the region methods stories, So how per recent two of the year I became clear, what this Work especially big horizons are not will open So how it is forbidden study regulation, not scientific and pedagogical work in the field of the subject itself. FROM this time I start teaching in universities in stories VKP(b) and Leninism" [2].

AT 1930-1933 Ginzburg taught the history of the CPSU (b) in VTUZ at soap-making factory them. M. Vakhitova, then went to work at the university. On July 13, 1933, the director of the university, Professor NB Vekslin, asked the Regional Committee of the All-Union Communist Party of Bolsheviks to approve ES Ginzburg as an associate professor of the socio-economic department and "assign her to KSU as a full-time employee." A few months later, Vekslin signed a submission to the university sector of the Narkompros RSFSR about approval Ginzburg in rank Associate Professor at the Department of History of the All-Union Communist Party of Bolsheviks and Leninism. The presentation was accompanied by a detailed description, which began with a certificate of trustworthiness: "Comrade. Ginzburg — party member, in the Bolshevik way, linking his scientific and pedagogical work with everyday active participation in work Tatar party organizations. Tov. Ginzburg in flow 8 years leads work in Kazan universities - first in quality assistant (in rank Pedagogical University Assistant was approved by the GUS), and then as an independent teacher. In the Kazan State university comrade. Ginzburg has been independently teaching the history of the CPSU(b) and Leninism for three years now. During this time, Ginzburg has shown great pedagogical skills and the ability to make students work and assimilate material. AT the first years of his scientific and pedagogical work Comrade. Ginzburg worked in areas methods stories. Per this period she was written a number of articles for questions teaching history and political education in the schools of modern capitalist countries. Tov. Ginzburg worked above German and French materials... Per recent years comrade Ginzburg participates in the research work of the Kazan Institute of Marxism-Leninism. She prepared the material (1-1.5 printed sheets) for 1st volume of the "History of Tataria", published by the historical section of the Institute of Marxism-Leninism (submitted for publication). Tov. Ginzburg accepted participation in compiling stable textbook on historical rii of Tataria, writing the chapter "Tataria in the Revolution of 1905- 1907" (submitted to print). AT currently comrade. Ginzburg works in the East Party Department of the Regional Committee VKP(b), preparing to printing article "Kazan ." party organization during the period of the 7th Party Congress before the Chekhouchredilov intervention" (for collection "Tatar party organization in 1918 G."). On the basis Total declared The directorate of KSU asks for the approval of ES Ginzburg in the rank of associate professor" [3].

On April 8, 1934, ES Ginzburg was approved with the rank of associate professor in the specialty of the history of the All-Union Communist Party of Bolsheviks, and from May 25, 1934 G., in connections With education independent department on the history of Leninism, began to act as head of this department. But in the fall of 1935, Ginzburg was forced was leave university [4].

Personal files of ES Ginzburg, kept in the archival funds of the Kazan University and the Pedagogical Institute, her scientific publications — confirmation of the talent of the historian, one of those whose creative destiny was rudely trampled- on the.

* * *

[one] Singalevich FROM. P. (1887-1954). AT 1938 G. was arrested in connections with his SR the past was forced name all their acquaintances, in volume including and ginzburg, members non-existent organization (consequences for E. FROM. this is not had, t. to. to to that time she is was already condemned).

[2] CGA RT . - F. 1337. - Op. 31.—D. 55.—L. eighteen. Personal a business E. FROM. Ginzburg.

[3] There same.— L. 5.

[four] AT 1952, at the request of the exiled Ginzburg, a certificate was sent to her about volume, what With September 1935 G. she is worked in Kazan university in positions associate professor on stories VKP(b) and Leninism.—CGA RT. - F. 1337. - Op. 31.—D. 55.—L. 35.

REVOLUTIONARY OR HISTORIAN?

AT books about Nicholas Mihaylovich Lukin (1885-1940) - biographical data, analysis of the work of a scientist, story about his public activities [1]. He was born
21 July 1885 G. in Moscow teacher's family, studied at the Faculty of History and Philology of Moscow University, 1915 served assistant professor at the university. In 1918, Lukin was an elected member of the Socialist (later Communist) Academy, and in 1929— a full member of the Academy of Sciences of the USSR. Appointed director of the Institute of History of the Communist Academy (since 1932), editor of the journal "Istorik-Marxist" (since 1935), director Institute stories AN USSR (With 1936 G.).

In a personal personnel record drawn up in March 1930, it was stated that Lukin knew French, English, Greek and Latin, participated in the work of international congresses of historians, in 1936 he reported that he was author 6 monographs and 51 articles (this is only those that were recognized them in quality main) [2].

Following Soviet historiography, IS Galkin even in the title his books about Lukin on the first place put his revolutionary, not scientific activity. It seemed that this was evidence of trustworthiness, loyalty to the regime. Indeed, Lukin had been a Bolshevik since 1904, acted as a party propagandist, cooperated in "Social Democrat" and "Pravda". AT 1923 He wrote a Marxist textbook on modern history for universities and provincial Soviet schools. In the 1920s, he did not hold such high administrative posts as MN Pokrovsky, but he was the same legislator in the field of studying foreign history as Pokrovsky — in the study of domestic.

Opening investigation file no. 20642, I thought that most likely Lukin was arrested as a relative of Bukharin. or because, what his scientific conclusions not coincided with the market requirements of the moment. Getting to know the case understood, what all more difficult.

Lukin arrested 22 august 1938 of the year. On the certificate of arrest Lukin — note: Arrest agreed on phone with com. Vyshinsky. 21.8.38" Then at his apartment, in official office and on the dacha was produced search. On the apartment (Leningrad highway, d. 40, sq. 16) two NKVD operas Sobolev and Krasnobaev confiscated Lukin's party and trade union tickets, passport, notebooks, letters, 25 folders with manuscripts. All this, together with the arrested person, was taken to the Lubyanka. Filled out the questionnaire of the arrested person: academician, executive editor of the journal "Marxist Historian" Russian, member VKP(b) With 1904 Wife — Tatyana Nikolaevna, teacher of English language in air force academy.

Lukin was introduced to the certificate-justification of his arrest. It consisted entirely of slanders knocked out of people who knew the academician. Investigators actively interrogated Lukin Konkin, Panteleev and Koshelev.

Arrested NN Vanag (January 1937): "I know Lukin NM as a member of the Trotskyist-Zinoviev counter-revolutionary terrorist organization. In his cr/r activities, Lukin was associated with the following terrorists known to me: Tomsinsky, Seidel, Friedland and myself, Vanag... I know that Lukin led an active k/r activity at the institute of the Komacademy, led a terrorist group from among the researchers Western historians" [4].

Arrested FROM. G. Tomsinsky showed (June July 1936): "I know that Lukin was organizationally connected with Vanag and Friedland and that he is a convinced supporter Trotsky" [5].

Arrested GS Zaidel: "I suspect that for communication With foreign c/r groups used Academician Lukin NM, who often traveled abroad for personal congresses and congresses" [6].

Professor EB Pashukanis: "I know from Milyutin in 1935 G., what views right shares and included organizational academician Lukin' [7].

"Professor Kunin D. G.: "Despite on the then, what Lukin - member VKP(b), he entirely and fully shares installation right on fight With leadership VKP(b)... Spare center right was created in composition Frumkin, Lukin, Figatner, Melnichansky and Mikhailov... Return to capitalist system - here credo N. M. Lukin" [8] Lukin understood, what accused in terror and cooperation With right, t. e. With Bukharin and others. But because Bukharin was shot 13 Martha 1938 G. Why remembered again about connections With right — after all public process

73

over them was completed a few months ago and the newspapers trumpeted about them complete rout?

On August 24, 1938, after the first interrogations, Lukin found himself in the inner prison of the NKVD. An informer from among those arrested was placed in his cell. He reported to the judge Konkin that Lukin categorically denies the accusations of terrorism, but his "attitude towards the Soviet government is hostile."

Between topics Lukin continued meet With protocols interrogations already dead his colleagues, where contained fictional accusations in his address. Alone not withstood torture and signed all, what them suggested to others enough It was one call on the Lubyanka, To give "required" testimony, third willingly did this is of good will. Frightened Ts. Ya. Shapiro "remembered" that she always Lukin not trusted. BUT. G. Medvedev, employee institute (in 1918-1923 gg. served in Cheka) showed:

"After the assassination of Kirov, a large number of employees of the Institute of History were arrested as enemies of the people: Anatolyev (former secretary of the party committee), Paradisov (member of the party committee), Zeltser, Rubach, Vanag, Piontkovsky, Frid- lyand, Dalin, Dubrovsky, Bibikova, Popov, Zabirov, Frolov and others. Lukin, as director of the institute, aroused political distrust... Recently Popov, an employee of the archeographic sector of the institute, came to me and said that in the archeographic sector there is a group very connected- people among themselves — Morokhovets, Speransky, Rozhkova, Ustyugov. This Group leads myself closed, stands close to Volgin and in his time was close With Trotskyist Nevsky ... According to Popov, this group is set up sharply anti-Soviet."

There are no records of the first interrogations in the investigation file Lukin. Maybe, at first he he resisted as best he could, denied the slanders, emphasizing their absurdity. But after passing mine godfather path, Lukin broken. 9 October 1938 G. he became give "confessions" Bolshevik I have never been ... was in a group of so-called. "left communists" (t. e. together With Bukharin)... On the path active fight against the Soviet power I got up in 1928 when was recruited into the right-wing organization by Bukharin... Bukharin and I have known each other since childhood, and after the October Revolution we lived for a while in the same family... Bukharin gave me the task of training cadres for the organization of the right. In pursuance of this Ryazanov and I, Lukin, in 1929-1930. decided to organize a "special institute of history" at the Academy of Sciences, where bring up their reliable frames for successful fight against the party. Ryazanov e xpressed a proposal to involve specialists in this matter as well: Grushevsky, Platonov and others... The Trotskyist group Friedland".

Calling names, Lukin, apparently knew that these people, with whom he worked together, were no longer alive. Thus, he actually slandered himself, admitting his connection With "enemies people."

16 november 1938 G. convict Panteleev announced to Lukin about graduation consequences [9]. But in early December Lukin had a heart attack from unbearable experiences. While he was in the prison hospital, two informers from those arrested concocted a statement that Lukin was completely not exposed. Consequence resumed — now already with the aim of convicting the sick scientist ... "in espionage activities."

A little bit recovered from disease Lukin called for interrogation on January 19, 1939. Lukin denied the accusation of espionage: Spyware work I never not engaged, I ask you to believe me as a person who has repented of his crimes. He was informed that the investigation into his "case" had been completed and that he was participating in an "anti-Soviet right-wing Trotskyist organization and anti-Soviet and terrorist work, ie in crimes Art. 58-8, 11-58 UK RSFSR". Through day, 21 January 1939 G., Jr convict Koshelev decided that since the charge had been brought, the material evidence (folders with Lukin's manuscripts, books by Zinoviev, Osinsky, Lukin himself from his library) "have no value", and signed Act about them destruction.

On January 24, 1939, the indictment, which noted that "there is no material evidence in the case", approved Chief investigative parts Kobulov.

The court session of the Military Collegium of the Supreme Court of the USSR in the case of Lukin took place only on May 26, 1939. military lawyer Alexeev, in quality members - his deputies, Detisov and Dmitriev. Meeting began in 13.00 in indoors military colleges in Moscow (st. 25 October, d. 23). Chairman announced prosecutor- conclusion, emphasizing in particular: "Defendant Lukin is guilty myself recognized but denies presented to him an indictment on the practical preparation of terrorist acts against the leadership of the party and the Soviet states".

Lukin said what Bukharin — his cousin brother,

what his sister was wife Bukharin and "confessed":
In the period 1928-29. I lectured at Moscow State University on the history of imperialism in Western Europe, smuggling Bukharin- interpretation, throwing out Lenin's critique of imperialism in Western Europe".

The presiding judge was not satisfied with this. He tried to prove meddling Lukin to terror taking advantage of it "confessions" in time consequences.

Chairman: Vanag informed you that, having been called to an appointment with Stalin, he armed himself with a revolver. on the subject killings t. Stalin?

Lukin: This he to me not spoke.

The chairman read out the relevant testimony of Vanag.

Lukin: These testimony are fictional. We went to the Kremlin together with Bubnov, from whom we learned that it would not be Stalin, but Zhdanov, and therefore Vanag, who would receive us, knowing what Stalin us accept not will be, talk about murder his not could...

Chairman: You know Kunin?

Lukin: Kunin is the ex-husband of my first wife. met we With him in 1936 year on the Christmas tree at my daughters... About the murder of comrade. Stalin, I did not speak to him, but in the conditions of the festival (on the tree) we about this talk not could.

Chairman: Were you in the cell with Adamovich?

Lukin: Yes, sat.

Chairman: What you to him did you say?

Lukin: I told him that in my testimony to the investigating authorities I slandered myself, about which I sincerely regret ...

Member of the Court Detissov: When did you break ties with Bukharin?

Lukin: Household ties were broken by me in 1930, official - from 1936 G. ...

As you can see, at the trial, Lukin, who came to his senses, behaved with dignity. In his last, concluding speech, he said: "I ask the court to take into account that, in view of my morbid condition, I could not endure physical impact, due to what I slandered on the myself and slandered others I would not want to die without proving that I did not commit such an accusation that was brought against me. I admitted and I admit that I vacillated from the general line of the VKP(b) Party, did not believe in the victory of collective farm construction, this most I theoretically sympathized "right" ...

but I practically did not carry out any task of this organization .

At 2:00 pm the court retired for lunch and deliberation. At 15.30 was announced sentence: ten years corrective labor camps,
5 years deprivation any political right after departure in a concentration camp and confiscation of everything personally owned by Lukin property.

Lukin's wanderings around the concentration camps did not last long. 16 July 1940 of the year he died from second heart attack, not survived exhausted heart.

Years have passed. The memory of Lukin began to fade, his works were withdrawn from public libraries by order on censorship from eight December 1938 G. From party, he was expelled on August 26, 1938 as arrested by the NKVD. No one thought to stand up for their director, whom more recently hurried to greet and opinion whose opinion was considered the main one in deciding the working and scientific questions.

May 19 1956 to the Chief Military Prosecutor's Office country addressed Maria Solomonovna Markovich. She reported that she knew Lukin from 1922 and although the marriage between was not formally registered with them, but her civil conscience compelled her to apply for a retrial deceased in camps reporter.

The slow rehabilitation machine began to move. Consequence became gather materials about Lukin, studied
"confessions" containing slander-accusations against him. Biographical data of Lukin were requested from the Central Party Archive, from libraries — his main scientific works. The investigator found out that all those who slandered Lukin or rehabilitated or them "affairs" are in sts rehabilitation.

On January 25, 1957, the investigator invited Ts. Ya. Shapiro, a witness in Lukin's "case." She stated that she had worked with Lukin since 1934, that she was an enemy of the Soviet regime he not was, what in 1937 year, afraid arrest, spoke of Lukin as a "non-party member" and only later became convinced that Lukin was not an enemy. Written feedback about Lukin was presented by 24 January 1957 G. corresponding member AN USSR MV Nechkin. "I can attest, she wrote, "that NM Lukin always acted as a genuine Bolshevik ... His arrest aroused regret and bewilderment among the staff of the Academy," no one could understand or guess reasons... He was genuine a historian-researcher who always thoroughly studies documentary material".

March 16, 1957 Military Collegium of the Supreme Court The USSR rehabilitated NM Lukin due to the complete absence in his actions composition crimes.

Now let's turn to creativity Lukin. More in 1919 city, in most height civil war, was published his book about Robespierre. If we treat it as an attempt to explain the present by historical events, then a lot of analogies [10].

In his book, Lukin featuring the Girondins as Compromisers unable to lead movement, admiring Jacobins although and criticized per indecisiveness the first stages of the revolution. The parallels were very obvious. turns out, mortal executions demanded still the Girondins and foreign sends (in Russia: Cadets, Compromisers SRs and Mensheviks and interventionists). That there is terror Jacobins how and red terror Bolsheviks was forced reciprocal measure. They are resorted to to him in progress civil war, to by ourselves not become victims white terror a also because, what "without ." applications organizational violence to the Girondin-monarchist coalition, the Jacobin republic, squeezed into a ring domestic and external enemies finished would inevitably " [11].

Lukin claimed what initiative terror emanated from the people, the Parisian sections and popular societies. Not worth it would study criticism old works Lukina, but you can't not mention, what N. Molchanov led information about the social composition of the victims of the Jacobin terror in 1792-1793: noblemen - less than 9%, peasants—28%, workers — 30% [12]. In Russia, the Red Terror is punished primarily the peasants. So who are the "enemies of the people" if terror main way on the representatives people?

Lukin sang the terror of the Jacobins and in subsequent their works. He proceeded from provisions Leninist articles
"The Threatening Catastrophe and How to Fight It": "The great bourgeois revolutionaries of France ... made their revolution great by means of terror against all oppressors, both landowners and capitalists!" and tried to back it up with facts [13]. Lukin's conclusions based on statements Marx Engels and Lenin, reduced to to that what
"Without the establishment of fixed prices and a system of requisitions of surplus grain and meat, the Jacobin government could not it would be better to supply food neither to its one and a half million army, nor to those city sans-culottes who bore on their shoulders the whole burden of the struggle against the counter-revolution in 1793-1794 years." [14]. Here It was justification

and the activities of food detachments, and food requisitioning, and other extreme measures taken by the Bolsheviks during the years of civil war.

Lukin adhered to similar views in his book on the Paris Commune, published in several editions. 1871 G., where reproached Communards in passive defense and excessive conscientiousness, which became the reasons for their defeat.

In 1928, on the recommendation of MN Pokrovsky, Lukin was put forward in valid members academics Sciences, but when voting took place at a general meeting of academicians in January 1929, it turned out that communist candidates AM Deborin, NM Lukin, and VM Friche did not receive the required number of votes. This result was received by the public resonance and was rated how opposition Act.

5 February 1929 G. Lunacharsky spoke in Izvestiya with threats in address academicians: Our time — era very serious, fiery, and With fire this not recommended to joke nobody. Even people bleached most venerable gray hair and decorated signs differences, acquiring per scientific merit. Even in volume case, if these scientific merit are outside no doubt and recognized representatives revolutionary thoughts". 13 February 1929 G. took place re-ballot, under strong pressure Deborin, Lukin and Fritsche were . academicians. Lukin thought important production holistic Marxist worldview. Becoming at start such general publications, as "World History", he wrote about the importance of systematizing the history of mankind's past in chronological order [15]. These views Lukin defended in reports and at international congresses and numerous discussions domestic reviewers. spring 1930 A discussion took place at the Institute of History of the Communist Academy about G. Zinoviev's article on the history of the German Social Democracy, published in the 16th volume of the Great Soviet Encyclopedia. Lukin was among those who criticized Zinoviev per ignoring opportunism in German social democracy, embellishment of "leftism" Kautsky [16]. According to Lukin, important not Search truth, and then how much material confirm sayings of the classic. Such an approach was characteristic of the then state of historical science, and Lukin was no exception .

At end 1930—early 1931 gg. were held discussions Bourgeois historys West in USSR" and Position and tasks Western European scientific front", Lukin accepted in them active participation. Actually, in those for years there was not a single scientific conference, dedicated new and latest stories West, on the which Lukin would not have made the main report or the final word.

At the end of December 1928-beginning of 1929 the first all-Union conference of Marxist historians was held in Moscow. Lukin delivered a report "Problems of Studying the Epoch of Imperialism". His main conclusion: "The era of imperialism is precisely characterized by the fact that the process of pulling countries backward to advanced countries is done with dizzying speed" - called controversy, a then and condemnation [17].

In during the discussion "Bourgeois Historians of the West in USSR" (December 1930 G.) Lukin, along with With others, demanded critics non-Marxist ideological views. it necessary because, emphasized he, what part of the bourgeois historys spoke against collectivization, and some "become ." active participants anti-Soviet organizations like academicians Tarle or Platonov. Lukin urged to exposure Whole row bourgeois historical concepts, especially concepts those historians who turned out to be related With counterrevolutionary and wreck organizations." Of course he recommended in every possible way support that group non-party reviewers, which tied up their fate With proletarian the state. Subject his sharp critics become works of professors Vipper, Petrushevsky, Kareev, Tarle. Lukin demanded the consolidation of the Marxist cadres of historians and them merciless fight co everyone alien to Marxism-Leninism. Nobody from criticized not said neither the words. Tim not less, Lukin emphasized the importance of this "discussions" which became start "revelations of class companies those or other representatives bourgeois historical science" [18].

In February 1931, the department of the history of the international labor movement and the Comintern of the international Leninist school began to discuss the state of historical science, proceeding from from Togo, what "direction ." all work done in the past did not decisively correspond to the tasks that the party set for the communist historians of the West. In time discussions were are heard requirements "studies" of individual historians. Preparing the transcript of the speech, Lukin made a characteristic insert: "Finishing mine report, wrote he - me express wish that participants upcoming debate, leading resolute, relentless struggle with all anti-Leninist installation in our historical works, not turned Bolshevik self-criticism in indiscriminate accusation some comrades, in negation Total Togo really valuable that was done along the line stories West. Otherwise drafting catalog our transgressions maybe in significant degrees obscure basic task discussions — task to help resolute turn historys West in service side political requirements parties and Comintern" [19].

FROM one hand, Lukin was against "development", With another - swore in fidelity political exchange rate ruling parties. Lukin accepted measure self-defense. AT the country went political judicial processes above scientific intelligentsia. editable them magazine "Historian -Marxist" was subjected to sharp, edgy criticism, it turned out decree Central Committee VKP(b) about tasks scientific workers (March 1931 G.), in which stressed the task of fighting per partisanship and intransigence to currents hostile to Marxism . The Presidium of the Komacademy adopted a resolution "O ." position and tasks on the front history of the West, in which along with With G. E. Zinoviev, in political mistakes accused AT. P. Volgin, Lukin and F. BUT. Rothstein. Lukin, maybe, know about letter Pokrovsky (16 July 1931 G.) in which express decisive protest against critical parts project resolutions "for there are being built on the all famous and leadership holding theoretical posts old comrades monstrous accusations without slightest attempts these substantiate claims..." After all exactly Pokrovsky shortly before this resolution emphasizing: "By Parisian Commune 1871 of the year we we have the only in world literature strictly Marxist work... Lukina [20].

Apparently Lukin all this is seemed disrespect. He published article Per Bolshevik partisanship in historical science. To the results of the discussion on the western section historical front" [21]. AT her criticized and essentially rejected bourgeois historiography (especially social democratic) per proof "the eternal existence of capitalism", the lag of the "western section of the historical front" in the field of studying the post-war period in methodology was self-critically noted .

In 1933, at the VII International Historical Congress in Warsaw, Lukin actively defended the methodological foundations Marxism and them role in development historical science, "exposed" Kautsky and his understanding of imperialism. In 1934, by decision of the Council of People's Commissars, he was appointed editor of a textbook on modern history, became a member of the main editions Big Soviet Encyclopedias.

27 February 1936 G. Lukin, the first director only what created Institute stories AN USSR, spoke to employees With program speech. He pointed out what opening Institute related with party and government regulations on the teaching of history and the development of historical science. "These Events,- spoke he began... reform teaching in primary and middle school, creation history departments in Leningrad, in Moscow, a then and in Saratov, Accordingly, proper staging historical education in our Union, complete revolution in preparing frames. But all these activities were would unfinished, if would they not also touched upon historical research institutions"[22].

Among edits surrendered employees Institute in print in 1937, were "Anthology on the new history" (part 1), edited by Lukin and AV Efremov; collection of materials "Varlen (life and activity) ", edited by tion Lukin; were planned historiographic collections, a textbook on modern history for universities. The plans remained unfulfilled. The combination of Bolshevik revolutionary spirit and fidelity to scientific principles proved futile.

[one] Lukin N. M. Favorites works in Zx volumes. 1960.-T one; Europe in Modern and Contemporary Times / Sat. articles in memory of Academician NM Lukin.— M., 1966; Galkin ISNM Lukin — revolutionary scientist. - M., 1984; Dunaevsky VA, Tsfasman LB Nikolai Mikhailovich Lukin.— M., 1987.

[2] Archive AN Russia.—F. 350.—Op. 3.—D. 231.—L 9-12; TsGAOR.— F. 5143.—Op. 1.—D. 450.— L. 1-2 .

[3] Lukin N. (N. Antonov). The newest story Western Europe. - M., 1923.- Issue. one.

[four] Professor N. N. Vanag was shot eight Martha 1937 G.

[5] Professor FROM. G. Tomsinsky was shot in 1937 G.

[6] Professor G. FROM. Seidel was shot in 1937 G.

[7] Professor E. B. Pashukanis was shot four September 1937 G.

[eight] Professor D. G. Kunin was shot one august 1937 G.

[9] More before this FROM. Zinich hastened declare: "Enemies people — Friedland and Co., and then Lukin, for a long time sabotaged the work on the textbooks... pest Lukin sternuously planted "theory", what Institute stories AN USSR not must study textbooks, that this is the business of the schools themselves, at best, the business of individual employees Institute.— Historian-Marxist.—1938.—No. 6.- S. 200.

[ten] Lukin, later (in 1934 G.) who wrote special article "Lenin and the problem Jacobin dictatorship, know what Lenin saw in Frenchman-

The experience of 1789 and 1871 is "the most valuable material for testing the strategy and tactics of the Russian and international proletariat in its present and f uture revolutions."— See: Lukin NM Selected works.—M., 1960.—T. 1.—S. 322.

[11] There same. FROM. 68-69, 112.
[12] Molchanov AND. Montagnards. M., 1989.—S. 52.
[13] Lukin N. M. Favorites works.— T. one — FROM. 366.
[14] There same.— FROM. 125.
[15] There same.— T. 3.— M., 1963.— FROM. 432.
[16] Marxist historian. -1931.-T. 18-19.—S. 128.
[17] Proceedings of the First All-Union Conference of Marxist Historians.— M., 1930.— T. 2.— S. 49; Resolution of the Presidium of the Communist Academy on the situation and tasks on the front of the history of the West // Proletarskaya revolution.- 1931.- No. 4-5.-S. 184.
[18] Historian-Marxist.— 1931.—T. 21.—S. 44-47, 86.
[19] See: Dunaevsky B. A. Soviet historiography new stories Western countries. 1917-1941 g.— M., 1974.— S. 317-318.
[20] cm.: Sokolov O. D. M. N. Pokrovsky and Soviet historical science. — M., 1970.- S. 100, 253.
[21] Marxist historian. -1931.-T. 22. environment discussions characterizes shorthand report meetings Presidium communist academy 28 May 1931 G. Here several fragments from Lukin's speeches: After all if would we agreed With comrad Feigelson, who said what Lukin, Friedland, Seidel and all company just done now try proceed to studying pre-war imperialism and in practice nothing, beside manure, here No, then organizational conclusions asking themselves yourself because what it is forbidden leave these of people at guides...". Discussion very often reduced to fishing individual mistakes individual comrades because the whole row participants discussions his the most important and first task sink Togo or another friend, having strong to him more mistakes..." - Archive AN Russia. - F. three hundred fifty.- Op. I. - D. 423.—L. eight, 13. Lukin recommended "to participants... debate, leading resolute, irreconcilable fight co all anti-Leninist installation in our historical works, not turned Bolshevik self-criticism in indiscriminate accusation some comrades, in negation Total Togo really valuable what was done on lines stories West." — Dunayevsky AT. BUT. Decree. op. - S. 317-318. However, cooking materials for discussions to publications already after exit letters Stalin Lukin removed this is wish from text, So how any opposition "revelations" began to be regarded how manifestation rotten liberalism".
[22] Dunaevsky B. A. Decree. So. 320-321 .

AGAINST NOSTRADAMUSOV XX CENTURY

Vladimir Ivanovich Nevsky (Feodosy Ivanovich Krivobokov. 1876-1937) is known as a participant in the revolutionary movement in Russia, a propagandist of Leninism, historian, director of the Lenin Library [1]. He considered himself a member party leader since 1897, since working in the Rostov Social Democratic mug, in autobiographies wrote not about scientific research, studying at the natural faculty of Moscow University, but about party work in different cities of the country, meetings with Lenin and other Russian emgrants in Geneva, arrests links, shoots. FROM 1903 G. Joined to Bolsheviks never not left the party, was a professional, worked underground all the time, ... moved lots of searches and arrests set up an illegal printing house in 1903, ... wrote a lot in an illegal (before 1917 G.) and in legal press, ...in general always carried the work of an ordinary worker, "and as the best minutes of his life, he recalled life from hand to mouth, on false documents but With faith and enthusiasm [2].

Lenin saw Nevsky as a reliable and faithful companion. After October 1917 G. that some time entered in the Soviet government, even served as People's Commissar of Railways. Then in different years he — member of the Presidium of the All-Russian Central Executive Committee, rector of the Sverdlovsk University, head of the department for work in the countryside under the Central Committee, member of dozens commissions and boards, delegate many party and Soviet congresses and conferences.

Since 1920, Nevsky began to work actively in Eastpart, briefly headed his Petrograd bureau and edited the Red Chronicle magazine. "I ... being a mathematician by training,— wrote he,- Already after graduating from the Faculty of Mathematics, he devoted himself to a very narrow specialty — history of the revolutionary movement in Russia and related bibliography" [3]. In February 1925, Nevsky was appointed director of the Lenin State Library and held this post for exactly ten years until his arrest.

Nevsky — author several dozens of propaganda, popularizing works on stories revolutionary move-

zheniya, Bolshevism and the Soviets, philosophy. The list of his writings included 570 titles. Among them were publications that have retained their significance even today (for example, the reference book "Figures of the revolutionary movement in Russia. Bibliographic dictionary compiled by him. From the predecessors of Decembrism to the fall of tsarism"), others became an integral part of Soviet historiography. Such are Nevsky's works "From Zemlya i Volya" to the group "Emancipation of Labor" (M., 1930), "Soviets and armed uprising in 1905" (M., 1932), "Essays on the history of the Russian Communist parties" (Pg., 1923. Ch. one),
"Working traffic in January days 1905 of the year" (M., 1930).

All who wrote about Nevsky Note his great capacity for work, erudition, knowledge of European languages, devotion case, to whom he served. Historiographers emphasized modesty his research claims. AT foreword to "Essays on stories RCP" (With. v) Nevsky noted: Book named "Essays" and reader perfectly understands why: we more So few studied our history, at us more So few illuminated the most important moments our history we have published so few materials and documents that more long away before Togo time when can will be write history our parties."

Orthodox historiographers criticized those works of Nevsky, which testified to his doubts, searches truth, independence thoughts. To him were accused of "erroneous" provisions that the Emancipation of Labor group was ancestor revolutionary Marxism in Russia, what only on the III congress RSDLP happened
"first distinct decor how organizational, and ideological principles of Bolshevism", as well as "non-critical exaltation roles Plekhanov". praised same his for "Bolshevik firmness and conviction, consistent criticism of Menshevik views", for the fact that Nevsky in his work "The Third Party Congress" (Moscow, 1927; the book went through five editions) "put forward and substantiated an important thesis, according to to which the Bolsheviks have always advocated champions of the revolutionary unity of the party, while the Mensheviks opponents" [4].

AT special merit was put Nevsky sharp criticism "idealists" and "mechanists" as well as the circumstance that his article "Dialectical Materialism and the Philosophy of Dead Reaction" was printed as an appendix in the second edition of Lenin's book Materialism and Empirio-Criticism, and her positively much appreciated myself Lenin [5]. AT this article Nevsky spoke against works BUT. BUT. Goddanov, at the same time pointing on the them "idealistic" Influence at "Theory historical materialism" N. AND. Bukharin. Philosophers were quite satisfied with Nevsky's argument: Bogdanov is an idealist philosopher, his main idea of the unity ve buildings and development most different system - "com- plexes" - regardless from the material from which they are created his theory systems (biological or social), existing on general laws — metaphysical and abstract, a because torn off from practices co- socialist construction; finally wrong Bogdanov's views and Bukharin already because, what about them With responded with approval "bourgeois sociologist" P. Sorokin [6].

In his historical research, Nevsky, like Pokrovsky and other Marxist historians, proceeded from class assessments. "The peculiarity of the historian, - he wrote, be able to find there is a genuine spirit of class relations in the source, to force the source to speak in a language understandable to us, draw from under its most diverse form the very essence of social, class relations and the very source and its form" [7]. Nevsky believed that only he and his colleagues, Bolsheviks with pre-revolutionary experience, who had mastered Marxism-Leninism, were able to point out the truth, rejecting historical writings based on other methodological premises. In articles and reviews, Nevsky, not embarrassed by harsh epithets, spoke about the works of A.S. Lappo-Danilevsky, AT. AND. pechets, philosophers L. P. Karsavina, N. O. Lossky and others.

Not needs talk about volume, what ideas Bogdanov received a long time ago international confession (after all he stood at beginning synthesis disciplines, without what unthinkable breakthrough in any area human knowledge) or About, what now recognized the moral significance of the Christian philosophy of Karsavin, in center which God and human personality. One from most famous works Nevsky toy pores became his article Nostradamus XX century, in which indiscriminately criticized outgoing then non-Marxist journals. Karsavin, Lossky, M. Gershenzon and other ironically were called "priests Russian academic philosophy, a them "medieval ." mass" were considered as "accidental dislocations of any aging weirdos." Them attachment "to most remote sources theology" explained not personal mental, and social reasons in basis which — anti-Sovietism and idealism. "Whatever the modern bourgeois scientist,- wrote Nevsky,— per philosophy, history, psychology, ethics, he in final account comes to Mrs.

God and, no doubt, the criticism of socialism" [8]. Nevsky continued these arguments in the article "Restoration idealism and struggle With new bourgeoisie, where came to conclusion what attempt parts intelligentsia build
new awareness", taking advantage of NEP, founded on idealism [9].

Nevsky was a passionate bibliophile, collector of manuscripts and books. To him so liked this is Occupation that in 1928 he refused the honor of becoming rector of Moscow State University, preferring the position of director of the library. Nevsky could not be denied a certain independence, aspiration "Dare ." his judgment have" [10].

According to R. Medvedev, Nevsky was arrested after he forbade the removal of "undesirable" political literature from the library funds (he did not obey even when the NKVD officers presented him with a written order from Stalin). "I'm a caretaker" Nevsky declared. "The Party has instructed me to keep all this." [11]. But it is unlikely that this small Fronde came cause arrest.

His arrested in night With 19 on the twenty February 1935 of the year. At searched were withdrawn (and later gone) 76 books,
24 document With personal notes Lenin, 94 personal folders archive, correspondence, archival materials (2066 l.), manuscripts memories about Lenin, "Essays on history of the RCP (b)"—2nd volume and other, mauser, personal the documents. AT investigative deed Nevsky also not indicated cause-
us of arrest. The indictment stated : Consequence on cause anti-Soviet organizations right in november 1936 G. It was established, what convicted for counter-revolutionary activity to five years political insulator in 1935 year Nevsky AT. AND. hid my criminal activity how participant this organizations and not betrayed everyone famous to him participants organizations right." Further, it was reported what Nevsky was re-engaged to the investigation, since the incriminating of LB Kameneva, N. N. Vanaga , former Deputy Nevsky on the construction of the library
by E. G. Kulikov, secretary of the Moscow Committee of the All - Union Communist Party of Bolsheviks N. BUT. Uglanova, P. BUT. Galkina testified about training them assassination attempts on the Stalin and Kaganovich. Then should conclusion, what how terrorist Nevsky subject to court With application law from one December 1934 May 24 1937 Nevsky signed for the indictment conclusions.

Nothing new in comparison with the indictment contained the minutes of the court session. Chairman court 25 May 1937 G.

87

was Ulrich, members —

H. M. Rychkov and D. I. Kandybin. Meeting lasted a little more hours (began in 17 h. 44 min., ended in 18 hours 50 minutes). Nevsky was rendered mortal sentence. He acknowledged myself guilty only in volume, what sharply criticized some party resolutions. From given testimony on the preliminary exploration, he refused. Yes, on interrogation 23 november 1936 G. Nevsky said what "illegal center right stood on the positions terror that Bukharin, Rykov and Tomsk included in compound leadership of the counter-revolutionary organizations right." (Extract from this protocol figured among the testimonies sent out participants Plenum Central Committee VKP(b) in February 1937 for proof of guilt "right"). BUT on the court said that indication, written them personally on the the name of the people's commissar domestic affairs, It was made after long conversation co convict Glebov, which the assured his, what is this necessary in name interests parties and for condemnation of Bukharin and Rykov. He denied herself possibility existence all-Union and Moscow organizations "right" said what not led none conversations With Uglanov and not knows how explain testimony Vanaga and Galkina about volume, what, supposedly he them inspired terrorist thoughts." AT last word Nevsky, judging on protocol record, recalled the facts of his biography. "He is with 1897 yes is member parties and neither once not went out from party ranks. At royal mode he was repeatedly judge and was in exile. He was organizer uprisings in Petrograd and to him, certainly, ashamed anything hide from the court. He did not participate in terrorist organizations and neither in one opposition also not participated. From Zinoviev and Kamenev he refused more before revolution, because I saw that they have personal interests. He criticized the government and the party for allowing the total destruction of livestock for sabotage purposes, but now he sees that these people have been removed from responsible posts. He had a great influence on youth and admits that he does not need it was so sharp to criticize the policy of the party and the government, for this is harmful echo on the youth... He wrote to Stalin about the outrages committed by people who did not take part in the revolutionary movement, like Pyatakov, Yagoda and others, that the latter were corrupting, flattering, harming and abusing their position. He is not the organizer of a terrorist group and terrorist assignments Galkin not gave. He know what Bukharin, Rykov and Tomsk are organi-

congestion of the right, but did not know that they had contacted the Zinoviev-Trotskyist organization."

AT deed stored reference about execution AT. AND. Nevsky May 26, 1937. Neither the explanations in the last word helped on the court, neither negation guilt. Of course the verdict was handed down even before the trial, and the process of the trial itself was only a necessary formality. The materials of the court session did not contain convincing accusations against Nevsky and certainly did not give grounds for so ferocious sentence.

Little is explained and contained in the investigative volumes accusations in address Nevsky co sides frightened and broken physically and psychologically people. For example, LB Kamenev reported on August 14, 1936: "Nevsky. My characterization of his hostility and bitterness is based on personal meetings with him in 1932-1934. He is more Total spread on the topic about strangulation thoughts in the party about the lack of democracy. He personally attributed responsibility for this to Stalin and treated Stalin with hostility. To this was added anger for being removed from the leadership old members Central Committee. He spoke to me often sharply about a group of new students, meaning by this not only students in the field of history, but also their political associates. Of these, I personally met only Paradisov, who was reallyd to the leadership resolutely hostile. "I wanted would write- spoke he,- about volume and friend, but it is forbidden: at us after all think forbidden" [12].

AT investigative deed — several statements Nevsky on name people's commissar domestic affairs. 24 October 1936 G. he wrote what recognizes myself guilty in accessories to the counter-revolutionary organization of the "Right" and is ready to testify. At the same time, he is named among the participants of the organization "right" P. BUT. Galkina, historys N. N. Vanaga, PI Anatolyeva, PP Paradizova, mentioned that he was connected with the former secretary of the Moscow Party Committee N. BUT. Uglanov, although neither Bukharin, neither Uglanov for him no authority. "No one seduced me... My inner mood included me in the organizational illegal system right."

Yegor Fedorovich Kulikov, who worked as Nevsky's deputy during the construction of the Lenin Library, testified that Nevsky was known to him as an active member of the "right" organization. "He had his own counter-revolutionary group, which was part of the organization of the right. From participants groups Nevsky to me known Paradisov and Anatolyev... Nevsky especially viciously treated to Sta-

Lin and instilled hatred for Stalin in the members of his group. Kulikov called Nevsky, Paradizov, and Anatolyev people who "could commit a terrorist attack." At a confrontation in March 1937 G. Nevsky these testimony Kulikov did not confirm. "I affirm— Nevsky said, that he had never been involved in terrorist activities. Your views from Kulikova not hid but I to him not spoke, what ready kill Stalin and Kaganovich".

Attached to the "case" were reports from the seksots, Nevsky's cellmates. On October 6, 1935, one of them reported from the Suzdal political isolator that during the walk Nevsky declared what his and row others persons arrested those people,
who should have been in jail themselves. Another on March 6, 1937, he reported that Nevsky praised the investigation under the tsarist regime, comparing it with the course of his own investigation, and added that "the investigation is being conducted by five investigators, maybe good guys, but illiterate, and that he often them upsets."

On January 31, 1937, Nevsky's wife, Lyubov Vasilievna, wrote to the People's Commissar of Internal Affairs: "Last night, the daughter of VI Nevsky, thirty-one years old, died of transient consumption. A big request to give the opportunity to VI Nevsky to see his daughter for the last time and say goodbye to her. VI Nevsky is in Butyrki." There is no information in the file about what was the reaction to this request. It wasn't up to that, because just at that time Nevsky was actively "processed", So what eight February he wrote on the name Yezhov:
"I I undertake to give sincere and frank testimony about everything I know about the counter-revolutionary terrorist activities of the organization of the right. Please believe me."

The next day, February 9, 1937, Nevsky announced that since 1929, since his work as the head of the chair of the history of the revolutionary movement at RANION, a group of young historians formed around him: Paradisov, Anatolyev, Rubach, and others. "I disagreed with holding in life some the most important installation parties. As an example — attitude and practical implementation of party policy in the field of education, science, freedom of discussion and criticism. He showed that he had a bad attitude to Trotsky Zinoviev and Kamenev better — to Bukharin, whom he did not consider a counter-revolutionary .

This statement by Nevsky is accompanied by testimonies of historians Paradisova and Anatolyeva[13]. First arrested 2 February 1935 of the year and soon swear to 5 year old conclusion. In 1937, Paradizov's "case" was reviewed, his judged again. AT last word he said that his connection with Nevsky and Anatolyev was expressed only in conversations of an anti-Soviet nature, but there was no talk of terror.

Anatolyev was arrested together with Paradizov on February 2, 1935 and also charged to 5 years in the camps. Then a gossip followed, and as a result, on June 19, 1937, Anatolyev was shot, a day earlier than Paradizov. On repeat court Anatolyev showed what in 1927-1929 years at the Institute of History of the Komakademiya there was "the dominance of anti-Marxists", because they in chapter With Nevsky united to the section of new Russian history. "I completely deny the testimony of VI Nevsky about my belonging to the counter-revolutionary organization of the right. They are fictional from beginning to end. I was absolutely unaware of any connection of Nevsky and his entry into the organization of the right.

AT deed available document, how would confirming Nevsky's "connection" with Trotsky. This is a retelling of Nevsky's letter to Trotsky dated April 30, 1927 (note in the text: found during a search of Trotsky's apartment): "In the letter, Nevsky stated that he shared the addressee's pessimism, explaining that there were grounds for this , ob- Denia over life leads to the conclusion that "the country is strongly to the right." AT the confirmation this thoughts pointed out on the

"the ever-growing bestial anti-Semitism, wholesale drunkenness, the growth of the peasant bourgeoisie, some phenomena on the theoretical front ... events in the West, our economic phenomena ("decrease prices") and t. P., conversations workers, peasants, them thoughts, behavior".

AT then time, when from arrested knocked out ridiculous "confessions", there were meetings, articles were published in which Innocent, public opinion was preparing to condemn the "enemies" and approve the actions of the authorities. Yaroslavsky on the pages "Historian-Marxist" (1936.-
No. 4. — P. 3-16) attacked his recent like-minded people: "... On the historical front ... such double-dealers, such renegades and participants in counter-revolutionary organizations as Nevsky, Zaidel, Rubach, Malyshev , Prigogine, Kiparisov, Anatolyev, Paradisov, Friedland, Vanag, dalin, Lozinsky, Tomsinsky and other, ... converging on the denial of the greatest role of Lenin and Stalin ... and especially those who tried to blur and hush up the greatest role of comrade. Stalin as a brilliant successor great affairs Lenin... BUT after all in them hands... was

the entire journal "History of the Proletariat", ... they "were in leadership magazine Marxist Historian.

Shortly before the appearance of this article, on April 15, 1935, about two months after Nevsky's arrest, a "closed meeting" of the Presidium of the Communist Academy was held. The reaction to the January (1935) letter Central Committee VKP(b), sent out in party organizations in connection with the murder of SM Kirov. The main report was made by party historian MA Savelyev, who stated that that during the "first quarter" of 1935, 40 researchers were dismissed from the institutes of the academy, which is especially "unfavorable at the Institute of History, in the ... these double-dealers, counter-revolutionaries from the Nevsky-Anatolyev company, what Nevsky is _ "soundrel pest" [14].

5 May 1954 of the year Love Vasilevna, widow Nevsky, contacted military prosecutor's office With request refise a business husband. At verification turned out his, a also Paradisova and Anatolyeva innocence. "O ." frivolity of testimony Vanaga and Fridland, wrote investigator, checking "case" and them depravity testifies that fact, what to number participants counter-revolutionary organizations and _ terrorists they unfounded attributed, except Nevsky, and a number of other persons which not being nothing compromised, are in the present time featured figures Soviet science" (there were in mind BUT. M. Pankratova and M. AT. Nechkin). found out what investigator-executioner Nevsky - Zinovy Glebov, 1903 of the year birth, was myself arrested fourteen September 1938 G. and in January 1940 was shot per falsification investigative affairs, application methods physical impact on the exploration, blackmail arrested.

Academician AND. AND. mints on the request convict prosecutor's offices to give review about Nevsky pointed out what With him not worked and advised apply to A. M. Pankratova. 25 April 1955 of the year Pankratova in recall about Nevsky noted:

"AT. AND. Nevsky I know how editor parties. We worked together in Communist academy in 1929- 1932 gg. He was member of the Presidium academy and entered in of the editorial board of the collection "History of the proletariat of the USSR", which I edited... Personally I know more other PI Anatolyev, who wrote under my leadership a large work on the history of the Marxist organization in Russia in the 80s, never completed it ... I only remember about Nevsky that he was a soft and delicate person century and very industrious. He was beautiful propagandist and a well-educated man, even before his arrest, he was popular among the intelligentsia as an old Bolshevik and responsive human".

Military Collegium of the Supreme Court of the USSR June 1, 1955 fully restored in civil rights name AT. AND. Nevsky.

* * *

[1] Chesnokov VIVI Nevsky as a historian of the Russian revolutionary movement // History and historians.— M., 1965; Pushkareva I. Revolutionary, historian of the revolution // Communist.— 1976.— No. 8; and others, as well as: Figures of the USSR and the revolutionary movement in Russia. Encyclopedic dictionary Pomegranate - M., 1989.
[2] Figures USSR...- FROM. 564.
[3] Story USSR.- 1967.—No. 1.—S. 107.
[four] There is nothing and to say that, in fact, representatives of the Mensheviks were also supporters of unity. In March 1917, many local organizations of the RSDLP called themselves united, despite the decisions of the Prague Party Conference of the Bolsheviks. (1912) about separation and the demands of the leaders of Bolshevism after the legalization of political parties in February 1917 for a separate functioning.— See: Essays stories historical science in USSR M., 1966.—T. IV. - S. 365; Communist.- 1976.— No. 8.- S. 86.
[5] Lenin AT. AND. Full coll. op.— T. eighteen.- FROM. 17.
[6] Klushin VI The role of VI Nevsky in the Marxist interpretation of history (1918-1925 .) years)//Philosophical science.— 1970.— No. 1.- S. 130-137.
[7] Nevsky AT. AND. Essays on stories RKP.— FROM. 524.
[eight] Under banner Marxism.— 1922.— No. four.- FROM. 98.
[9] There same.— No. 7-8.— FROM. 122-126 .
[ten] AT 1930 Nevsky wrote a letter to Stalin, objecting to the destruction of the Chudov and Ascension monasteries, referring to the fact that the preservation of monuments — part of party politics.— History of the USSR.— 1967.—No. 1.- S. 108-110.
[eleven] Banner.- 1989.—No. 2.— FROM. 201.
[12] Kamenev did not fail at the same time to cast a shadow on his enemy Yemelyan Yaroslavsky. He "suddenly" remembered the conversation with I.A. Teodorovich, which the spoke to him: "your mistake not in 1925 a in 1917, when you dropped your objects about the impossibility of a socialist revolution in a country like Russia. Kamenev: "Teodorovich told me that he was on good terms and saw each other often. With Yaroslavsky, which the often helps out his from trouble, in connections With his, Teodorovich, editing "Katorga and links." On the my astonishment, how he co their own sentiments finds common language with Yaroslavsky, Teodorovich answered me: "Of course, Yaroslavsky appears to you very one-sidedly. In fact, he is not what I think, he himself is critical of many things, and after the blow he received about his history of the party, he is very angry with Stalin and, although he admitted his admit, he begins to understand where this regime is leading, which he himself supported. These words of Teodorovich were confirmed by Zinoviev's message to me. (I don't know where he got it from) that Yaroslavsky's wife, Kirsanov, in connection with Stalin's criticism historical works Yaroslavsky, configured very evil against Stalin and not shy sharp express yourself about German in his circle."

From these and other testimonies of Kamenev it is clear that he was answering the specially asked questions of the investigators, who "just in case" collected dossier on the Yaroslavsky and others persons.

[13] Pyotr Pavlovich Paradizov, born in 1906, member of the Bolshevik Party since 1926, worked as a researcher at the Institute of History of the Communist Academy, was the author of several works on history working class in Russia. P. P. Paradisov was shot
June 20, 1937 Paradisov's letters to the family from the Chelyabinsk detention center see: EN Nikitin. Archive of the historian PP Paradizov // Archaeographic yearbook per 1988 year.—M., 1989.—S. 237-252.

Pavel Ilyich Anatolyev, born in 1897, Bolshevik since 1919, researcher employee of the Institute of History of the Communist Academy, author articles about working movement in Russia in XIX century, stories strikes, etc.

[fourteen] Archive AN Russia.—F. 350.—Op. 1.—D. 997.—L. 6, 8-10.

CHOICE FATE And FATE CHOICE

Investigative a business Sergei Andreevich Piontkovsky (1891 .) — 1937) takes three volumes. Actually, all his life is located in protocol first volumes No. 3257. Two other — this is identical texts diary editor per 1927- 1934 gg [1].

The first volume opens warrant No. 8636 from 7 October 1936 G. on the arrest and search FROM. BUT. piontkovsky, living in Moscow on address: square Sverdlov, d. 2/4, apt. 313. Co. time arrest Piontkovsky It was 45 years. FROM him lived his retired mother Elena Grigorievna and wife - Elizabeth Mikhailovna Chermenskaya. At During the search they seized: party and trade union tickets, two diary folders, notebooks, books, leaflets, copies of documents. AT resolution about arrest, signed chief 5th branch secret political department M. L. Gatov, Piontkovsky accused in volume, what he "is member of the counter-revolutionary Trotskyist-Zinovivist terrorist group organizations. By order Trotskyist-Zinovivist center, in particular Prigogine, led training to commit terrorist attack above comrad Stalin." From Togo same document should have what next "counterrevolutionary"
"enemy of the people" was exposed by other active members of the named organization - Prigozhin, Friedland, Vanag and Tomsinsky. Needless to say, historians were beaten out of ridiculous, but necessary by the investigation, confessions-slanders in order to create the appearance of "disclosing" another "terrorist" organizations."

Another scene was coming up in the theater of the absurd, from the stages of which a sepulchral eerie cold blew. The script was written in advance, the roles were distributed, the actors were prepared, the tragic ending was almost a foregone conclusion. After all, the enemies must to be all more and more: class struggle on measure promotion to socialism escalates So learned leader, a he, how known not is wrong.

To Piontkovsky were applied measure impact and through month after arrest editor "confessed" what he "double-dealer", led organizational Trotskyist counterrevolutionary_ _ work, being participant counterrevolutionary

Noah illegal Trotskyist groups on the historical front led Mintz, Elvo and etc."

Minulo several days Piontkovsky a little came to myself and refused from knocked out "confessions".

From protocol interrogation 16 november 1936 G.:

Gate: Consequence has data about volume, what you are active member counter-revolutionary Trotsky-Kist-Zinovievskaya organizations. Recognize whether you this is?

Piontkovsky: It's monstrous In no case can I admit the accusation, because not only am I not a member of a Trotskyist counter-revolutionary organization, but I have not participated in any anti-Party groupings in the past and have always actively advocated the general line of the CPSU (b).

Gatov was not embarrassed by such a turn of affairs: senior comrades constantly instructed the Chekists that the enemy was cunning, cunning, dodgy, so he prepared a plan for further processing of the arrested person, relying on forced slander others historians - "members organizations."

Evidence of counter-revolutionary intentions and deeds, the historians' commitment to Trotskyism, the contempt also looked for in his diary. Here is the required passage — diary record per 23-29 October 1927 of the year. "In the evening lectured at the GMTU on October revolution - piontkovsky noted, — was reading era wars and February, took apart and compared to the forecast of the revolution given by Lenin and Trotsky during the war and their assessment of the February Revolution. During the lecture, a group of children began to whisper and laugh. I suggested that they stay after the lecture and explaining what was the matter, rather than whispering and thus making me nervous. After the lecture, they enthusiastically told me that I was reading tendentiously and at all not So, how It follows that I am tendentious in two respects: I paid too much attention to Trotsky's mistakes during the war and at the moment of the February Revolution. Trotsky, as one of them told me with the greatest fury, did not individual flow time. Therefore, to talk about his mistakes during the war and at the time of the February Revolution is completely unnecessary. I said that I rank Trotsky higher than they do, and I consider, of course, that Trotsky represents an undoubtedly sharply expressed and delineated trend social democratic thoughts".

The investigator underlined the last sentence, and after reading out, Probingly looked on the Piontkovsky.

— Yes,- said reporter.- Wording in diary

various, but no connections With Trotskyist organization at me not It was and no.

Gateow posted new cards - indications editors N. Elvova and his wives M. Bychkova, G. Fridlyand, S. Tomsinsky, A. Prigozhin, provocateur Y. Elkovich. The compromising material collected was like a firing squad. Thus, Elvov called Piontkovsky's statements about the party "slanderous"; Friedland included him in the "Trotskyite terrorist groups Prigogine"; last
"confessed" that at a meeting with Piontkovsky in early January 1935, he agreed to take part in a terrorist group. But here same did disclaimer: Keep in mind Comely, myself I fire I won't." Elkovich assured that already in 1919 Piontkovsky was a "Zinovivist" in his political moods, that he collected documents from the opposition and therefore they saw him as a specialist who could in the future "illuminate in the proper spirit the entire history of the struggle of the Trotskyist-Zinovivist organization against VKP(b)".

Reason Investigator Piontkovsky did not listen, but he already clear saw, which before him opened up abyss, and then, what a business stitched white threads. Yes, in 1931-1932 in conversations With Mintz, Elvo, FROM. Dubrovsky, B. Grave, they "started from the fact that on the historical front-those conditions are created under which it is impossible to work, that these conditions hinder the development of theoretical thought, what creative Work is replaced treasury", But where same here slander, counter-revolution?

Bychkova claims that during the meetings, the named historians, in volume including and he, led 'anti-party conversations" and there was an "organizational connection" between them. However, she said nothing about the content of their conversations in June 1935. could remember. And no wonder. Returning after a long stay in the camps, Bychkova in 1958 said that in time interrogations answers per her composed investigator,
"Wrote Wrong" content these protocols were simply fabricated. She admitted that only a few times was visiting Piontkovsky with her husband, that the contemptuous set "unbearable tasks" for her, demanding to characterize reviewers, which she is nearly not knew.

What was left for Piontkovsky to do? Shocked by the lie and almost despairing, he writes a statement addressed to the commissioner state security I. Agranova: "I beg You, t. commissioner, call me and personally interrogate. I I am accused of the gravest crimes for a citizen of the Union. Accessory to Trotskyist terrorist organizations.

I deny this accusation and ask you, and in your person the Soviet government, to carry out another investigation into this case. On the statement, Agranov's resolution: "To Molchanov." Then Molchanov - Gatov: "In business." And that's it. The voice of one who cries in wilderness socialist legitimacy." Nobody and no need It was listen to him.

accusatory conclusion on cause Piontkovsky was prepared less how per two month. 3 December 1936 his year signed prosecutor Union BUT. Vyshinsky. Captain GB Gatov brought consequence before end. What need It was "prove", then and "proven"... characteristic detail: closing indictment nearly verbatim coincided With resolution about the arrest. Piontkovsky accused in, what "was a participant counter-revolutionary Trotskyist-Zinovivist organizations carried out one December 1934 of the year assassination of Kirov and preparing in recent years (1934-1936 .) years) terrorist attacks against leaders VKP(b) and Soviet governments; entered in compound combat terrorist groups etc. n. active actions", led terrorist Prigogine; gave agreement Prigogine on the participation in terrorist activities and accepted from him exercise recruit from numbers students several persons, able to be performer terrorist attack above t. Stalin." Summary, of course. It was otherwise: "Due to stated, Piontkovskiy FROM. BUT. subject to court Military colleges Supreme court Union SSR With application law from one December 1934".

After statements Military collegium Supreme Courts of the USSR accusatory conclusions, a happened this is the 5th of March 1937 of the year,- it It was awarded Piontkovsky. Through two days began hearing affairs, process was closed. To the question of the chairman, Does Piontkovsky recognize myself guilty editor answered: "Not, not I admit." He said what participant terrorist was not an organization, was not a double-dealer, the content of his own them testimony now thinks wrong. "On the all over preliminary investigation his condition it was like this - transmits the words accused protocol,- what he signed statements with which he did not agree. Piontkovsky denied testimony about yourself Prigogine, Friedland, Tomsinsky, Elvo. Let's resort again to protocol. "With everyone listed persons him never no personal accounts not It was. Explain, why they all give incriminating his testimony, not maybe". Only, With how Piontkovsky agreed,— this is with imprecise wording diary.

In his last speech, Piontkovsky once again emphasized that he is not a Trotskyite, but the author of several articles against Trotskyism, that he had no terrorist intentions. "I can still do a lot of good for the Soviet government. and I beg court to give to me possibility honestly work for good parties and socialist motherland."

The court did not find such an opportunity, however, and did not look for it. With a completely different purpose, the Military Collegium of the Supreme Court, consisting of the military lawyer V. Ulrich, military lawyers I. Nikitchenko and N. Rychkov, gathered for a meeting. In 55 minutes - a exactly so many last meeting, - it was only possible to stamp the decision taken in advance. Sentence same read: "Piontkovsky Sergei Andreevich to capital punishment — execution by firing squad with confiscation of all personal property belonging to him. The verdict is final and not subject to appeal. decrees Central Executive Committee of the USSR from one December 1934 subject to immediate execution." AT night With 7 on the eight Martha 1937 G. Piontkovsky not became.

On May 10, 1956 Andrey Andreevich Piontkovsky addressed to main military prosecutor countries With a request to reconsider the case of the deceased brother. He pointed out that the information about German may to give historys BUT. M. Pankratova, II Mints, EN Burdzhalov, EN Gorodetsky, GN Anpilogov, who knew convict.

Reviews have been preserved in the rehabilitation case. Let's reproduce some of them. Burdzhalov, deputy editor-in-chief of the Voprosy istorii magazine, who studied under Piontkovsky in 1929-1933, wrote: "All of us, communist students, knew SA Piontkovsky as an educated Marxist, a profound researcher and a good teacher.. In the person of SA Piontkovsky, we saw an example of a Bolshevik historian, a fighter for Leninism in politics and science." According to Anpilogov, Associate Professor of Moscow University, "he was a good scientist — bold and sharp in judgment, outwardly seemed rude, but in essence - a simple, attentive and sensitive scientist-communist. Academician Pankratova: "I knew Professor Piontkovsky as one of the greatest specialists in the history of the USSR... among historians, Professor Piontkovsky was considered one from most orthodox reviewers, and his arrest in his time called bewilderment, So how none information about volume, to he was tied With Trotskyist elements at us not It was".

Other reviews were also very positive. But this is now, twenty years later. BUT then writing about

Piontkovsky or silenced or used his name in a stamped ostracized set. Belated repentance, although others did not even know it ...

On June 7, 1956, the Military Collegium of the Supreme Court ruled acquittal conclusion in connections With revision "cases" of SA Piontkovsky. An unbiased consequence established nonsense in accusatory imprisonment and testimonies of the accused. "Prigozhin testedified during the preliminary investigation that he learned about Piontkovsky's participation in the anti-Soviet organization from Friedland, but Fridland did not speak about Piontkovsky in this regard... another case Elvov, in addition to Piontkovsky, named Mints, Sidorov, members of the anti-Soviet organization, Rubinstein and Dubrovsky, but these these individuals are currently well-known figures in Soviet historical science... Tomsinsky has been rehabilitated, Elkovich convicted per falsification, Gateow shot for crimes."

In same month that same instance sentence 7 March 1937 in relation to Piontkovsky was canceled and the case was dismissed due to the lack of corpus delicti. A copy of the document was sent to the historian's wife, Elizaveta Mikhailovna Chermenskaya, which together With topics reported another lie: they say, SA Piontkovsky died in camp on April 14, 1940. This was required by the instructions. The totalitarian regime hushed up the truth about mass executions innocent of people, because and practiced
"softening" messages about of death in camps on illness.

This is all that the investigation file reported. And it is completely unclear who Piontkovsky was, why did he "receive" such close attention from the NKVD? Why so tragic ended his life?

The name and works of Sergei Andreevich Piontkovsky were well known, especially during the formation of Soviet historical science. Piontkovsky was among the first members Eastparta, approved in early September 1920 by the decision of the Politburo of the Central Committee of the RCP (b) [3]. Since May of the following year, he has been a professor at the Department of the History of the Communist university them. I. M. Sverdlov and at the same time, deputy editor of the journal Proletarian Revolution. In 1922 Piontkovsky — full member of the newly opened scientific research institute at the Communist University in Petrograd. He worked at the Institute of Red Professors, the Communist Academy, the Russian Association of Scientific Research institutions public science, 2nd Moscow State University Moskovsky institute stories, philosophy and literature. AT 1934 year resolution SNK USSR and Central Committee VKP(b) he was introduced to the group for compiling a textbook on the history of the USSR.

Authority Piontkovsky — teacher and scientist was high enough. MV Nechkin in the late 1920s, sharing their impressions about the examination session at the 2nd Moscow State University, told about such case. On the blackboard She posted a list of literature needed to pass the test on the history of Russia in the 19th-20th centuries. It indicated work AT. AND. Lenin. "On the next same day early in the morning me wake up call on phone.

— it He speaks student, I at you rent offset. There Your list is posted on the board. Is it possible to replace Lenin with Piontkovsky?

— Piontkovsky?

— Yes.

Categorically object. Student dissatisfied.

— But why not? After all, Piontkovsky is in his course about then same writes."

Wide popularity Piontkovsky brought his first major work on the history of October - "October- sky revolution. Its premises and course", published in 1923. She is survived several publications, was translated into foreign languages. A copy of the first edition of this book was in library Lenin in Kremlin [4].

In 1923-1926. three editions of the Reader on stories October revolution" piontkovsky, in 1925 year — reader on stories civil wars in the USSR. At the same time, and again in several editions, his essays on the February days of 1917 and the history of the labor movement in Russia were published [5]. In those years, there was, perhaps, not a single major historical journal in the country in which articles and reviews were not systematically published. and notes Piontkovsky [6]. Under his collections of documents, memoirs of the White Guards are published as editors and with a preface, together with I. Mints he edits the series "The Civil War in Essays", together with M. Mebe Lem and V. Nevsky "Library on the history of the peoples of the USSR" [7].

In 1928, Piontkovsky, as a delegate with a determining took an active part in the work of the First All-Union Conference of Marxist Historians with a loud [voice]. Then he was elected a corresponding member of the Communist Academy of Social Sciences. In 1928-1936 three editions come out "Essays stories USSR XIX-XX ve-kov" — a revised course of lectures given by Piontkovsky at Moscow University, the Institute of Red Professors, the Moscow Institute of History, Philosophy and Literature. In 1931, Piontkovsky published a generalizing historiographical work devoted to criticism of bourgeois concepts of the history of Russia. As one of the authors, he took part in writing the fourth volume on stories party, published under general edited by E. M. Yaroslavsky.

The works of Piontkovsky were positively evaluated in the press. Naturally, they could not do without criticism, which, however, the longer it went on, the more it took on a politicized and unbridled character. A wave of tendentiousness began in the late 1920s: the stage of "an all-out offensive of socialism along all fronts" began, and, consequently, the class struggle intensified. Adversaries were looked for everywhere and, of course, found. Of course, someone, at the behest of his heart, followed the guidelines of the totalitarian regime, paying tribute to dogmatism, a somebody on the revelations built his own career, insured himself against possible accusations of this or that otherwise bias.

Here are some examples of criticism of Piontkovsky's works of those years. Book Piontkovsky (Essays on stories Russia in the XIX-XX centuries.— A. L.),—— summarized in a review of it V. Rakhmetov,— spineless. The author ... does not agree with the existing truths, in particular, with the generally accepted scheme of Pokrovsky, and disagrees with Lenin on a number of issues, ... disagrees with revolutionary Marxism-Leninism in a number of fundamental questions." AT 1932 year Tolstikhina and Miller, reviewing in the journal "Historian-Marxist" the work Piontkovsky, saw in them "a whole system of political and fundamental historical mistakes" — depiction of the revolution as a spontaneous process, belittling the leading role of the Bolshevik Party; distortion of the Leninist theory of the development of the bourgeois-democratic revolution into a socialist one; replacing the history of the class struggle with the history of individual counter-revolutionary generals and t. d. AT guilt editor put then, what he "nowhere" did not come out with a detailed criticism of his mistakes in the press ".

The chapter on the civil war, written by Piontkovsky for the fourth volume of the History of the All-Union Communist Party of Bolsheviks, was particularly well received. So, BUT. Abramov, AND. Schmidt pointed out that this chapter "from beginning to end is a continuous perversion stories civil wars, for in her 'greased role party, not illuminated leading the role of the Central Committee, Lenin and Stalin, the legen d about the role of Trotsky has not been exposed. In the same label-accusatory spirit and with the same claims, another team of historians , A. Andropov, N. Radkov, BUT. Soloveyko, AND. Fedin, E. Fokin. The reviewers were not concerned with the essence of the issue, not with the argument, with the identification of real shortcomings. in the works of Piontkovsky, a an apology for the Bolshevik mode, "thin neck" leaders" ⁵ . Other difficult was to wait in conditions when, in the words of I. Babel, "ideologies became more, how oxygen."

At first, Piontkovsky reacted to criticism in his address rather calmly. AT 1928 year he wrote down in diary:
"Day after day, as always, there is almost nothing to remember about thread should, all mundane work - lectures, seminars, enemies, someone scolded my book, I scolded, someone scolded another again will scold - all, how always, and all how usually". On the review Rakhmetov responses So:
"It is difficult to imagine anything more illiterate. misrepresented data, misrepresented thoughts, attributed to what I did not think and did not write, and barked at the most desperate way." Piontkovsky thought what her inspired Mintz, and then in his hearts added: "In general, all our historians - crooks.

Two years later, in 1930, Piontkovsky is disappointed and depressed. happen:
"ten years, how I already in Moscow, writing books, a results - per ten years not choose me neither in one from academics. Meaning, ideologically I more not turned in ideologist, not fully digested. My history is now being scolded, they say it is not Leninist and in general. And honestly, right now, I all time read Pokrovsky, not praising yourself must to tell, what all same on comparison With him I am both in the sense of facts, and in the sense of their illumination, and in the theoretical sense, of course did his book step forward in areas stories... BUT what same to me farther do? I don't know how to do anything. I can give lectures, write books, go to the cinema, and yet I have to do chores not will take on the shallow party I not I can work and more not will give. Position tragic."

Indeed, who was any Soviet professor? Civil servants who are completely dependent on those in power. They can be kicked out of work, leaving no prospects, they can scold or consign to oblivion their previous works. What to do next? It was also a problem for all the creative intelligentsia, who could "create" in a totalitarian state only With his permissions, neither on the iota without departing from the general line. And she constantly hesitated...

In February 1932, Piontkovsky wrote that after numerous revisions, he developed a fear of the audience. Yes, teacher was afraid talk, since the students were looking for biases in his lectures. He understood that numerous "revelations" could lead to physical destruction. And bitterly noted: "They say that I turned gray during this month. The devil knows, it's very difficult, having been 13 years in party, agree With topics what you all
For thirteen years he was in the Party only the mouthpiece of the hostile classes. agree with this wording. — it's like admitting myself hardened pest social fascist and counterrevolutionary. No, I will never agree with that."

Completely torn and exhausted by shameless criticism and overwork, on October 24, 1932, Piontkovsky wrote in his diary that all his books had been cursed and spat on, that they had stopped printing and it began to seem to him that that his whole life — a total mistake. "I didn't have to do history, not had to do science, there was no need to take intellectual work in the field of ideology as an indisputable legacy...". And then followed figurative conclusion: "AT ." result elaborations I found myself like a fish stranded. Turn into dry good animal I can't And in the water, too, is no longer allowed- yut" [10].

AT 1936 year attacks on the Piontkovsky intensified. I. Frolov called the third edition of "Essays on the history of the USSR XIX and XX centuries" Piontkovsky "ideological marriage,
"irresponsible", "anti-scientific, anti-Leninist book" and "advised" hand it over in archive. After all in her guiding party instructions to historians were not taken into account, and the author himself was a member of the group of N. Vanaga, whose textbook was so disliked Stalin. BUT. Klinov emphasized anti-historicism
"Essays" saw in them illustration Togo, what happens, if you do not take into account Stalin's instructions "in the matter of raising teaching stories on the due height" [11]. Maybe, after these furious reviews, Piontkovsky did not leave thought about ambulance denouement.

Then It was two class default: name forbidden — "enemy of the people", the works rested in a special depository. From the second half of the 50s, references began again: the taboo was lifted, editor rehabilitated.

Now they wrote about him as the compiler of the first scientific and historical collection documents about October 1917 G.

(E.A. Lutsky), a who gave a correct description of "the enormous role of the leader of the Bolshevik Party and the head of the workers' and peasants' government VI Lenin in ensuring the success of the October armed uprising in Petrograd and the creation of the Soviet states" (M. P. Iroshnikov). G. D. Alexeeva, VM Vodolagin, EN Gorodetsky, AG Chernykh called the book Piontkovsky "October revolution in Russia. Its background and course" was the first generalizing work of Soviet historiography of the early 1920s. on this topic. L. V. Cherepnin thought faithful position work Piontkovsky

"Bourgeois historical science in Russia" (it, alas, was replete with harsh judgments and categorical statements in address featured Russians historians.— BUT. L.) About, that the pre-revolutionary historiography in country to end 20s was "driven ." in dead end" and dies, how that

"the class it represents and expresses." As written from a Marxist position, he considered the book of the historian Brief feature article working movements in Russia" V. N. Laverychev [12].

This list can be continued. But evaluative statements about individual works of Piontkovsky did not give an idea about his creativity in in general. His kind

The "white spot" was the biography of the scientist. Moreover, attempts to publish such an article all the time came across on the tangible resistance.

For the first time I received an offer to write about Piontkovsky in early 60s gg. Then in Institute of History AN USSR G. Alekseeva collected a collection of Bolshevik historians. At me before now since stored unpublished article about editor With brief recommendation FROM. M. Dubrovsky:

"Comrade AL Litvin's article on SA Piontkovsky can certainly be published. Made the most necessary corrections. May 17, 1965 G.".

However, the general line again wavered. To the manual came team Brezhnev. Collection It was thrown out of all plans, because the fate of many Bolshevik historians was tragic a write about this became unfashionable and the word "repression" began to disappear from biographical essays . Necessary whether talk, what all attempts somewhere "attach" this material were unsuccessful.

In 1975, the Department of the History of the USSR of the Kazan Pedagogical Institute, where I then worked, prepared a collection of articles on domestic historiography. My article about Piontkovsky was recruited, read proofreading... and followed call in local censorship (oblite). There

reported what this article not will be published, acclaim, to me not will be allowed promote views
"a Jew and a Menshevik since 1905" and that this has already been reported in Department propaganda and agitation regional committee CPSU. I wanted justify: brought extracts from evidence about the birth and baptism of Piontkovsky in the Orthodox Church, spoke, what in 1905 year to him It was fourteen years and he could not then be an active Menshevik ... Soon it became known what getting ready my personal a business and They want to condemn me in the party order for spreading Menshevism...

I had to submit the article for review to the most authoritative ideological authority for party bodies. - Institute of Marxism-Leninism under the Central Committee of the CPSU. Its employees the doctors historical science P. BUT. Golub and LM Spirin gave a positive review with an important conclusion for me at that time: "The article is methodologically sustained and from the standpoint of modern Soviet historiography right evaluates role and meaning works one of the first Soviet Marxist historians. instance of this "protection letter" dated January 19, 1976 with all signatures and Email's seals I gave in department of science regional committee parties. Personal business did not take place, but also article not was published.

Gone more ten years. AT Institute stories USSR AS USSR prepared a collection of articles to the 90th anniversary Academician II Mints. Compiled and edited by VD Polikarpov proposed to me participate in German articles about Piontkovsky. Material entitled "Among the first historians October" was edited, prepared to the set. And suddenly I receive a letter from Polikarpov with a request to urgently respond to the comments of the "black" reviewer, who recommended not to publish the article. What confused him? Links on the work Piontkovsky start 20s years, in which the books of LD Trotsky, NI Bukharin and other, then still unrehabilitated political figures. I, not delaying, took per feather and wrote that in my material other provisions of the historians were quoted. As a result, the aforementioned collection under the title "The Historical Experience of the Great October Revolution" (M., 1986) was published without an article about Piontkovsky. It was published only in 1990 in the first issue of the journal Questions of the History of the CPSU. The article was written with careful wording, defaults: more once test fate is not wanted.

Why same, but, return Piontkovsky from

was the absence so long? It seems that the answer to this question can be found in the creative bio graphy of the scientist. After all, there were no formal obstacles: Piontkovsky, as already noted, was rehabilitated in civil and party terms as early as 1956. There is probably some more important solution reasons Togo, why Piontkovsky, in Stalin's expression, "fell out of the cart." They shot him Dubrovsky gave 10 year old Gulag term, left alive, Mints was not touched. A game of chance? investigation error? Or fate in the form of a totalitarian regime, which, like a mythological creature, devoured their children?..

Let us trace the life and creative path of Sergei Andreevich Piontkovsky.

He was born on October 8 1891 in Odessa in the family of a professor-lawyer. Childhood and youthful years future the pass in Kazan, where With 1899 G. his father, BUT. BUT. piontkovsky, Occupation department criminal rights in university. Lawyers he known for his work in which advocated cancel mortal executions and conditional release the accused. Died Andrew Andreevich in 1916 G., not living up to time revelry violence and collapse their humane ideas. AT 1910 G. Sergey Piontkovsky received certificate maturity per full eight year old well in 3rd Kazan gymnasium, a in 1914 G. finished Faculty of History and Philology Kazansky university and was abandoned for the preparation of to professorial rank on department Russian stories under leadership professors N. N. Firsov.

The surviving documents testify to the participation of Piontkovsky in the student movement. In 1912, he was one of the organizers of a gathering of university students. A year later, he became the chairman of a literary circle that united representatives of the "left parties" [13], at the same time he spoke at a student meeting against the inspiration of the "Beilis Affair" by the Black hundreds. In 1913-1914. Pravda was sent to Piontkovsky's address from Petrograd. As a student, he belonged to that part of the democratically minded youth who rushed to an active public activities, but whose path in revolution was difficult [14].

Piontkovsky not straightaway became communist: With Martha 1917 and until the end of 1918— Menshevik-internationalist or, as he himself wrote in his biography,— Menshevik-Unionist [15]. In June 1918 Piontkovsky wrote in the newspaper Rabochaya Volya published by him in Kazan, that "at the moment" the worker Class must understand, what struggle per power

"a fruitless and harmful task" [16]. He resolutely opposed the outbreak of the civil war and the Bolsheviks who fomented it, believing that it was premature to talk about a socialist revolution in [Russia]. In his autobiography, Piontkovsky reported about this time: "From the moment of the revolution, he was engaged in social activities. Was a member executive committee Council workers deputies Kazan... wrote in newspaper "Working a business", was member editorial board
"Kazan working newspaper", "Banner of the Revolution". He was a participant in the October events in Kazan. After the victory of the armed uprisings in city he continued work in the Kazan Soviet, was a comrade (deputy) commissar of labor of the province, headed the department of distribution working strength.

Dragged him in and scientific activity. AT December 1917 Piontkovsky passed the master's exam in Russian history, in March of the following — on political economy. At the same time, the Council of the Faculty of History and Philology extended his stay at the university for another year. - to prepare for a professorship. However, a lung disease forced him to interrupt his studies in science and send Xi on the koumiss treatment in Ufa province.

Piontkovsky left Kazan in June 18th. unrolled civil war, temporary capture Czechoslovak legionnaires and
komuchevsky People's Army of the Urals and Medium Volga region not allowed to him come back home. Near of the year he spent in Tomsk and Vladivostok. AT autobiographies Piontkovsky wrote about this time:
"From September 1918 until the autumn of 1919 he was a member of the executive committee Council trade unions in Siberia, and from April to July 1919, in addition, he was a deputy chairman of the Vladivostok provincial council of trade unions ... In Siberia in 1918-1919 he published workers' magazines and cooperated in them. Edited "Work Path" in Tomsk (came out No. one) and Seaside worker" in Vladivostok (issued No. 1-2). He wrote in the Sibirsky Rabochiy (all the mentioned publications were of the Menshevik direction.— BUT. L.), published in 1918-1919 years in Irkutsk" [18].

Kolchakism made a heavy impression on Piontkovsky, therefore, returning to Kazan, in September 1919 G. he entered in RCP(b) [19], wearing topics most on loyalty another dictatorship - Bolshevik.

In Siberia and the Far East, Piontkovsky collected material for his first published works on the history of civil war. war. They are — "Year in kingdom Kolchak",

Our Far East. Japanese intervention in Siberia" - were published in Kazan in 1919-1920 under pseudonym Espe (according to the initial letters of the author's first and last name). So in Kazan newspapers 1917—1918 gg. he signed his articles, a later some reviews.

The main source of Piontkovsky's book "A Year in the Kingdom of Kolchak" were Siberian newspapers, magazines, impression. BUT most interesting — intelligence on the activities of trade unions, sickness funds, labor exchanges, workers' cooperatives, etc. Piontkovsky's data on the functioning of workers' newspapers and purely economic strikes of workers were later supplemented by the facts of their political speeches against Kolchak's mode.

In 1920 Piontkovsky's second book, Our Far East. Japanese intervention in Siberia. The work was of a scientific and propaganda nature, and its positive meaning was in trying reveal role Japan in interventions show her futility. AT basis and this book lay a narrow circle of sources — Siberian periodicals of that time. Piontkovsky did not touch upon the event row interventions and was inclined believe The main reason for the landing of Japanese troops in Primorye is the traditional competition for markets and sources of raw materials.

AT end 1919—beginning 1920 gg. Piontkovsky acquires in Kazan an experience party-Soviet and trade union work, acting as the head of the propaganda department of the provincial committee of the RCP (b), a member of the Presidium of the Kazan provincial trade union council and the Kazan Council of Workers, Red Army and peasant deputies. Narya- du With teaching activities in Higher Institute of Public Education and the Workers' Faculty of Piontkovsky University often spoke before population cities with lectures: "The program and charter of the party", "Why do we have It's hard to live." On April 20, he was a delegate of the 3rd All-Russian congress professional unions.

At the end of the summer of the same year, Piontkovsky moved to Moscow. Related this is It was, apparently With topics what in June 20th VV Adoratsky, who worked together with Piontkov- skim in Kazan university, received letter from
MH Pokrovsky with an invitation to come to the capital to participate in compiling chronicles October revolution and showdown archives white guard rulers — Kolchak, Denikin and others. Piontkovsky went on the call of Adoratsky how professional reviewer. Last help-

passed, as they together carried heavy bags with Kolchak's documents from the building of the Cheka on Lubyanka and transported wali them in archive [20].

Pokrovsky helped friends and in device on the new place. A note from 26 august 1920 G. on the name head of houses Soviets BUT. P. Platonov read: "Tov. AT. AT. Adorati and FROM. BUT. piontkovsky, members RKP, performing responsible work on behalf of the Chairman of the Council of People's Commissars on disassembly white guard documents, desperately need in indoors for housing. I beg You render named comrades all-round assistance, otherwise they won't be able to do what they've been given comrad Lenin order" [21] Main place work for Piontkovsky With autumn 1920 G. became Eastpart, where him also accepted on initiative Pokrovsky and Adoratsky [22].

Piontkovsky entered compound second subcommittees Eastparta, engaged in history RCP(b) after February 17th.

Piontkovsky was then in his thirtieth year. He was full of energy and hopes. First years stay editor in Moscow are extraordinarily fruitful: Piontkovsky published various archival materials and numerous reviews, taught classes on the history of Russia in the 19th century. from the lecture group communist university name I. M. Sverdlov. Together With Pokrovsky edited the first numbers magazine "Proletarian" revolution" and also stubbornly looked for and systematically sent in Kazan the Bureau Eastparta the documents, relating to stories local organizations RSDLP. AT July 1922 in Petrograd communist university for "Conducting work in the spirit of revolutionary Marxism" opened a research institute. Piontkovsky entered in initiative group on his creation, a then was approved his valid member.

The formation of new branches of historical science - party history and the history of Soviet society - took place simultaneously. AT Eastparte Piontkovsky worked less than a year: in May 1921 he handed over his affairs to MA Savelyev. But per this short term he passed good school. It was then that the circle of his scientific interests was determined. Owls: the history of the October Revolution and the Civil War, the Russian working class, the class struggle and the revolutionary movement, historiography. The central place in Piontkovsky's work was occupied by the history of the first years of Soviet power. He was among the employees of Eastpart attracted Agitprop department Central Committee RCP(b) to creation work on stories October revolution, a also training educational Literature [23].

Above their first books on stories Revolution Piontkovsky began work With end 1920 G. AT autobiography written April 29, 1921, he reported: "By order Commissions stories parties (available in mind Eastpart.— BUT. L.) writing book size 12-15 printed sheets under name "Proletarian" revolution." Book will be finished in June-July month" [24]. Parallel was conducted Work on compiling readers on stories October revolution (edited her Pokrovsky) [25].

Pokrovsky's monograph and reader on the October Revolution were published in 1923. They were preceded by a number of publications in magazines, in volume including article about roles Lenin in the October Revolution [26].

In articles about the February days and events of July 3-5, 1917, published in Petrograd, published around the same time, Piontkovsky came to the conclusion that the second Russian revolution was a necessary stage on the way to the realization by the proletariat and the peasantry following it of their own goals and its own class program, and the execution of the July The demonstrations led the Mensheviks and Socialist-Revolutionaries to "political death", they became "parties of open reaction and counter-revolution" [27]. It is easy to replace it can be said that he proceeded from the Leninist characterization of the behavior petty-bourgeois parties in then time.

AT 1922-1923 gg. along with With fragments from preparing for printing works them It was published more twenty reviews and annotations on the Soviet publications and memories White Guards, as well as a review of the literature, which can be considered how peculiar historiographical addition to readers and monographs about October revolution. He positively assessed the work of Trotsky and Bukharin, critically — Milyukov and did conclusion, what systematic study stories revolution not is underway. Most of the works, in his opinion, were "written by direct participants and may serve example Togo, as understood her move representatives public classes like perceived move events in volume or otherwise camp" [28].

In historiographical works, Soviet scholars assess Piontkovsky's contribution to the study of the history of the October Revolution and reveal the erroneous propositions contained in in his first books 20s [29] years _ The formula about the "two-facedness" of the October Revolution is subjected to the greatest criticism. revolution (With one hand, revolution

111

socialist, on the other - bourgeois). Piontkovsky expressed his point of view as follows: "Two forces took part in the October Revolution: the proletariat and the petty bourgeoisie — peasantry. It was imposed on the October Revolution my indelible seal. She is was immediately and proletarian and bourgeois. October the revolution was two-faced, but these two sides of its face, like the two-faced Janus, were closely connected friend With friend and unthinkable alone without other" [30]. AT those years this point vision shared by L. N. kritzman, M. N. Pokrovsky, BUT. AT. Shestakov A. I. Yakovlev [31], about this wrote in their first work on October TO. Zetkin [32]. Pokrovsky and in 1927 year supposed gal, what October revolution represented yourself
"binding of the socialist revolution, ... and the national and bourgeois revolution." And that there is no doubt that against Denikin and Kolchak we were helped to fight back bourgeois Democrats [33].

From analysis text "Anthologies" and success Piontkovsky's works make it clear that the formula "about the two-facedness" of October was taken by him as a common place in historical literature. and . repeatedly repeated.

Otherwise saying formula "about duplicity October" Piontkovsky was taken how something given, famous in historical literature. However this given had change properties mine appearance and outlines. Through four of the year in from this to 10th anniversary October essay Piontkovsky asserted: "Proletariat brought before end bourgeois revolution, while at the same time putting into practice its main revolution revolution socialist." AND, finally, in 1935 he wrote: "October the revolution was proletarian in motive force, socialist - by goals. proletariat, the poorest peasantry created the October Revolution. The proletariat, making its main revolution against bourgeoisie and exploiters, the most casually destroyed leftovers feudalism. The main decisive in October was transition of power from hands of the bourgeoisie in arms proletariat" [34].

Evolution views Piontkovsky happened on measure of approval in Soviet historical and political literature then dominant concepts about October revolution how revolution socialist. Although Now it's clear what unbiased de-ideologized study character Togo, what happened in Russia in October 1917 of the year, more to be. And then dot vision historys start 20s hardly will be be called only "erroneous" and methodologically wrong.

In 1924-1927. Piontkovsky's essay on the February Revolution, which reveals its bourgeois-democratic character, was published in four editions, the role of RSDLP(b) in leadership masses. Historian wrote:
"The position of the Bolsheviks in the February days was clear. It was a position not to muffle the movement, but to deploy it. growth and growth... Leaders who do not trust the masses, leaders who fear the masses — Such is the position of the Mensheviks and Socialist-Revolutionaries in the February days"[35].

In the works of those years, Piontkovsky acted as an apologist for the Bolshevik policy. Together with Pokrovsky and others, he joined in the criticism of Trotsky's works on the history of October, and then - Zinoviev and Kamenev. His remarks were traditional for the time: Trotsky exaggerated his role, Petrograd garrison, slogans in days October and t. P. So same, how and Pokrovsky, participated in praise activities Lenin and Bolshevik party in 1917. In the article "Lenin in the Council of People's Commissars" (Piontkovsky was the first began write about Lenin how Chairman SNK, his roles in creation Petrogradsky VRK) he assert that "Lenin was not only the initiator of the creation of the Council of People's Commissars, but he entered into all the details of its internal structure and practical activities. He organized the work of the Council of People's Commissars, its apparatus, technique and organization"[36]. Piontkovsky considered the creation of the history of the Bolshevik Party as the main force that led the proletarian revolution, the struggle against all attempts at restoration to be the most important task. pre-October relations in years citizens- which war, the construction of socialism in the period of the new economic policy.

From cohorts official Soviet historys he stood out perhaps, one — professional meaning documents and active publishing work. Actually, With publications documents started his scientific activity in Moscow. Already in first room "Proletarian" revolution" (1921 G.) appeared compilation documents from archive Kolchak. Piontkovsky took apart department archive police and printed materials from work history movements in Russia first addressed to study fund Council of People's Commissars. He introduced in textbook turnover resolutions party congresses and articles Lenin, the first decrees Soviet authorities, text peasant kaza, memoirs participants October events in Petrograd. Prepared reader on stories civil wars in Russia long years was the only collection where Soviet the documents can It was see in

Comparison with the documents of other regimes that functioned on the territory of the country in 1918-1921. Piontkovsky cited many of them in the section on the Civil War of the Fourth volumes Stories VKP(b)".

AT further Piontkovsky planned edition a series of documentary collections dedicated to the activities of the RCP(b), party and Soviet construction, trade unions, economy countries, a also position in become a counter-revolution. special meaning he gave collection and after publications documents primary party organizations, which outlined would move October in factories and factories, in barracks, eat, village." AT 1928 G. under editorial Piontkovsky and With his preface came out compilation documents "Tips in October", in success years — memoirs and documents collections in history civil wars and stories peoples USSR.

AT special view historiographic literature Piontkovskiy single out memoirs. He high much appreciated memories N. TO. Krupskaya, D. read, AT. Williams, AT. BUT. Antonova-Ovseenko, F. F. Raskolnikov about revolution, very critical treated to memoirs leaders non-proletarian parties and White Guards [37].

In the 20s. Soviet historical-party source studies were created. At his origins stood H. H. Avdeev, V. AT. Adoratsky, FROM. N. Valk, M. H. Pokrovsky. To Piontkovsky should rightfully be attributed to him. That For many years, theoretical source studies proceeded from the assessment of sources, primarily taking into account their class origin. Sharing this point of view, Piontkovsky, more than any of his contemporary historians, gave this aspect paramount meaning.

AT 1926 G. under editorial and With preface Piontkovsky was released one from first bibliographies in history October revolution. AT literature, dedicated this topic, he especially single out works Lenin, thought his first editor October. Piontkovsky high much appreciated also work associates Lenin, for these "leaders and leaders political fights proletariat per power, leaders fights per retention authorities and per building socialism" were also the first historians of the new world [38].

At the same time, it is impossible not to notice that the official attitude towards many of Lenin's associates, which began to change from the mid-20s, immediately had an opportunistic effect on labor. yes reviewers. Piontkovsky's works were no exception. If a in 1923 G., overlooking literature about October revolution, he, for example, high much appreciated separately work N. AND. Bukharin and L. D. Trotsky then from similar review, tagged 1926 year, they simply drop [39].

Proceedings piontkovsky, in volume including on stories working class Russia, echo modern to him stage and state of the art historical science. BUT she is already was in power narrow utilitarian class approach, dogmatism, a priori truths. A sacred attitude quickly formed to Leninist texts, scientific arguments began to be forced out party installation, political labels. surveying somehow historical literature, Piontkovsky noticed what historys take diagram, given in works Lenin, his conclusions about meaning October and illustrate these provisions specific material. One- nako and myself he did So same.

The archives preserved the minutes of the meetings of the directorate of the Institute of Red Professors of the Communist Academy. Among them is the plan for a seminar on history proposed by Piontkovsky on the 1931/32 training year. It set the task of proving to the audience that "history is definite view class awareness", what need
"against the background of revealing the class essence of individual historians, representatives of individual classes, to give an idea of the main problems of the Russian historical process . "
[40] As a historian, he believed that the dictatorship of the proletaria without the coming of a dictator was unthinkable. Piontkovsky, with his works, defended and justified what happened in October 1917, glorified Lenin and stopped before Stalin's apologia.

Piontkovsky studied at a pre-revolutionary school and university, with professors who began their scientific career at the end of the 19th century. But in his diary entries see through hatred to "bourgeois reviews" FROM. AT. Bakhrushin,
MM Bogoslovsky. The exception for him was his teacher, Professor Kazansky university N. N. Firsov,
"amazing old man", but not a Marxist... For Piontkovsky historiography subdivided on the bourgeois reaction, and proletarian Marxist revolutionary. By his your opinion last received from pre-revolutionary only printed material Yes technical skill operate historical documents. After October history has become "combat tool proletariat" [41].

But it would be wrong to assume that Piontkovsky is only floated on downstream wholly was at time in captivity. He by no means idealized the "new" society. educated, from professorial families, owned many weak

Vyansk languages, as well as German and French, having been on a scientific trip to Italy and Austria, Piontkovsky was quite contemptuous of the emerging party nomenclature. After a vacation in Kislovodsk in the summer of 1928, he wrote in his diary that he had met with the average response workers. "Party dignitaries do not interfere even during their holidays with ordinary party punks. In no country, perhaps, has the aristocracy been placed in such strong and highly privileged conditions as in our country. He was disgusted by the cruelty and punitive omnipotence of the often insignificant people who were in power. In the same place, in Kislovodsk, he accidentally witnessed a conversation between two Chekists. One from them told With enthusiasm how shot in basement former officers and went, squelching in blood.
"I got scared, the recalled what if he starts shooting someone again ... "And he described this Chekist. "At all puny, liquid, only in eyes some bloodthirsty devilry".

Piontkovsky, who was a supporter of the class views of Pokrovsky, when attacks began on the latter him, trying to protect him. "Mistakes in Pokrovsky's books— he asserted, do not belittle the role he played in the history of the development of Marxist historical science in our country. Pokrovsky's books are a stage in the development of Marxist historical thoughts" [42].

Yet conformism often prevailed. In a diary entry dated February 24, 1930, there are arguments about the obsoleteness of Pokrovsky's views, that "he outlived himself," as new materials and new ideological attitudes appeared. Now, the writer believed, it was necessary talk about the only leader - Stalin.

Piontkovsky himself apparently decided to keep up with the new ideological trends. In 1928-1930. there was a defeat of the historical department of the Academy of Sciences. The ideological support of various "fabrications" was taken over by the Communist Academy. One of the first blows was dealt by Pokrovsky in a report at a conference of representatives of Marxist-Leninist institutions on March 22, 1928. On October 10, 1930, at a joint meeting of the section of the industrial capitalism Institute stories Comacademies and Society Marxist historians spoke Piontkovsky with the report "Great Russian bourgeois historiography of the last decade". This report was not made honor him. He sharply criticized the works of SV Bakhrushin, R. Yu. Y.U. AT. Gauthier, BUT. BUT. Kiesevetter, FROM. F. Platonov,

MK Lyubavsky and other scientists, because "throughout the revolution they defended the interests of the owners". AT works historys Piontkovsky discovered
"zoological nationalism Moscow Labaznikov" and regarded them "as the last resistance of the bourgeoisie, the last convulsions of a dead man." "Our task," he said, "is is to help them die quickly, die without trace and remainder" [43]. These conclusions supported by SA Golubtsov, AV Shestakov and other participants of the meeting .

similar discussions passed in Leningrad, Kyiv and Minsk. These performances at a time when Platonov, Lyubavsky and others were arrested, it is difficult to regard otherwise, how hit in back slandered colleagues.

Piontkovsky wrote in his diary 1 November 1930, shortly after his pogrom report that he was fired from the Institute of History and deported from Moscow to Kharkov, which was revealed anti-Soviet conspiracies reviewers, economists and engineers, which was hard for him. That's all. Nothing about the report. Perhaps Piontkovsky, speaking with frantic, labeled criticism, somehow wanted to declare his political loyalty to the regime, which needed little such assurances? May be. At least the certainty that Piontkovsky defended the provisions of the report sincerely, no. But fact there is fact, and he is black gloomy page in biographies scientist.

December 11, 1930 Piontkovsky noted that he was working on book on historiography. His Occupation question will this book stone under construction socialism" and how soon it will become obsolete. He complained that the extremely It is difficult to participate in the building of socialism by writing books. Justified whether he this my a book? thought whether that avoid continuous study, publicly participating in them? Difficult to tell. However they his not passed.

Full despair, pain lines find in diary entry per 3 February 1932 G. "On the ideological the front is coming desperate study. I never neither in what oppositions not was, a generally all we most sincere way betrayed parties, and suddenly we (speech goes also about Elwove and Mince.— BUT. L.) turned out to be Trotskyist smugglers, falsifiers stories parties and Bolshevism, one word, enemies working class. Us are working on from numbers in room in "Bolshevik" gave several articles in "Truth". Finally, two days contract all mine books, articles, notes, bibliography working through in the ICP, they found a plethora of mistakes, turned my entire ten-year activity into one ink blot, and proved like two and a half that I am a Right opportunist with Menshevik-Socialist-Revolutionary bends."

Last record in diary dated 23 March 1934 It refers to being summoned to a meeting of the Politburo Central Committee of the All-Union Communist Party of Bolsheviks, together with other authors of textbooks for secondary schools. About the fact that Molotov presided over the meeting, Bubnov delivered a "disgusting report", and Stalin's words were heard in "reverent silence": textbooks these nowhere not fit." After this they were called by the nervous Bubnov and "shouted" who and what textbooks will be write...

On March 19, 1936, Piontkovsky gave his last public lecture at the Sverdlov Higher School of Propaganda at Central Committee of the CPSU (b). AT volume same year she is was from - given under name "Servdom Russia in fight with the revolution in Europe. In the autumn of that year, after him came. Further reader known.

On the conscience willingly butchering dictatorship millions of victims. He was cursed, fell into disfavor, anyone who believed objectionable to the good of the revolution. Such people were found among those who built and strengthened the regime, and among those who stood in opposition to it, and among those who remained silent. Piontkovsky was active, in plain sight, for many years he was We walked next to Pokrovsky, whose school was destroyed in the mid-30s, showed professionalism, and therefore — was potentially dangerous. Perhaps his archival historiographic research also played a role. Assurances of loyalty did not work then. The principle of "what would you like?" could save body, but not soul. But in given case and it did not help. Maybe the ancients are right: "To each person destiny create his morals"?

* * *

[1] In 1963 Andrey Andreevich Piontkovsky (1898-1967), lawyer, corresponding member AN USSR, specialist on criminal law, appealed to the Military Prosecutor's Office with a request to hand over to him the personal diaries of his dead elder brother. On March 4, 1963, military prosecutor B. Repin decided that "in terms of its content, the diary of SA Piontkovsky was directly relations to cause not It has and nothing does not contain anti-Soviet in itself. A.A. Piontkovsky received a copy of the diary. I read excerpts from it when I was visiting him in 1964, when I was collecting materials for an article about the fate of the historians. Later, I was able to identify the text of this diary with a copy stored in the archive, and only after that it was possible to draw a conclusion about its authenticity. (a diary printed on the typewriter, edits No). AT text

essay wide used this, more not published, source.
[2] Gateow M. L., employee NKVD, 22 February 1939 G. was death for abuse of office. When reviewing affairs in 1956 G. grounds for rehabilitation not found.
[3] Eastpart Bulletin.— Gosizdat, 1921.— No. 1.— S. 18. In the composition of the board East Party included: B. B. Adoratsky, H. H. Baturin, A. S. Bubnov, VA Bystryansky, VI Nevsky, MS Olminsky, SA Piontkovsky, MN Pokrovsky, DB Ryazanov.
[four] Piontkovsky FROM. BUT. October revolution in Russia. Her prerequisites and move. Popular-historical essay. - M.-Pg., 1923; M., 1924; M., 1926. See also: Piontkovsky SA Histoire populaire de la Revolution d'Ostobre—Paris, 1927; Library AT. AND. Lenin in Kremlin. - M., 1961.—S. 226.
[5] Piontkovsky FROM. BUT. Reader by history of the October Revolution. - M., 1923; M., 1924; M., 1926; He same. civil war in Russia (1918-1921 .) gg.). Reader.— M., 1925; He same. February days of 1917.-L., 1924; L., 1925; L., 1926; L., 1927; He is. Brief essay stories working movements in Russia (With 1870 G. on 1917 g.).- L., 1925.
[6] Only in the journal "Proletarian Revolution" in 1921-29. more than twenty of his works were published. See: Proletarian Revolution. Systematic and alphabetical index 1921-1929— M., 1931.- S. 148-149.
[7] Tips in October//Sat. doc.—M., 1928; Shulgin AT. AT. 1920 g.-L., 1926; AT this series came out: Chaadaeva O. Kornilovshchina. - M. - L., 1930; Kornatovsky N. Northern counter-revolution.— M., 1930; Pukhov A. Kronstadt rebellion.— M., 1931; This library published: Zeltser V. and Gaisinovich A. Pre-reform economy.— Kharkov, 1930; Simonov FROM. Pugachevshchina.-Kharkov, 1931; and etc.
[eight] cm.: Proceedings first All-Russian conferences Marxist historians. - M., 1930. - T. 1.—S. 417-418; T. 2.— S. 616. At the same time, SA Piontkovsky joined the commission for the study of the history of the proletariat of the USSR, set up by decision of the conference.— See: 50 years of Soviet historical science. / Chronicle.—M., 1971.—S. 130.
[9] Historian-Marxist.—1928.—No. 7.—S. 224, 228; 1932.—No. 1-2.—S. 193, 200; Bolshevik.—1931.—No. 22.—S. 75; 1932.—No. 1-2.—S. 123.
[ten] Last record in diary dated Piontkovsky 23 Martha 1934 G.
[eleven] Historian-Marxist.—1936.—No. 3.—S. 121 137; Struggle classes.— 1936. — № 5.—C. 117, 120.
[12] Lutsk E. BUT. Playback text decree "O ." earth" in Soviet publications// Problems source study.— M., 1963.— T. XI.— C. 27; Iroshnikov M. P. Creation Soviet central state apparatus.— L., 1967.— FROM. eleven; Alexeeva G. D. October revolution and historical the science in Russia (1917-1923 .) gg.).- M., 1968.— FROM. 165; Vodolagin AT. M. October armed uprising in Soviet historical literature.— M., 1967.- S. 29; Gorodetsky E. N. Soviet historiography Great October. 1917 - middle 30s years.—M., 1981.—S. 174; Chernykh BUT. G. AT. AND. Lenin — historian proletarian revolution in Russia.— M., 1969.— FROM. 308-309; Essays stories historical science in USSR. - M., 1966.   T IV. - S. 164.
[13] BUT. Arosev recalled: "We have heard for example, what there is some other organization among gymnasium students. We went to one of its members FROM. Piontkovsky. FROM him talk AT. Scriabin (later V. M. Molotov. - A. L.) and I in some darkish room near the kitchen in twilight time. Piontkovsky sat on the chest, watched

at us through pince-nez with lively, sharp eyes... and asked in detail us about program our classes. From conversation Nothing came of it, since it turned out that he, Piontkovsky, was somehow worried about then position, what our organization not refused from revolutionary practical action, but together so was composed of various revolutionary socialist elements." — Arosev BUT. How we entered in revolutionary work. - M. - L., 1926. - S. 66. Kazansky chief of police thirty October 1913 G. reported to office governor what student Piontkovsky refused from positions owner literary Cup. This demanded from him father, Professor BUT. BUT. Piontkovsky (1862-1915), who at that time was elected to the dean of the faculty of Law and did not want his son to somehow compromise him.— CGA RT.— F. one.- Op. 4.- D. 5481.—L. fifty.

[14] In 1914, Piontkovsky graduated from the Faculty of History and Philology of Kazan University with a diploma first degree and was left to prepare for a professorship in the department of Russian history. Piontkovsky studied with Professor HH Firsov and, as a student, was awarded a gold medal for his scientific work "The Main Social Trends in Russia for 1811-1812 and Expression of these currents in journalistic and literary works of that time. But spring 1914 G. Firsova forced submit in retired and returned to the university only two years later, in the spring of 1916. Piontkovsky in this is time was engaged under leadership Professor DA Korsakov, who in the report for 1915 noted the diligence of the graduate student, but found that his source study preparation leaves much to be desired, and also that "Piontkovsky is under the influence of random contemporary views."— CGA RT.— F. 977.— Op. 1.- D. 2364.- L. 17.

[fifteen] Archive AN Russia.— F. three hundred fifty.- Op. 3.— D. 249.— L. four.
[16] working will.- Kazan, 1918-12 June.
[17] CGA RT.— F. 271.—Оп. 2.—D. 153.—Л. 35.
[18] There же.— Ф. 3682.—Оп. 2.—D. 405.—Л. 158.
[19] RTSKHIDNI.—F. 17.—Op. 9.—D. 1911. Questionnaire of the party census. filled fifteen January 1927 G.
[20] Adoratsky AT. Memories of occurrence Istparta // Proletarian Revolution.— 1930.— No. 5.— FROM. 164. The archives of Kolchak and his government were transferred in 1920 to the archive of the October Revolution .
[21] Soviet archives.—1966.—No. 5.—S. 7.
[22] Pokrovsky MO occurrence Eastpart // Proletarian revolution.—1930.—No. 7-8.—S. 139.
[23] See: Ivanova LV Formation of the Soviet scientific intelligentsia (1917-1927).- M., 1980.-S. 73, 134, 137; Nosov A., Yusupov E. Lenin's heritage and questions of the methodology of the history of the Great October Revolution.—Tashkent, 1984.—S. 232, 233.
[24] CGA RT. - F. 3682. — Op. 2.—D 405.- L. 158.
[25] RTSKHIDNI.— F. 17. — Op. 60.— D. 88. — L. 27. 16 november 1922 G.
Pokrovsky reported to the Agitprop Department of the Central Committee of the Party: "Having looked at the manuscript readers on stories October revolution, compiled by Comrade Piontkovsky SA, I find that, in terms of plan and content, it corresponds to the tasks that were assigned to it. Therefore, it can be submitted for printing so that the proofs, as they are printed, are sent to me for final editions."— There same.— L. four.
[26] Piontkovsky S. Lenin in October days 1917 // _ Young Guard.—1923.—No. 9-10.—S. 88.
[27] Piontkovsky S. July 3-5 //Sovremennik.—1922.—No. 2.— P. 17; See: Lenin AT. I. Full. coll. op. - T. 34.- S. 44.

[28] See: Piontkovsky S. Review of Literature on the History of the Proletarian Revolution in Russia//Print and revolution.—1923.—No. 2.—S. 99.

[29] Gorodetsky EN Soviet historiography of the Great October Revolution.— M., 1981.— pp. 174-175; Essays on the history of historical science in the USSR.— M., 1966. - T. 4. - S. 447-448; Historiography of the history of the USSR. The era of socialism. - M., 1982.- S. 65 92, and others

[30] Piontkovsky SA Reader on the history of the October Revolution tsii. - S. 183.

[31] cm.: Kritzman L. Heroic period great Russian revolution (the experience of analyzing the so-called "war communism"). - M., 1925. - S. 30-34; Pokrovsky MN Counter-revolution in 4 years. - M., 1922. - S. 11; Shestakov AV Essays on agriculture and peasant movement during the war years and before October 1917—L., 1927.— pp. 120, 162; Yakovlev I. About historical sense of October.— M., 1922.— FROM. fifteen. and others

[32] K. Zetkin wrote: "In essence, the revolution had to carry the proletarian-socialist grain." - Zetkin K. For the Bolsheviks // Communists West and Soviet Russia. - M., 1918.- S. ten.

[33] GARF.— F. 4655.—Op. 1.— D. 53 - L.. 10, 20.

[34] Piontkovsky FROM. BUT. Reader on stories October revolution.— p. 183; He same. October 1917 G.—M.—L., 1927.—S. 97; He same. History essays USSR XIX and XX centuries - M. - L., 1935.—S. 518-519.

[35] Piontkovsky FROM. February days 1917 city - L., 1924.—S. thirty.

[36] See: Piontkovsky S. Mistakes in the "Lessons of October" comrade. Trotsky // Proletarian revolution.—1925.— No. one; He same. Bolshevism and question about bourgeois-democratic revolution // communist revolution.—1926.—No. 24; He is. On the eve of the October Revolution // Communist revolution.—1927.—No. 19; He is. October 1917 g. - S. 101-103. For answers to comments addressed to you, see: Trotsky LD Stalinskaya school falsifications. - M., 1990.

[37] Piontkovsky SA Memoirs of the October Revolution // History of factories. - M., 1934.- Issue. 8.- S. 55-62.

[38] Piontkovsky S. Preface to the book: Danishevsky SL Experience of Bibliography October revolution. - M. - L., 1926.

[39] cm.: Proletarian revolution.—1926.—No. 2.—S. 234-235 .

[40] Archive AN Russia.—F. 350.—Op. 1.—D. 510.—L. 35, 36.

[41] Proletarian revolution. - 1927. —No. 2.—S. 114 121.

[42] Piontkovsky S. The struggle of MH Pokrovsky with Russian bourgeois historiography//Historian-Marxist.—1932.—No. 6.—S. 86; He is. memory scientist-revolutionary//Front science and technology.—1935.— № 4.— S. 9.

[43] See: Piontkovsky S. Great power tendencies in the historiography of Russia//Historian-Marxist.—1930.—No. 17; He is. Great Russian bourgeois historiography last decades // Historian-Marxist.—1930.— T. 18-19; He same. bourgeois historical the science in Russia. - M., 1931.

LAST SOCIAL DEMOCRAT AT VKP(b)

21 Martha 1930 G. in conference room Institute Marx and Engels solemnly celebrated the 60th birthday of David Borisovich Ryazanov (1870-1938)[1]. The meeting was chaired by the chairman of the CEC, MI Kalinin. Welcoming the hero of the day on behalf of the Central Committee of the party, the government and the Central Executive Committee, he read out the official resolution: "Noting the largest scientific merit comrade Ryazanov, the creation of the Institute of Marx and Engels — the only scientific laboratory in the world on Marxist studies, the history of the labor movement and the class struggle, as well as the discovery and publication of many works of the founders of scientific socialism unknown until recently ... to award DB Ryazanov with the Order of the Red Banner of Labor." And right there, to the applause of those present, he attached the order to the lapel of the jacket of the touched hero of the day.

Deborin made a report on the scientific work of Ryazanov. He features his colleague as "an outstanding revolutionary, ... a figure in the professional movement, ... a major scientist, researcher of a special scientific discipline - Marxist studies. Ryazanov was also welcomed: Katayama - on behalf of the Comintern, Lozovsky - Profintern, Budkevich - Revolutionary Military Council of the country, Yaroslavsky — editorial offices of the Pravda newspaper and the All-Union Society of Political Prisoners. Pokrovsky stressed the uniqueness Ryazanov, which completed in volume, what he did not go through "any correct school", but became a first-class scientist, and what kind of people — units. Steklov remembered, what when they met at Ryazanov more there was no venerable bald head and gray hair — it was "very beautiful youth With thick hair." Bach speaking on behalf of the Academy of Sciences, said that although in this institution Marxism was not considered a scientific discipline for a long time, now that admitted this is not the case. And a worthy representative of this science — Ryazanov ("world scientist, ... fierce to work, ... incomparable organizer"). Bukharin spoke about courage Ryazanov, which the in July days 1917 years, being non-party, supported the Bolsheviks, and in 1919, during time offensive Yudenich, did in Petrograd without succumbing to general panic[2].

In his final speech, the hero of the day repeated that he was self-taught and promised: "My voice will always be heard when it is necessary to defend the cause of the proletariat and the cause of communism." The Central Executive Committee of the USSR adop ted a resolution on the establishment of the Ryazanov Prize in order to encourage scientific research on the history of the development of Marxism and the development of scientific biographies TO. Marx and F. Engels [3].

February 16, 1931 (almost on the anniversary of the anniversary celebration) Ryazanov was arrested. Month there were interrogations. On March 23, the head of the 2nd department of the OGPU D. Dmitriev, having familiarized co investigative materials, defined:

"AT ." progress consequences on cause union the Bureau Central Committee RSDLP, it was established that a member of the counter-revolutionary Menshevik organization, Professor II Rubin, handed over to Ryazanov row Menshevik party documents for storage. It turned out that at the institute, under the guidance of stvom Ryazanov worked Menshevik elements, in 1926 he invited the Bundist Rubin Isaac Ilyich to work, who was condemned to exile. Ryazanov vouched for him and appointed Rubin head. office of political economy of the institute. Soon Ryazanov hired a member of the union bureau Central Committee RSDLP shera, member Central Committee Menshevik Cherevani and others Ryazanov patronized Mensheviks.

During the search carried out by the OGPU, the institute had Dozens found statements, in which family members of convicted Mensheviks through Ryazanov and with active his participation excite various intercessor- [4] ... In his testimony, Rubin noted that, gradually drawing closer to Ryazanov, he established in the doctrine of the latter views akin to Menshevism ... Ryazanov took for safekeeping in December 1930 a letter from a foreign delegation of the RSDLP, outlining a new tactical orientation for intervention. Documents motivating the need for a bloc with bourgeois counter-revolutionary organizations, proceeding from the same principle of accepting intervention...

The interrogated Ryazanov denied the charge against him: none documents from Rubina not was getting, that Ruby Menshevik not knew...

I decided: investigative a business on accusation Ryazanov, 61 years old, submit for consideration by the panel of judges OGPU.

16 April 1931 G. special meeting at collegium of the OGPU decided send Ryazanov in Saratov on the 3 of the year. Prior to this, there had been a search at the apartment (where

confiscated his correspondence, articles, instances Socialist messenger", letters

Radek, Nikolaevsky and others), as well as a confrontation between Ryazanov and Rubin, where the former refuted all the "confessions" of the latter.

23 February Ryazanov wrote in Politburo Central Committee VKP(b), that after conversations with the leadership of the OGPU and the prosecutor's office Prokofiev, Guy, Dmitriev, Krylenko to him the charge became clear. "It boils down to Rubin's testimony in presented to me his letter. It turns out that shortly before Rubin's arrest Allegedly gave me for safekeeping a sealed envelope with papers that are of interest to the history of the RSDLP, with a request to keep thread it and give it back to him after he is released. None links — t. Guy — on the everyone famous passion mine
"collect", or — t. Krylenko — on the mine "kindness" and "carelessness" not may obscure all the wild absurdity of such a vile slander. I would have to be a paramount idiot to deposit the documents from Rubina..."

Ryazanov admitted that he received some kind of sealed packages (in foreign envelopes) with a request to hand them over to someone. He handed them over to the OGPU to Yagoda and Evdokimov, and generally story his relations With Rubin "fabulous known Menzhinsky and Yagoda. I, along with other comrades, appreciated Rubin as a very knowledgeable economist and beautiful translator..." [5] Central Committee, which the more
On March 10, 1930, he welcomed in my person "a tireless fighter for the triumph of the ideas of the great teachers of the international proletariat Marx, Engels, Lenin" ... can be sure that I soul or the body is not guilty of the act that my former employee raises against me in the most vile way, "assured Ryazanov.

However, oath assurances did not touch any of those who until recently uttered toasts in his honor. Ryazanov was sent in Suzdal insulator. AT investigative deed
No. 553901 stored script his letters from eleven April 1931 to the board of the OGPU [6]. He complained of deteriorating health, poor nutrition, asked to be transferred to Moscow, given books for reading, allow date With wife, Anna Lvovna. He was allowed to receive parcels, was given a writing paper and sent away ... Then, one after another, decisions followed special meetings OGPU -fifteen December 1933 G. term his expulsions was extended more on the 2 of the year;
March 5, 1934 was followed by a ban on residence in the Moscow and Leningrad regions for a period of 2 years. Finally, on January 21, 1938, the Military Collegium of the Supreme Court USSR swear Ryazanov to higher measure take that-

knowledge . On the same day the sentence was carried out [7]. AT. BUT. Smirnova claimed what massacre With Ryazanov, the progress of which was closely followed by Stalin (all the materials of the investigation were reported to him), was one of the first menacing signals of the total offensive of the regime on science. ku [8]. By your opinion R. Conquest, court above "Mensheviks" in 1931 served as a favorable occasion to involve the old Bolshevik Democrat Ryazanov and exclude him from the party, claiming for his unlawful association with the Mensheviks These statements necessary correct: the reprisal against Ryazanov was not one of the first acts in the destruction of social scientists, it was part of the process them condemnation and discredit; and Ryazanov not was released, how thinks conquest, certainly, if not count, what link there is freedom.

Since the second half of the 1920s, the tendency to intimidate the intelligentsia—engineers, military men, historians, economists, and foreign specialists—has consistently increased in the country. If the beginning of the 20s was marked by the trial of the leadership of the Right SR party, then the beginning of the 30s — over the "working peasant party", the "union bureau of the Central Committee of the RSDLP" and other mythical organizations invented by the OGPU and the Central Committee of the party. In the person of Ryazanov, one of the country's oldest Social Democrats was condemned. This was a warning not only to academicians, scientists, social scientists (after all, the directors of the institute were tried Marx and Engels), but and old Bolsheviks. Ryazanov formally was member VKP(b) With July 1917 He was well acquainted with Lenin and practically with all the leaders of the Second International. Of course, distinguished by independent judgments (often different from Lenin's), not afraid to criticize the Central Committee, known for his ironic attitude towards Stalin, he could not survive. Suffice it to recall certain facts from the biography of Ryazanov, to make sure in this.

David Borisovich Goldendach (Ryazanov) was born in Odessa, studied in gymnasium, although and not finished her. In 1887, at the age of seventeen, he became interested in the ideas of the populists, then became a social democrat. During overseas trips tried to publish Marxist literature. In 1891 he was arrested and after a preliminary 18-month conclusions swear to four years prisons. Sat in Petersburg "Crosses" then was exiled to Chisinau. In 1900 he emigrated, in 1903, after the Second Congress of the RSDLP, he published the polemical pamphlet Broken Illusions. AT 1905-1907 gg. created unions in Odessa and Petersburg. Was arrested and again emigrated. AT 1909 G. worked lecturer in propaganda school "Vperyod" on Capri, then at Lenin, in Longjumeau. Participated in the Zimmerwald Conference. But most importantly, he collected manuscripts of works, letters from Marx and Engels, contacted with their relatives and also with BUT. Bebel, E. Bernstein, F. Mehring, K. Kautsky [10]. After the revolution, Ryazanov led the Petrograd trade unions, became organizer Institute Marx and Engels, one of the founders of the Communist Academy, collectors Soviet archives [11]. Ryazanov was compiler and editor essays Marx and Engels, Plekhanov and Lafarga, author many original essays on history Marxism.

He was a member of the Presidium of the Second Congress of the Soviets, but then, together with Kamenev and others, supported the idea of creating a homogeneous socialist government, for which he was sharply criticized by Lenin and Trotsky. Ryazanov opposed Lenin on the VII congress RCP(b) in March 1918 on the issue of concluding the Brest-Litovsk peace. He declared himself as about supporter world revolution and accused Lenin in volume, what that did bet only on the Russians peasants.

"Lenin wanted to use the slogans of Tolstoy," Ryazanov said, "having modified them in accordance with the epoch he was going through. Tolstoy recommended arrange like a peasant, like a fool, Lenin — like a peasant, like a soldier. In his opinion, pursuit save Soviet Russia how center of revolutionary propaganda for the international proletariat explained desire "arrange ." in Russia
cell under spruce", under protection German bayonet" [12].

On the VIII congress parties (March 1919 G.) corrosive Ryazanov discovered what Bukharin, speaking With (how it was then called) "great-power opposition" to the national section of the program of the RCP (b), borrowed This idea from Stalin [13]. Equally critical was Ryazanov's speech at the Ninth Party Congress. He ridiculed the speech of Rykov, who, together with Trotsky, defended the idea of statehood. trade unions and spoke against exile from the trade union work of Ryazanov, who opposes stateization. Objecting to Rykov, Ryazanov (not without sarcasm) suggested giving the trade unions the opportunity to engage in security right workers and them upbringing [14].

The 10th Party Congress, which met in March 1921, ended with the rejection of the policy of war communism and the proclamation NEP. AT then same time Lenin brought barely whether not before absurdity idea unity party, special resolution

consolidating, contrary to the principles of democracy, the right of the Central Committee to exception own same members. Too much strong there was fear caused Kronstadt speech and sympathetic reaction on the him workers and peasants. Ryazanov did not fail to compare Lenin 's call for unity with an attempt Pugacheva reconcile their supporters: "AND speaker's speech (Lenin) and speech Samara comrad (Milonova) reminded to me one from our predecessors of the XVIII century - t. Pugachev. When started fractional disagreement... Pugachev addressed to their associates with a heartfelt word: "Gentlemen generals, it's full of you argue. Not trouble, if would and all Orenburg dogs jerked feet under one crossbar, trouble, if our males will gnaw among themselves. Well, make up!" Ryazanov believed that the Central Committee, while stubbornly fighting dissidents, was itself "cultivating" and growing "workers' opposition " [15].

The 11th Party Congress was the last one led by dil Lenin. Ryazanov took part in the discussion of his report, very figuratively submitting position in the party: "All comrades who have to ... criticize the policy of the Central Committee find themselves in a difficult situation. Our Central Committee — a very special institution. They say the English Parliament can do anything; he can't just turn man in woman. Our Central Committee where stronger: he already not one revolutionary man turned in baba, and number such bab incredible multiplies." According to Lenin, Ryazanov noted, it turns out that the communist the consignment for work in new conditions absolutly not fit." Ryazanov thought what So will be before those until the Central Committee ceases to stifle inner-party democracy [16]. At the XIII Party Congress, Ryazanov spoke out against the transfer of Marx's ashes to Moscow, at the XIV he stated a decrease in the theoretical level in the work of the party and said that the party's policy was "not always correct, and often very erroneous, in peculiarities per last thing time" [17].

Ryazanov always was configured on the criticism. His caustic remarks, mockery of authorities irritated apparatchiks and party oracles. Judging on his speeches on the congresses, he few was considered With statutory prohibitions and spoke out So, how thought necessary. He knew yourself price, how alone from the best connoisseurs history of Marxism. Maybe, can to tell, what his upbringing, image thoughts behavior were quicker social democratic than the Bolshevik type. It was Ryazanov on one of assemblies in middle 20's when Stalin tried to "theoretically" substantiate possibility building socialism in one separately taken country, cut off his publicly:

"Stop, Koba, don't make a fool of yourself. Everyone knows, that the theory is not yours element" [18]. Stalin said nothing, but, of course, remembered. After all, there were legends about his vindictiveness, a on testimonial Kamenev, for Stalin "higher ." pleasure — reveal enemy get ready, ok take revenge and then calmly sleep" [19].

So same independent judgments Ryazanov allowed himself in articles, books and publications edited by him. He originated dil from rights scientist doubt in everyone not considering while dealing with authorities. "If it is possible and should be critical to Marx and Engels, and I showed this is in several works, which Mehring honored with the most flattering praises, - wrote Ryazanov, if legends can be refuted, created with the light hand of Marx and Engels, then not less sacred right It has Marxist destroy the legends created by the anarchists. And I succeeded in showing that a series of the most stupid insinuations and the most filthy slander with which they tried to sully Marx's party honor, which were taken on faith by Bernstein and Mehring, are simply sucked out from finger" [20]. Ryazanov also established that row provisions Marx on stories Russia based on conclusions editor H. M. Kostomarova [21].

AT In 1923, Ryazanov published a work plan for the institute Marx and Engels, which included editions of the works Marx and Engels in 32's volumes; Plekhanov - in 26 volumes; Kautsky - in 21st; Lafarga - in 4th tomac 22_ -. This plan was supported [23]. And in 1930 G., when the situation in social science changed, Stalin was canonized as a classic, the attitude towards social became sharply hostile, history was rewritten and modernized, Ryazanov still in the introduction to the "Archive of K. Marx and F. Engels" limited tasks publications study stories Marxism and I and II Internationals [24]. He probably thought it natural controversy about able public Sciences (1928), speaking in defense of works written without the use of Marxist methodology. Ryazanov spoke flatteringly about the high scientific research culture of the works of D.M. Petrushevsky, although he met the objection of Gorin, who believed that only commitment Marxism [25].

In science, everyone was equal for Ryazanov, and in politics he hated party games. Not applying for high positions, he was primd how in big questions So and in personal values. So, in November 1928, Ryazanov wrote to Pokrovsky, chairman of the government commission on celebration 100th anniversary Chernyshevsky: "Not Considering it is possible for me to perform together with A. Lunacharsky, I, to my regret, have to refuse to participate in the evening dedicated to the memory of Chernyshevsky" [26]. Then, noting the precarious position of Bukharin, he carried phrase, which remember: "AT ." Politburo Marxists don't needed" [27].

I must say that Ryazanov expressed his opinion about Chernyshevsky at a meeting of the Society of Marxist Historians (1928). Piontkovsky, who was present, admired Ryazanov's erudition: he is "a marvelous old man. Such abyss knowledge No neither at whom. Such wild memory, remembers everything, and most importantly, what delights and amazes - this is the most complex of information ... This old man managed to throw a lot of valuable thoughts during a discussion speech, and about influence Chernyshevsky on the Russian historiography, and on Klyuchevsky in particular, and on the significance of the illegal press for 60s years for development legal thoughts, and on the analogy between Chernyshevsky and Blanqui in the sense of ideology. Wonderful interesting thoughts" [28].

Ryazanov not was going to readjust in please political conjuncture and was, on essence, doomed. AT de cabret 1930 of the year Stalin in conversation co listeners Institute of Red professorships set before them task beat on everyone directions." He proposed them not forget Ryazanov, after all "Institute Marx and Engels at us on the fly away" [29]. How not once noticed Ryazanov, Always easier find monks, how arguments." So what he hardly whether surprised when against him started wild political campaign. AT guilt to him put statement, as if "Leninism nothing new not gives for development Marxist teachings" [30]. Note what "accusation" not It was deprived grounds. When, in 1928, the then ordinary teacher of philosophy M. B. Mitin introduced in IKP report Lenin and Stalin, like successors philosophical teachings Marx and Engels, then received comment Deborina, Luppola and Karev that the title is incorrect. Lenin's only work on philosophy is Materialism and empirio-criticism" — not a philosophical treatise, but popular critical notes, and Stalin did not write anything at all on philosophical topics [31].

By your opinion Ryazanov, "if Leninism is really a new, higher stage of Marxism, if Marxism is really ...removed Leninism how "Hegelism" and "fire-"

Bachianism" were removed by Marxism, then — provided that our young philosophers really understand the meaning of the words they use— it is necessary that the new party congress liquidate not only my "Menshevik" view of Leninism, but immediately withdraw from circulation Stalin's book "On Lenin and Leninism" Lenin's views on the dialectical method from 1894 to 1914 were subjected to significant change... Only after acquaintance with the correspondence between Marx and Engels, Lenin began a new, deeper study of materialist dialectics... He at results that enabled him, in contrast to Plekhanov, to clarify and improve the understanding of Marx's dialectics... These the results were used by him in his excellent article on Marx ... therefore there can be no question of Leninism as a new, higher method of scientific research in comparison with the method of Marxism ... One can only speak of the dialectical method Marx Engels and Lenin" [32].

Ryazanov, certainly, know what self concept "Leninism" did not meet Lenin's enthusiasm; that newspaper articles by G. Zinoviev or the young historian V. Sorin in 1923, insisting on understanding Marxism as interpreted by Lenin [33], the weather did not; what was the more popular statement: Marxism in science, Leninism in tactics; that the term "Marxism-Leninism" was introduced into the propaganda turnover in middle 20's a Stalin saw in Leninism
"Marxism of the era of imperialism and the proletarian revolution". At Ryazanov It was his opinion.

AT letter, written in Presidium Comacademies
On February 8, 1931 (a week before his arrest), Ryazanov was indignant at the philosophical discussion, its devastating results. criticism Deborina, urged Seriously evaluate his works, since no one has yet proved that they "represent in fact, in essence, Menshevik idealism ... Deborina and his group blame in denial
"Leninism in Philosophy as a New and Highest Stage in the Development of Dialectical Materialism". When such an accusation is made by philosophical infants who think that Marxism is just as easy, by decree of the ICP, to rename in Leninism, how Petrograd decree CEC to Leningrad, and Tsaritsyn - to Stalingrad, you can still understand. But when this is does Presidium comacademies, he first must prove, what Leninism there is "whole worldview" that he "removed" or "buried" Marxism in areas philosophy, rights, economy, history, he first must subject destroying criticism

all the works of Lenin, proving the exact opposite. If a we building — and must build — socialism in one country, then "it would be a hopeless utopia to build science in one country and for one country." Ryazanov was very critical of the activity of the Presidium of the Communist Academy as the "brain of the party" and asked to be removed from the Presidium [34].

thirty April 1931 G. compound presidium Komakademia has been revised. It consisted of: M.H. Pokrov- sky (chairman), SB Pashukanis and VP Milyutin (deputies). Director Institute stories — Pokrovsky, deputy for academic work — Dubynya, for scientific work — Lukin. Director Institute of Philosophy — Adoratsky, his deputies — F. BUT. Gorokhov, M. AT. Mitin (in connections With this Adoratsky was dismissed from the post of director of the Historical Party Institute of the Red Professors [35]). But it all happened already after arrest Ryazanov.

In an unpublished letter to Pravda, he continued to make excuses, mind and present. Ryazanov wrote that back in 1919, when the Socialist Academy of Social Sciences began to work, and it was proposed to rename it in communist he objected: "I not Bolshevik, I not Menshevik but if you think myself Marxists, then you should not shy away from the word - socialist". Ryazanov gave a fragment of his speech at the XIII Party Conference, where spoke about to yourself: "I not old Bolshevik, I am not a Leninist, but I know that even the St. Petersburg comrades feel ... that I he is more closely connected with them than many of the old Bolsheviks, who received the name of old fools from Lenin. He reminded what edited With Bolsheviks in 1905 G., was reading lectures in longjumeau, wrote in "Star" and not in "Truth" Trotsky. "How, finally, explain, that L. Trotsky in his bulletin found it necessary to give a specific description of the activities of the institution headed by Comrade Ryazanov: Marx and Engel Institute sa remains still in counterweight institute Lenin and Istpart the only institution where Marxist thought burns and shines, where the theoretical weapon of the proletarian revolution is restored, refined, honed and partially forged anew. How to explain? Why does the Volga flow into in Caspian sea?" [36].

The arrest of Ryazanov discouraged his contemporaries. Piontkovsky called it absurd and wild. "Everyone knows Ryazanov," he wrote in his diary. "Kautsky knew him very well, know all pillars II International, his everyone knows guiding layers communist parties and social democracy of the whole world... For the time being, we feed only on rumors about this case, but the rumors themselves evoke colossal sadness. David Borisovich, this extraordinary old man, an exceptional brawler, with a violent head and violent temperament, a man of great knowledge, a witty man, who is accustomed to seeing the revolutionary movement on the podium, in the All-Russian Central Executive Committee and in the All-Union Central Council of Trade Unions, at trade union congresses, as one of the indispensable participants in the Russian revolution..." (diary entry dated February 24 1930).

Piontkovsky, paying tribute to the class-party perception of events, wrote about Ryazanov as a "petty-bourgeois" democrat, so and not become Bolshevik and that his inherent independence turned him into an oppositionist.

In periodicals, from the high stands, and after the arrest of Ryazanov, the his defamation. Presidium Comacademies in a special resolution called Ryazanov "a direct conductor of social democratic influences in our midst, an agent of counter-revolutionary Menshevism" [37]. On March 7, 1931, the Presidium of the Society of Marxist Historians decided to expel him from the society for "defending the Menshevik views on Leninism, denying its special role as Marxism in the era of imperialism, deliberately separating historical research from the demands of the Party and the Comintern." Ryazanov was charged with the fact that he worked at the institute representatives "bourgeois professors", that he opposed the liquidation of RANION and defended academic historians [38].

Of course, Ryazanov's arrest and reprisals against him are not accidental. R. A. Medvedev associated them with the trial of the so-called "Union Bureau" of the Central Committee of the RSDLP (Menshevik cov) [39]. This process took place from March 1 to March 9, 1931. 14 people were accused: VG Groman, member of the Presidium of the State Planning Committee of the USSR; VV Sher, Member of the Board of the State Bank, then Deputy Head of the Archives of the Institute Marx and Engels; H. H. Sukhanov, writer; AM Ginzburg, economist; MP Yakubovich, responsible worker People's Commissariat USSR; AT. TO. ikov, writer; II Rubin, Professor of Political Economy, Head of the Cabinet of the Institute of Marx and Engels; and others. The chairman of the court was HM Shvernik, members: VP Antonov-Saratovsky and MK Muranov; public prosecutors N. AT. Krylenko and G. TO. Roginsky; lawyers - AND. D. Braude and N. AT. Kommodov [40].

AT past many from accused really were

in the Menshevik Party, but then, as specialists, they worked exceptionally honestly in their official places. They were accused of deliberately distorting plans for the development of the national economy, "wrecking" and launched to various terms of impr isonment. The "bourgeois professors" who worked at the Ryazanov Institute included two: Vasily Vladimirovich Cher and Isac Ilyich Ruby.

RA Medvedev found many absurdities in the conduct of the process of the "Union Bureau" [41], but, apparently, it would be more accurate to say that the process itself was falsified from beginning to end. and haunted political goals. One from convicts, M. P. Yakubovich, spent in Imprisonment for 24 years, remained alive and lived until his death in 1980 in Karaganda disabled home. ten May 1967 g. this former nobleman and revolutionary wrote To the Prosecutor General of the country: "No 'Union Bureau of Mensheviks' has ever actually existed... The OGPU investigators never sought in no way to reveal the real political connections and the real political positions of the accused. They had a ready-made scheme of wrecking organization... The extraction of "confessions" began. Some succumbed to the promise of future blessings. Others who tried to resist were "advised" by physical methods impact: beaten (beat on face and on the head, on the genitals, they threw them to the ground and trampled feet, lying on the earth strangled per throat, bye the face was not flushed with blood, etc.), were kept awake on the "conveyor line", put in a punishment cell (half-dressed and barefoot in the cold or unbearably stuffy and hot, without windows), etc. For some enough It was one such threat impact. For others it applied in different degree, in dependencies from resistance everyone...

After assassination attempts on the suicide me already more
 not hit, but but in flow long time not were allowed to sleep. I reached before such states cerebral overwork, what to
 me became all on the light all equals: which any shame, which whatever slander on the myself and others only would
 to fall asleep. AT such mental able I gave consent to any testimony ... what to me prompted investigators... For a few days
 before start process the first "organizational meeting" of the "Union Bureau" in the office of senior investigator DM Dmitriev and under his chairmanship ... At the "session" the accused met with each other and coordinated (rehearsed) their behavior in court ... I knew Krylenko for a long time, even from the pre-revolutionary times. Knew close... Krylenko said to me

something like this: "I have n o doubt that you not personally guilty of anything. We both do our duty to the party. I considered you and still consider you a communist. I will be the prosecutor at the trial, you will confirm the data during the investigation of testimony. it — our party duty with you..." [42].

Yu. A. Shchetinov, who specially studied the sources, both Soviet and emigré, did not find a single document which the confirmed would version OGPU, and came to the conclusion that, apparently, they do not exist in nature [43]. Comparison texts testimony, published in the verbatim record of the process, with the original kept in the investigation files (there are 58 volumes), testifies about careful editing first [44].

And yet, given the necessary critical correction testimony former employees Institute Marx and Engels, consider what they said and what they accused his former director.

VV Sher (born in 1883), member of the RSDLP since 1905, secretary Moscow Council workers deputies, not times before revolution seated in royal prisons showed that in institute Marx and Engels he began work in January 1930, when he was "cleaned out" for his Menshevik past from the State Bank, where he had previously served. Ryazanov knew about it, but took his on the work. family they were on work in trade unions With 1906 of the year. AT institute Cher worked in the archive; like all employees, had access to documents. The archive was not used as a repository for illegal documents. He spoke with Ryazanov as with an old acquaintance; probably Ryazanov knew "that there is a Menshevik organization, working in Russia", but With Sherom about that's for me spoke [45].

II Rubin (born 1885) declared that he had been a member since 1904 Bund, a Menshevik-internationalist. Worked in party publishing houses worked in institute Marx and Engels, head of the cabinet of political economy from November 1926. On behalf of Ryazanov, from the beginning of the 1920s, he was engaged in the translation of the economic works of Marx and Engels. Relations with Ryazanov were good. During Rubin's arrest in 1923, Ryazanov came to visit him, brought literature, and even offered to bail him. Ryazanov did not know about his "connections with the Mensheviks" and about the documents that he, Rubin, hid in his office. acclaim, emphasized ruby, "moral responsibility for what I in their party purposes used institute and used personal location to to me Ryazanov -

falls entirely and exclusively on the me". He noted that his "relationship with Ryazanov was not very close." Before his dismissal from the institute in December 1930, Ryazanov took from him several documents on the history of social democracy for safekeeping, however, "if Ryazanov had been aware that I had been taking an active would not have taken the document from me in any way." Ryazanov knew about his possible arrest, and therefore denied taking any documents from him, because for this it was necessary to be "a paramount idiot."

From the testimony of Sher and Rubin it is clear that both of them were important to Ryazanov primarily as excellent specialists, and not people with a Menshevik past. The case with the transfer of some documents to Ryazanov for safekeeping is unprovable: one said that he had given the documents, the other is what not took and even in eyes not saw. themselves the documents stayed not found.

The lack of evidence did not stop prosecutor Krylenko, who, in the indictment, specifically has stopped on the relationships Ryazanov With Sher and Rubin and made a conclusion as terrible as it was absurd: "...When I asked question Rubin what other prerequisites formed the basis of his proposal to Ryazanov, what other moments played in the agreement of Ryazanov to the concealment of documents, that sympathies alone are not enough here— logic should suggest only one answer here. Moments of a different kind, moments of organizational connection, must have underlain this closeness. to Ryazanov, a not only personal sympathy.

Rubin was pleased to remain with his formulation. But it is quite clear to me that the situation that was there spoke about more close communications, spoke not only about consent Ryazanov hide the documents, but spoke and about acceptance them all measure to to that to these documents were not found. These documents exist, it is completely clear. it — writing document. it — written directive about interventions..."[46].

The prosecutor's fantasy was boundless: Ryazanov, it turns out, took document, because he was with Rubin one organizations. Document nobody not saw, not read, he was not attached to the indictment. But Rubin, the only one who knew about him, during interrogation (under threats, beatings or what?!) "confessed", and therefore the document took place, and the Menshevik Bureau welcomed the intervention .

It is forbidden not agree With remark Solzhenitsyn, that in the trials of that time only a bullet was absolute, and evidence of guilt — relative. Solzhenitsyn called the process of the Allied Bureau of Mensheviks "stuefyingly smooth." chatting With Yakubovich, writer figured out what during the investigation, Yakubovich "received" arrested persons, for example, II Rubin, into the Bureau. At first, Rubin refused, but he was "investigated" in the Suzdal prison. There he met with Yakubovich and Sher and asked first: "How could you think that I — member of the Union Bureau? And Yakubovich answer (answer amazing, here a whole century of the Russian intelligentsia): "The whole people suffer— and we, intellectuals, must suffer". Yakubovich is not could on the court refuse from their deceitful testimony. After all, this would be "a denial of the entire life goal for which Yakubovich lives, of the entire path by which he tore himself out of erroneous Menshevism into correct Bolshevism." And more: After such scandal not will give to die, they will not simply be shot, but will be tortured again, already in revenge, driven to madness, a body and without Togo tortured. For such a new torment - where to find moral support? in how glean courage?" [47].

Ryazanov not acknowledged myself neither in how guilty his failed to "include" in the "Union Bureau of the Mensheviks". He denied his guilt and success six years, when he worked in Saratov as a consultant in the library of the Saratov University, and when his again arrested and accused of links with the mythical "right-wing opportunist Trotskyist organization."

Probably, while working in Saratov, at the university, he repeatedly recalled answer Chernyshevsky officer arrived to him in exile and offered to apply for pardon: "It seems to me that I was exiled only because my head and head boss gendarmes Shuvalova arranged in different ways "But is it really possible to ask for pardon about this?" Ryaza could also answer his executioners - new He was and remains a Marxist historian, whom Pokrovsky called the first to start work in this [direction]. He was and remained a European-style social democrat who could not (and did not want to) hesitate together With general line VKP(b).

* * *

[one] A transcript of the celebration has been preserved and a special commemorative compilation articles. - RTSKHIDNI. - F. 301.—Op. 1.— D. 167; On the combat Post. / Sat. Art. to 60th anniversary D. B. Ryazanova - M., 1930.

[2] Surpassed everyone perhaps, Clara Zetkin, which wrote in her jubilee collection: "On the plinth of a magnificent monument to the creative scientific work of the Soviet state, a name Ryazanov.
[3] This premium never and nobody not was awarded. Soon about she was completely forgotten, since the name of Ryazanov was ostracized for many years.
[four] Ryazanov was approached for help by hundreds of scientists, not only former Mensheviks. AT investigative deed stored lots of letters to asking him to help in alleviate the fate. These are letters from historians Lyubavsky, Petrushevsky, Platonov and others. EA told me that you are allegedly saving academic colossi from Marxism, to which I remarked: "It is not clear he's obviously save Marxism from Pokrovsky, a You mix these two things".- Herald AN USSR.— 1991.— No. 11.—S. 103. Ryazanov was known for his harsh speeches against the punitive policy of the Bolsheviks in different years. In 1922, he spoke out against the persecution of clergy of different faiths, at a meeting of the All-Russian Central Executive Committee on August 3, 1922, Ryazanov demanded cancel all mortals sentence SRs and others convicts for "counter-revolution." Bulletin of the Russian Academy of Sciences.—1922.— No. 4.— S. 103-113.
[5] II Rubin taught political economy at the Institute of Red Professors and reputed popular professor.
[6] "For six weeks now, I have been transferred to Suzdal, where I am sitting in a damp cell facing north and located opposite various services," wrote Ryazanov.
[7] D. B. Ryazanov was rehabilitated 22 Martha 1958 G. And only exactly 32 years later, on March 22, 1990, Ryazanov was reinstated as a valid member AN USSR, not fair excluded from her
3 Martha 1931 G.
[eight] Smirnova AT. BUT. The first director Institute TO. Marx and F. Engels. D. B. Ryazanov // Questions stories CPSU.—1989.— No. 9.- S. 84.
[9] Conquest R. Big terror.- Riga, 1991.— Book. 2.— FROM. 398.
[ten] Even before October 1917, Ryazanov's works on the First International were published. and published two volumes works Marx and Engels per 1852-1856 gg.
[eleven] Archive AN Russia.—F. 350.—Op. 3.—D. 256.—L. one; Figures USSR and the revolutionary movement of Russia / Encyclopedic Dictionary Pomegranate.— M., 1989.— FROM. 639-640.
[12] Seventh extra congress RCP(b). Stenographic report.- M., 1962.- S. 73, 75, 91.
[13] "Ta wording, which he (Bukharin. - A. L.) repeats for comrade Stalin — workers' self-determination classes — as an objective criterion, So same insolvent, how and formula rights nations for self-determination...," said Ryazanov. See: VIII Congress of the RCP(b)// Stenografich. report. - M., 1919.- S. 59.
[fourteen] reflecting lunge in mine address, Ryazanov remarked: "You see what if I corrupt the trade union movement, then I I have been working hard since the time when Comrade Rykov did not distinguish between a cavalry saddle and a lathe.— See: IX Congress of the RCP(b) / Stenografich. report. 29 March -4 April 1920 city - M., 1920.- S. 207.
[15th] X congress RCP (b) / Shorthand. report. (8-16 March 1921 г.) .— M., 1921.— C. 45-46.
[16] XI Congress of the RCP (b) / Shorthand. report. (March 27 — April 2, 1922) .— M., 1922.— S. 69.

[17] XIII Congress of the RCP (b)./ Stenographic. report. (23-31 May 1924 г.) .— M., 1924.— S. 560-561; XIV Congress of the CPSU (b) / Stenographic. report. (18-31 December 1925 г.) .— M., 1926.—С. 688-690.
[18] cm.: Tucker R. Stalin. Path to authorities. 1879-1929.—M., 1990.—S. 433-434.
[19] cm.: There same.— FROM. 195.
[20] Ryazanov D. Essays on stories Marxism.— M.—L., 1928.— T. 1.- S. 5-6.
[21] There same.— M., 1923.— FROM. 529-530.
[22] Ryazanov D. Institute TO. Marx and F. Engels at VTSIK. - M., 1923. - S. 35-58.
[23] cm.: Volgin AT. P. Institute TO. Marx and F. Engels // Scientific worker.—1926.—No. 3.—S. 27-36.
[24] Archive TO. Marx and F. Engels.— M., 1930.— Book. 1.—S. 3.
[25] Herald Communist academy.—1928.—Kn. 2 (26).—S. 250, 262.
[26] RTSKHIDNI.—F. 301.—Op. 1.—D. 90. AT March 1929 G. Ryazanov refused to be vice-president of the USSR Academy of Sciences, probably not wanting to be a conductor party politicians.
[27] cm.: Cohen FROM. Bukharin. Political biography.- M., 1988.— FROM. 376.
[28] Piontkovsky wrote down in diary: "AT ." newspapers there is several articles about the anniversary of Ryazanov. It must be said that his anniversary is celebrated much worse than he deserved it. The old man is really funny, yelling wild voice, patronizes the Mensheviks collects exceptional rarities about Marx and Engels, publishes them, wrote a number of articles himself, knows exclusively a lot of and exclusively a lot of remembers, but he does not always think clearly and clearly, although he yells fuzzy thoughts terribly loudly.
[29] Questions stories CPSU.—1989.—No. 9.—S. 83.
[30] Pravda.—1931. -fifteen January.
[31] cm.: Avtorkhanov BUT. G. Technology authorities // Questions history.— 1991.—No. 2-3.—S. 127.
[32] RTSKHIDNI.—F. 301.—Op. one.- D. 90.—L. 66-70.
[33] Pravda.—1923.—3 January; Petrogradskaya truth. -1923.-30 August.
[34] RTSKHIDNI.—F. 147.—Op. 1—D. 33.—L. 56-57.
[35] There same.—L. 61.
[36] There same . - F. 301.—Op. 1.—D. 90 — L. 133-139.
[37] Proletarian revolution.—1931.—No. 4-5.—S. 183.
[38] Historian-Marxist.—1931.—T. 21 - S. eighteen.
[39] Medvedev R. O Stalin and Stalinism // Banner.—1989.— No. 2.— FROM. 183.
[40] See: The Process of the Counter-Revolutionary Organization of the Mensheviks. / Transcript judicial process, accusatory conclusion and sentence. - M., 1931.
[41] Banner.—1989.—No. 2.—S. 184-185.
[42] See: Stalin's regime of personal power. On the history of formation. - Moscow State University, 1989. - S. 94-95.
[43] There same.— FROM. 67.
[44] HH Sukhanov sent a statement from prison to the Central Executive Committee of the USSR, where he claimed that he "sacrificed his conscience by agreeing to play the comedy of the Menshevik trial", and told in detail how the "court performance" was staged .— See: Stalin's regime of personal power.—S. 70.
[45] Process counter-revolutionary organizations Mensheviks.— FROM. 147-148.
[46] There same.— FROM. 351.
[47] New world.—1989.—No. 9.—S. 123-127.
[48] Marxist historian. -1930.-T. 15.—S. 168.

MINGAREI SAGIDULLIN And "SAGIDULLOVSHINA"

Investigation case No. 3389 on charges of Mingarei Sagidullovich Sagidullin is not much different from a million similar.

Sergeant GB Vakhonin 6 Martha 1938 G. "installed" what "Sagidullin MS in the past since 1928 was the head of the "leftist counter-revolutionary nationalist organization in Tataria, which outgrew in 1931-32. into the Trotskyist rebel anti-Soviet organization
"Peasant ittifaq", for which in 1933 the board of the OGPU was sentenced to 10 years in prison. While in Dmitlag, Sagidullin, "as an undisarmed Trotskyist, carried out counter-revolutionary activities among the prisoners" and put task "overthrow ." Soviet power and the commission of terrorist acts against the leaders of the CPSU (b) and the Soviet government. Therefore, Sagidullin, who is in Kazan Prison No. 1, was charged with new charges.

When you read something like this, it's not the illiterate clichés of practiced phrases that strike you, it's not the senseless crackling of the accusation, it's not their sheer lack of evidence, but complete disregard for the person, for his rights. According to the canons of those years, the more threatening words the accusation contained, the more reasoned it should have been... although the latter less Total interested investigator.

He had his reasons. Yes, back in 1929 the first secretary Tatar regional committee VKP(b) M. Razumov said at the party plenum: "Sagidullin, under the necessary conditions, can be an excellent and useful party worker, but not in the Tatar Republic, because he was brought up in an oriental atmosphere, is a product of the national environment and he will never completely break away from this environment. can" [1] . The secretary of the regional committee, who considered himself an internationalist, essentially ruled out the possibility for Sagidullin to serve his people. For the sergeant of the GB, the defendant Tatar immediately became a "nationalist." The investigator did not consider what time new accusation against Sagidullina Razumov was already shot how
"enemy of the people" and his negative assessment did not play, seemed would, his former roles...

Sagidullin was not spared by A. Lepa, who replaced Razumov as first secretary of the regional party committee in 1933. Involved in the then unbridled beating of national cadres, in the implementation of the policy of Russification, the People's Commissariat of Education of Tatarstan , with the approval of the party authorities, declared: in its old, ossified forms; they tried to preserve the old Arabic and Persian terms, incomprehensible to the masses of the people, to revive dead words again and form new artificial terms on their basis; they tried to ignore the significance of the Russian literary language in the development of the Tatar language; At the same time they strove for internationalism, skipping over reality. It is known that these trends, which fought against the policy of the party and the Soviet government in the field of language development, were rebuffed by the Tatar party organization and were defeated . " [2]

The sergeant of the State Security Service knew that Sagidullin was a "nationalist", he was serving term, but to him not seemed absurd idea about volume, what, being in concentration camp he could prepare assassination attempt leaders parties and government...

According to Sagidullin, the questionnaire of the arrested person says: he was born on April 18, 1900 in the village of Verkhniye Suksy, Menzelinsky district, Ufa province, in a family of peasants - Nina is a poor man. AT February 1920 of the year entered in RCP(b) and then he wrote about himself: "I read almost all the books of the first importance on theory, stories and practice Marxism". FROM 1918-1920 Sagidullin - chairman of the village Komsomol cell, from the beginning of 1920 - at Komsomol work in Menzelinsky county, from October 1921 Mr. — head propaganda department, then secretary cantcoma parties. Then in Kazan he headed the United Sloboda district committee, he was favorably characterized as an enterprising worker who understood the national policy. In January 1925 Sagidullin became manage organizational department regional committee VKP(b). And then same has begun sunset his party careers. AT February 1926 G. he was asked to leave the republic for "incontinence" expressions.

Sagidullin left to Central Asia returned a year later and got busy historical and literary work. AT 1927 year, to anniversary October revolution appears his book
"Tatar workers on the paths of the Great October". The brochure was published by the Tatar Institute of Party History. Following the then class canons reference research-

The historian presented the events of 1917 according to the scheme: the Tatar workers acted together with the Russian workers, and the Tatar bourgeoisie was united in their aspirations with the Russian... Probably, he was one of the first who tried to anal yze the materials Muslim congresses of that time. And who was not afraid in 1927 to publish a group photograph of members of the Muslim Socialist committee, among which was and M. Sultan-Galiev, to to that time already excluded from parties.

In accordance with the political situation, Sagidullin proved with the help of various newspaper publications the fact of the participation of many Tatars — but not the masses of working people - in the process of transfer of power to the hands of the Bolsheviks, tried in every possible way to discredit the completely parliamentary idea of creating the Idel-Ural state. Although the documents show that the project of creating Idel-Ural was then supported by all the peoples of the region, it was not implemented.

Sagidullin's book was very loyal to to the authorities. But in her It was named a lot of names. And they are here same delivered auto RU trouble. Among staff members on creation Zabulachnaya republics" in Kazan At the end of February 1918, Sagidullin named Nigmat Enikeev. The very fact of proclaiming the firman on education state "Idel-Ural" in Kazan Zabulache (hence
"Zabulachnaya republic") was declared counter-revolutionary by 1927. On the basis of newspaper publications, N. Enikeev really acted then, in 1918, in Zabulache. Now he was afraid of this, he wanted to forget the past in every possible way. and filed complaint on the author books.

On February 10, 1928, the Tatar Regional Committee of the All-Union Communist Party of Bolsheviks discussed Enikeev's statement and adopted a voluntaristic decision, surprising in its ignorance: "1. comrade Enikeev Nigmata ... to rehabilitate. 2. tov. Sagidullin for the premises in issued brochure "Tatar workers on ways to October" surnames Enikeeva N. without availability on the fact of any documentary data and thereby compromising a member of the party, as well as the release this parts of the brochure without the consent of the members of the editorial board - to announce a reprimand. 3. Bearing in mind that comrade Sagidullin was repeatedly involved in group work, and having returned to the Tatar organization, as having filed an application for full retreat from group wrestling, what them performed not It was — to put before the OK the question of the expediency of secondment t. Sagidullina in order Central Committee VKP(b)" [3].

A little later, Sagidullin's book will be declared "vs- female sortie" and on the years hidden in special storage

Such same fate befell and his second brochure "On the history of the Vaisov movement" (Kazan, 1930). Sardar Vaisov was the leader of the religious sect of "God's warriors" who opposed the national and the political resistance of tsarism, they accused the Muslim clergy of supporting those in power. Vaisov proceeded from the old principle: all people are brothers, and therefore are equal to each other. He and his supporters dreamed of the revival of the Bulgar Khanate. Vaisov welcomed the October Revolution, recognized the power of the Soviets and, although he could not imagine socialism without Islam, opposed its most reactionary canons. His sermons and the squad of "God's warriors" enjoyed a certain popularity among part population cities. Chairman Kazan Cheka GM Ivanov later wrote: "When October came coup, then Vaisov telegraphed to a comrade Lenin that he was entirely for the workers' and peasants' revolution and offered his services to the Council of People's Commissars. In February 1918, when the Idel-Ural bourgeois Muslim republic (zabulachnaya republic), With the consent of the Council of People's Commissars, the Soviet Kazan released seven thousand rifles and money for the organization of the "green guard" of the Vaisov warriors to protect Soviet power from the counter-revolutionary troops of the All-Russian Great Shuro. His headquarters fit on the Hay area in rooms Bulgarian. The Muslim bourgeoisie, seeing in him a dangerous adversary, decided to take a desperate step. Here is a huge crowd people reduced agitators Shuro, with weapons in hand, rushed to the headquarters of the "Green Guard", defeated his and brutally tore to pieces Sardar Vaisova.
The "Green Guard" was disarmed and dispersed, and all the weapons fell into the hands of Shuro and were directed against the Soviet government." [4] Vaisov was buried on March 8, 1918, investigation real killers not found.

Sagidullin set the task of giving an outline of the history of the Vaisov movement, beginning his co second half XIX century, as a response to the peasant reform of 1861. The most interesting was the correspondence of G. Vaisov given in the brochure. and L. N. Tolstoy, data gendarmerie observation of the Vaisovites. Of course, in the spirit of the times, Sagidullin I saw in the Vaisov movement after October 1917 a reactionary phenomenon. But the study itself is little known earlier topics, comparison in the book of facts establishing general traits in outlook various of people

(Vaisov and L. Tolstoy), differed sharply from conjuncture nyh conclusions author.

Then it was typical for many professional historians and those who were looking for the truth. The facts known to them said one thing, but they drew conclusions for the sake of politics. Sagidullin was characterized by a sincere belief in the revolution, Lenin, for him politics Stalin represented
18th brumera", Thermidorian coup, the coming to power of Napoleon, emperor, dictator. He could not put up with it, he protested against the rules of this "game", which cost life whole generation party bonz.

In August 1929, the newspaper "Kyzyl Tatarstan" published pamphlet Sagidullina "Tribe sycophants", which criticized the sycophancy of leaders to superiors and rudeness on relation to subordinates. This, of course, did not please the authorities. The Tatar Regional Committee of the All-Union Communist Party of Bolsheviks was not slow to make a decision "On the mistakes of the editors of Kyzyl Tatarstan and Krasnaya Tatariya". The bureau of the regional committee discussed Sagidullin's article, stating that "the party has always fought against sycophancy." This general proposition did not in any way refute the specific data of Sagidullin's article. The bureau of the regional committee could not refute anything. That is why they resorted to a political discussion of the article: "...the article by Comrade. Sagidullina, as well as the articles of comrades Shatskin and Stan condemned by the Central Committee, are a disguised attack against the foundations of the Bolshevik Party. Declaring what TOADIES necessary search not among right and left, and among the middle and others, comrade. Sagidullin under the guise fight against sycophancy guides blows on the main cadres of the party and seeks to justify the struggle of the right and "left" deviators against the general line of the party. This article is at the same time a frank attempt to justify and renew the repeatedly condemned all Tatar party organization work on harassed authority parties in the masses. That's why article comrade. Sagidullina can only harm the cause of cleansing the party ranks from degenerate elements" [5]. Sagidullin received "last thing ." warning" and accepted solution leave from Kazan.

In 1930, Sagidullin became a student of the philosophical department of the Institute of Red Professors and moved to Moscow with his family. This institute was created on the initiative of Lenin back in 1921 and was, in essence, in its curriculum a postgraduate course for the training of social science teachers, teaching students only on Marxist program. By your opinion who studied in this

Institute of Professor Abdurakhman Avtorkhanov, the ICP set quite high academic requirements for applicants . The ICP was called the "theoretical headquarters" of the Central Committee party, which the gave a lot of personnel how Stalin so his opponents (Avtorkhanov BUT. Technology authorities. - M., 1991.—S. 18-20).

At the Institute of Red Professors, Sagidullin studied enthusiastically two With half of the year. finish not managed. Not gave. 21 December 1932 G. he was arrested and to ten years corrective labor camps. First was in the isolation ward of the Butyrka prison. After the announcement of the verdict, he was sent under escort to the city of Dmitrov, to the ITL (Dmitrovlag). The accusations brought against Sagidullin were senseless and cruel. As in many protocols, the accusations of that time did not contain material evidence of a "crime". Sagidullin was charged with: participation in the activities of the "nationalist counter-revolutionary insurgent organization "Peasant Ittifaq". Further I quote from the text of the verdict, turning Attention to the soulless, bureaucratic, illiterate language ... It turns out that Sagidullin in "Peasant ittifaq"
"entered through the Trotskyist organization in Kazan, in which he took an active part since 1928, being the liaison link between "Peasant ittifakom" and "Trotskyists". And he was also accused of "participating in the creation underground technology organizations (printing houses and t. etc.) and in the release of anti-Soviet leaflets, most of which he himself edited." It seemed would, in connections With the accusation of establishing the printing house should have been material evidence, but them not It was.

it It was time completion first five-year plans as then noisily wrote in the newspapers - building the foundation of socialism in country. Write and talk can It was about anything. The realities of those years look extraordinarily tragic. "The superhuman power of lies", according to B. Pasternak, could not somehow make human grief forgotten and made the policy of those days for industrialization and collectivization as flawed as the desire to satisfy hunger with human beings. It is now known that it was in those years that a mass deportation was carried out. population — dispossessed and evicted from places permanent residence more 200 million human. Not less ten million human become victims hunger 1932- 1933 gg.

When one person dies — relatives grieve about it, but when will millions? Officials tried to silence the ongoing politics terror violence and hunger. BUT those, who tried to think otherwise—isolate, intimidate, shoot. To make it easier to deal with imaginary en emies and to convince population in volume, what they exist and because of them — all the troubles, experts in provocations came up with parties and associations that should be crushed and then life will become better ... As in the fairy tale of Fazil Iskander— Let's all try cauliflower someday ...

Thus, the crisis in agriculture, caused by its real destruction, ruin villages, the eviction of peasants and robbery, exorbitant taxes, authorities explained
'wrecking activities major scientist-economists A. Chayanov, N. Kondratiev, who allegedly created the "kulak- kuyu party" — "Labour Peasant Party" to overthrow the Soviet regime. Naturally, the party created by the myth-makers had to have its supporters. in various regions countries. So in Kazan arose
"a business" about "kulak" group "Peasant ittifaq",
"terrorist and nationalist organization", the main "theorist" of which was declared Mingarei Sagidullin, and his closest associates Gilemdar Baimbetov, Galimzyan Aminov, wali Khabibullin. First, at the end of 1932-beginning of 1933, thirty human, then more about so many same.

An unbridled, slanderous campaign was launched in the newspapers against the "Trotskyist" Sagidullin under the derogatory headings "Sagidullism". Part of arrested some were accused of preparing an armed uprising, others - of support connections With them. AT result 5 che- Lovek It was shot, rest got various terms conclusions. Sagidullin— ten years.

During interrogations, Sagidullin, like Khanzafarov, admitted myself guilty only in volume, what in 1928-1929 gg. as if would
"consisted in an illegal counter-revolutionary Trotskyist organization," in which he was involved by the former chairman of Tatsovnarkhoz Shcherbinin. This organization, according to him, was headed by the "Trotskyites" Preobrazhensky, who were exiled to Kazan. Ter-Vaganyan and Sergey Safronov. Own same Sagidullin denied participation in the leadership of the Peasant Ittifaq. ten January 1933 of the year he wrote in Central Committee VKP(b) and OGPU: "Such monstrous charge, addressed to me, is in no way true, and I fear that, from this point, the investigation will take the wrong direction: to prove the unprovable. I've already done my part. Please check them carefully. A business goes about participation mine With end 1928 of the year

to the end of 1929 in the Trotskyist organization in Kazan. The accusation is presented without a calendar framework, outside of time. Further Sagidullin reported what With end 1929 Until May 1930, he was in the northern region, then he was preparing to enter the institute of red professors, studied in Moscow, and all this time "with no anti-party organization tied not was".

On the proposal of the OGPU, the issue of the "Peasant Ittifaq" was considered on February 9, 1933 at the party collegium of the Central Control Commission. Yemelyan Yaroslavsky, Secretary of the Collegium, signed performance about exception Sagidullina from parties. more, strange, what his expelled after, and not before the arrest, as was done in the order of things. "Dmitrovlag", where Sagidullin was sent and where, as a "Trotskyist", he was placed in one of the points remote from the railway, was the base for the construction of the Moscow Canal. — Volga. M. Sagidullin began working there as an editor of ki With law correspondence. 5 October 1933 of the year Sagidullin from camps wrote letter Maxim Gorky With request for help. Simultaneously repented: "AT ." 1928 year, when EA Preobrazhensky and Vaganyan settled in Kazan — Trotskyists - I joined to them mug, was reading Trotskyist literature, helped their work financially and organizationally. At the end of 1929 I moved away from the Trotskyists, began write and oppose them, and in the ICP I completely eradicated all vestiges Trotskyism but I before arrest hid about volume, what once upon a time adjoined to Trotskyist organizations and actively helped. Gorky gave this letter to Yaroslavsky. He formally unsubscribed: "There are no grounds for reviewing the case." Sagidullin was transferred to another camp - on Solovki.

In 1957, in connection with the rehabilitation of Sagidullin, investigators KGB Tatars started new verification his "affairs". They are interrogated remaining in alive his accomplices . Gali Kudoyarov said that Sagidullina knew from 1922 of the year and remembered his "Trotskyist" hobbies. Khanzafarov confirmed his acquaintance with Sagidullin with 1925 of the year and not remembered about his accessories to any anti-party grouping. He also said, what about "existence organizations "Peasant ittifaq" never not heard... Our guilt only in volume, what we opposed Stalin 's personality cult , anything else against Soviet authorities nobody from us not had."
Investigator KGB Tatars M. Aminov looking for in 1957 year data about facilitating in Kazan "Peasant ittifaka" and not found them. That's why in imprisonment he write-

sal: "So the way produced additional checking presence of a counter-revolutionary rebel organizations "Peasant ittifaq", which put supposedly its task is to carry out an armed uprising in the spring of 1933 of the year With help peasants, not is confirmed." But in volume, what Sagidullin was "Trotskyite" and led Active anti-party and anti-Soviet activity" in 1928 — 1929 years, he was sure. More Togo, when got up question about rehabilitation Shamiya Azanova, wives Sagidullina, arrested 16 October 1937 of the year and who has been in camps and special settlements before 1956 of the year, Aminov wrote down what Trotskyist activity" Azanova not installed. However, she know "about counter-revolutionary activities her husband Sagidullina, about how not reported... Because the guilt Azanova installed in misreporting, ...then in a t t h e present time it is appropriate to raise the issue before the judiciary authorities about retraining composition pre-steps Azanova".

AT 1957 year neither Mingarei sagidullin, neither his wife, Shamsia Azanova, not were fully rehabilitated. Investigators KGB Tatars not removed With him accusations in "Trotskyism" a With wives non-information on the husband." Khrushchevskaya "thaw" was only most start revision cases unreasonably repressed. AT Trotsky and Bukharin, those, who was convicted or betrayed ostracism together With them, rehabilitation not was carried out. Trotsky was removed from all public service in end 1927 and in 1929 deported from countries. After killings Kirov one September 1934 G. Stalin started big terror. FROM this time word "Trotskyist" has become synonymous "enemy people." For Stalin all they were still and terrorists. AT newspapers wrote about Trotskyism how varieties of fascism, they were sought out, arrested, shot. Trotsky wondered: if in country found so many my supporters, why in Kremlin Stalin a not I?

A case was opened against Sagidullin as a Trotskyist directly in camp and for completion consequences transferred to Kazan, where he how "Trotskyist" started.

From interrogation Sagidullina in Kazan 6 Martha 1938 of the year:

— You are a member of an anti-Soviet terrorist organization that existed in the Dmitrovsky camps where you served your sentence. Do you intend to give frank testimony to the investigation in your terrorist activity?

— Nothing to me about the existence of a terrorist organization not known and I in her participant not was.

Then the method of physical influence was applied to him by such masters of torture as Matvey Sheludchenko, Vasily Yurchenko and others. They also testified against him. This is a description of him, compiled from reports camp sexots. AT her to him attributed the words:
"Lenin features the League of Nations as a bunch of bandits. Now the USSR has entered in this league. Walking like this by, CC, guided usurper Stalin came down to such charms asical monarch socialism. it sounds paradoxically but topics not less, very it is probable that a socialist monarch will be elected in the not too distant future." It turned out that Sagidullin continued to criticize Stalin: "In general, interesting events await us, because it is no secret to anyone that no one likes Stalin. For example, Radek, which the all time sings to him laudatory hymns — doesn't love him the same as before. Radek does not love Stalin because he knows so much about him in order to love him. and respect". AT characterization should conclusion:
"In conversations with prisoners, convict Sagidullin constantly asserts that major political events will soon take place in the USSR and that major disagreements are brewing in the Central Committee of the Party."

Then Sagidullin was shown testimonies against him by prisoners: an artist from Tomsk, Konstantin Sobolevsky, and a journalist from Omsk, Nikolai Zhigulsky. The first, during interrogation on March 15, 1937, named Sagidullin among those who were ready to commit a terrorist attack and kill People's Commissar Yezhov, which the was going to inspect camp. Second
2 June 1937 G. assured convict on his same pointer:
Newspaper nationals "Kanal-Zarodary" edited featured Kazan Trotskyist Sagidullin Mingari. FROM him at me was frank talk, he opened to me, that he still is undisarmed Trotskyist, just detached in the camp from the organization and not having the latest political guidelines of their leadership. It was from him that I first learned about anti-Soviet sentiments... In addition, Sagidullin told me that the formation of camp units strictly according to nationalities contributes to the work of nationalist Dashnaks, Musavatists and Pan-Turkists".

And again from interrogation Sagidullina eight Martha 1938 of the year.

— You are an unarmed Trotskyist. Among the prisoners of Dmitlag, a also White Sea-Baltic camps, agitating the latter against Soviet power, introduced ideas Trotskyism praising at this sworn enemies of the people Trotsky, Bukharin, Radek and others. Do you confirm this?

— I may have misjudged on a number of points, but consciously counter-revolutionary agitation I not led. To so erroneous judgments I attribute his opinion about Bukharin, not remember to whom express me about Radek, since they were not yet arrested at that time. I have never fully shared the Trotskyist platform and have never been a convinced Trotskyist. My anti-party, anti-Soviet views treated to national question.

On May 10, 1938, Mingarei Sagidullin pleaded not guilty at a closed court session of the visiting session of the military collegium of the Supreme Court of the USSR. He called the testimonies of the false witnesses. The verdict was prepared in advance. Sagidullin was doomed.

On August 28, 1968, the sister of Mingarei Sagidullina, Shamsia, lived in samarkand, applied With application to the Attorney General countries: "In the autumn of 1937, my brother Sagidullin and his wife Azanova were arrested, recognizing them enemies people, condemned to ten years deprivation freedom. Prior to their arrest in Moscow, they lived on the street. Bolshaya Pirogovskaya, at home No. I not remember. On the day arrest at they had two children twins: boy Rafael, girl Louise, born in December 1925. In connection with their arrest, but to the best of my knowledge, the children were identified in children's house. Flat, remaining per them in G. Kazan, where they lived before . on the studying in Moscow, was occupied by the Ministry of Internal Affairs. I, being the sister of Sagidullin, fearing illegal repression, kept silent all these years, hoping that my brother was alive and would have to come back home. Together with him arrested and convicted long ago already returned and achieved rehabilitation, my but my brother did not return and I have no information about him. My brother has never been an enemy of the people, his family and he were victims of illegal repressions of certain leaders of our state, and I want this undeserved shameful spot take off With my brother rehabilitate him, and if he is not alive, tell me the time and place of his death."

The judicial flywheel for the rehabilitation of Sagidullin began to slowly unwind. Letters of inquiry were sent from the KGB of Tatarstan with requests to check and inform why Sagidullin excluded from party, was whether "Trotskyite" in reality, what is fate those, who his judged and slandered?

An additional check established that the witness against Sagidullina Nicholas Zhigulsky in 1922-1929 was tried more than once for theft and embezzlement, became a journalist in the camp. It turned out that if the chief Dmitlag FROM. G. Firin cooked "assault" on Yezhov and With this goal recruited 219 human former "counter-revolutionaries". Almost all of them were shot. An audit in 1956 established that this whole "case" was falsified, and therefore everyone was rehabilitated. The investigation found that Sagidullin's "testimonies" were simply brutally beaten out and his executioners were convicted in 1940 year.

27 On November 1968, Sagidullina's sister was invited to the Samarkand KGB, where she was informed that her brother was shot ten May 1938 of the year.

AT January 1969 G. Prosecutor's office USSR came to the conclusion about groundlessness condemnation Mingariya Sagidullina. Military Collegium of the Supreme Court of the USSR February 8 1969 yes established what "evidence guilt Sagidullina in anti-Soviet agitation... not available", what "Sagidullin is convicted, without sufficient grounds for that." Because the board decided: Sentence military colleges Supreme court USSR from ten May 1938 of the year in regarding Sagidullin Mingariya Sagidullovich on again opened circumstances cancel, a a business about German production stop per absence composition crimes." After receiving this rehabilitating document sister Sagidullina applied in KGB Tatars With asking to find out which property It was confiscated at brother's arrest and it is forbidden whether reimburse his price, on the what she is claims how relative and financially needy. From the KGB of Tatarstan Sh. Sagidullina was told that her brother really was swear to execution With confiscation of property, but since he was arrested in Moscow, in Kazan, no documents on this about not have. Examination, carried out Moscow Chekists showed the hall what in time arrest wives Sagidullina in Moscow "there was no property in the room, with the exception of literature", that "Sagidullin's property was not confiscated due to lack thereof", since at the moment arrest, he lived with his family in the dormitory of the Institute of Red professors.

sister Sagidullina it was announced orally. This episode investigative a business about Mingaree Sagidulline ends. But not may stay without answer many questions related to lawlessness, the destruction of people and the fact that those who did it did not suffer any punishment. The execution of several executioners meant little. After all, monuments to the ideologists and inspirers of the destruction of their own people still stand in the center of Moscow.

Mingarei Sagidullin belonged to to a new generation of historians who have no doubts about Marxism, devoted to Lenin and the revolution. He understood the development of the country after October 1917 as democratic, with the expansion of the rights of nations to life and place in society. 'Cause if you don't really pay Attention on the ideological frame of his two short books, it will become clear that the research topic he has decided is quite natural and not accidental. Evidence of the active participation of the Tatars in the revolution, an attempt to compare the teachings of Vaisov with the teachings of Tolstoy meant that all peoples have universal human values and they have equal rights to them. But he only began to search for the truth on his own, without sufficient professional education. His fate was criminally cut short in heyday creative opportunities.

* * *

[1] National question on the III plenum Tatar regional committee VKP(b), 3-10 november 1929 Kazan, 1930.—S. 107.
[2] Cit. from book: Davletshin T. Soviet Tatarstan. Theory and practice of the Leninist national politicians.- Munich, 1974.- S. 300.
[3] TSKHIDNI RT.— F. 292.— Op. 8940.—D. 328.— L. 12.
[4] CGA RT. - F. 823.— Op. one.- D. 2.— L. 2-3 .
[5] TSKHIDNI RT. - F. 292.—Op. 8641.—D. 322. - L. ten.

NAHAMKIS. HE SAME STEKLOV.

From the personal file of a law student of St. Petersburg University Nahamkisa Ovshia Moiseevich:
"Born August 15, 1873 in Odessa, of the Jewish faith. August 24, 1906 baptized in the Orthodox faith named George (Yuri) Mikhailovich. He graduated from the 3rd Odessa Gymnasium on June 14, 1891, from August 1891 to May 30, 1892 he was a student of the law faculty of St. Vladimir University in Kyiv, on May 30, 1892 he was dismissed from the university for non-payment of fees. In September 1908, he was accepted as a student of the law faculty of the St. Petersburg university. Graduated university in 1916 year since diploma first degrees."

In his autobiography, Steklov explained his long student life as follows: from Kyiv University was dismissed for not attending lectures, from St. Petersburg University for the first time - as a result of arrest and emigration. "On his return from the second emigration, he again entered St. Petersburg University in 1914 and finally passed the university exams in 1916 G., t. e. through 25 years after admission to the university. After that, he enrolled in the class of assistants to a sworn attorney in Petrograd, but he did not have to practice law in view of the revolution"[1].

He was a capable and enthusiastic person who took up early the revolution, the study and propaganda of Marxism, and found a way out for his stormy energy in politics, journalism, and scientific research. There was a lot in his life: solitary confinement in an Odessa prison, exile, escape from distant Yakutsk, meetings with Lenin, Plekhanov, N. Bauman, V. Zasulich and thousands of other people, comrades in revolutionary work and building a new state .

Steklov left behind many books written by him (the first appeared in 1902). The most notable of them were the biographies of NG Chernyshevsky and NA Bakunin, story International.

Steklov was correspondent "Sparks" "Proletarian" "Pravda" and many others magazines and newspapers. Was reading lectures in public law at Longjumeau, the school founded by Lenin. But Bolshevik became not straightaway. at first He did not accept Lenin's interpretation of the principles of organizational centralism, he also reacted negatively to the agrarian program proclaimed in 1903 by the Bolsheviks. The first acquaintance with Lenin's articles struck Steklov: "The author was completely unknown, a novice in the literary field. However, he spoke in the tone of a powerful person, he decided, pronouncing his sentences with such authority that only the most important figure who has per yourself already lengthy political and literary experience" [2].

The democratically minded intelligentsia considered their debt resist the authorities not join With her to any compromises. Serve, receive a state salary — could, grumble, express dissatisfaction, in free from work time — revered debt. But how and what to do for the people? "Vekhovtsy" talked about the abyss that separated intelligentsia and vulgar.

FROM reporter's precision and irony Steklov recalled how the Odessa Social Democrats campaigned in the 1890s years among workers. For example, the social democrat Kalashnikov picked up on the some construction site laborer and, not doubting his success, he began to agitate. "And now, stunned, crazed amazed savage nearly not who owned even articulate speech, Kalashnikov and his closest aides begin pumping up socialist sermons about exploitation, surplus value, class struggle, social revolution and t. d. unhappy, which the never not suspected the existence of such things, at first he was confused, and then became an ardent proselyte of new ideas. But the first application of what he learned from his new comrades was somewhat original. So, on the very first Saturday after settling in a new apartment in a bathhouse in old worn out boots, Oshmanets (name of worker what) returned from there in new patent leather low shoes. When asked where he got such lovely shoes, Oshmanets, smugly grinning answered: "BUT ." whistling-zero at one bourgeois. Enough them our blood drink!" spoke something about excess cost."

AT days overthrow autocracy in Russia, in February 1917, Steklov - in Petrograd [3]. Member of the executive committee of the Petrograd council, the first editor newspapers "News". Newspaper was body Petrosovet, and representative parties, included in his compound. remembering then time,

Steklov wrote: Izvestia o f that period expressed ... the character of a general, indefinite revolutionism, colored with a socialist tinge, opposing itself to the bourgeoisie, throwing out an internationalist banner and at the same time allowing, under common proletarian slogans, an unnatural cohabitation of profoundly different elements. , which sooner or late, when faced with vulgar practical prose, each had to speak in his own language and dispersed in various sides" [4].

Soon, both Tsereteli and Lenin began to criticize Steklov, primarily for agreeing with everyone. Steklov declared himself as a supporter of dual power and "revolutionary defencism", believing that the Soviets should control the power of the Provisional Government. However, on May 12, 1917, due to political differences with the leadership of the Petrograd Soviet and internal editorial intrigues and squabble he left fast editor.

Again he returned to Izvestia on behalf of the presidium II All-Russian congress Soviets and, having mastered Role "government publicist", remained there until June 1925 G. Then appeared his famous editorials- "glazing", then same (in 1923-1924 gg.) he together with Lunacharsky and others organizes and edits the Red field" and "New world". All this is time he member All-Russian Central Executive Committee and Central Executive Committee. Steklov was a member of the commission for the creation of the Constitution of the RSFSR of 1918, a delegate to many Bolshevik congresses, during the years of the Civil War he left the propaganda train - mi on the front, in 1919 G. was injured and nearly deaf after the explosion in building MK in Leontief lane.

In 1925-1935. Steklov edited the magazine "Soviet construction", for some time he worked as deputy chairman and chairman of the Committee for the management of scientists and educational institutions of the Central Executive Committee of the USSR. AT 1935 he came out on the retirement, With topics to proceed main business of life — publication of a multi-volume collected works of Bakunin.

Steklov's works, his speeches at scientific conferences, independent judgments went out per established and a track marked with red flags. The censors were vigilantly waiting in the wings, not forgetting that foreign historians Steklov's works among those in which there was a clear deviation from the Marxist concept (for example, works on the history of the Paris Commune), and which only because contributed something new in historical science [5].

In 1928, when the legend of the only true social and political doctrine was taking on more and more canonical outlines, and the number of its classics became strictly limited, Steklov spoke With anniversary report about Chernyshevsky. He featured Chernyshevsky As a thinker who, in his philosophical outlook, political principles and tactics, was a revolutionary communist and historical dialectic materialist, on the half a century publish much from about how learned Lenin. By his your opinion Chernyshevsky was
"the first to substantiate views in Russia, which received completed wording in doctrine Marx and Engels - revolutionary communism" [6]. Steklov was supported by Ryazanov. Pokrovsky, Nechkina, Mints and others spoke out against it, seeing in Chernyshevsky a revolutionary democrat and a peasant revolutionary. From the discussion in which Pokrovsky's point of view prevailed, [7] Chernyshevsky entered all historical textbooks as a revolutionary democrat.

Without going into a detailed analysis of the opponents' positions, let's pay attention to only one plot. Steklov met with Lenin at the very beginning of the century in Geneva. It was a time when Lenin had an unusually high appreciation of Chernyshevsky's work. N. Valentinov, who met with Lenin about in those same years, remembered what Lenin dragged on "to the revolutionary " dynamite " of Chernyshevsky, to his determiningness extremism left eye, Russian Jacobinism [8]. Maybe to be, that's why think, "plowed" Total Lenin, and received so sublime evaluation in report Steklov? Truth, under impact critics, Steklov then same recognized: "Of course, it is forbidden say that Chernyshevsky was finished Marxist and Bolshevik. But he was our forerunner both in politics and in philosophy, and in all others areas... Before Marxism he is not reached. AT this guilty Russian life, her backwardness, and may be, and premature the death of Chernyshevsky" [9] Among ideological predecessors Bolshevism Steklov called and Bakunin. "Can boldly say, wrote he, what if would she is (program Bakunin) was carried out, then revolution 1848 of the year not ended would so shameful collapse and captivated would yourself Slavic, on predominantly peasant peoples. But most wonderful side of the Bakunin plan is then, what he fast creature Soviet authorities and how would predicted in in general terms move great Russian October revolution 1917 year " [10]. AT then time views Steklov were recognized erroneous and rejected as invalid. But is everything he said wrong? After all, "condemning" methodological argument is not proof yet. The theoretical origins of Bolshevism are still insufficiently studied and it is difficult to say how true or incorrect the provisions are. Steklov.

In the early 1930s, certain provisions were also criticized. works of Steklov on the history of the First International and the Riga Communes. He denied conclusion Marx like the Commune was "that for a long time desired political form in which the economic emancipation of labor could take place. Steklov thought that one forms, which correspondents dictatorship the proletariat Commune not gave. Because he called her "solid mistake." Conclusions, made them in the early 1920s, Steklov confirmed and in February 1936, arguing what "will to authorities at Parisian the proletariat is not It was, and even Parisian Commune... in was largely the result of the stupid actions of the provocateur government" [11].

Leafing through Steklov's investigation file, I carefully looked for any accusations related With his works. Them not It was. But, maybe, they created him a kind of reputation at power has.

28 January 1938 senior lieutenant of state security L. Raikhman submitted a certificate to his superiors for consideration: "According to intelligence data, Steklov is hostile to the leadership of the party and the Soviet government. Systematically conducts counter-revolutionary propaganda, expressing his hostile attitude to politics parties." And then there are Steklov's "statements" collected and presented to the NKVD by the seksot (I took the word "statements" in quotes, So how nobody not tried to to establish their authenticity and belonging to Steklov). Steklov seemed to be saying: "Even these vile corrupt bourgeois constitutions provide voters with the right to write any candidate on the ballots, and we don't even have that. Under bourgeois constitutions, anyone is allowed to be elected, a at us at such democracy please vote for one candidate... Accusations of espionage and other counter-revolutionary activities used party As a pretext to eliminate dissatisfied with the current regime and politics parties. If a would Marx was alive in our days, then and his would pinched Stalin... AT this wave of arrests, no one can understand anything, who is being arrested and for what, however, another and expect It was it is forbidden".

talking about work newspapers "News" and her new editions,

remarked: "Let's see how these people, appointed by the Central Committee, will cope with the work. They'll ruin the job." Condemning the policy of the party, he asserted: "At present, scientific work can only be carried out abroad, books are not confiscat ed there. We have only books in science that ten editions of Stalin."

To these "statements" postscript: from messages 1937 and 1938 years. And resolution: to arrest and search. The date: 3 February 1938 G.

AT that same day Steklov was arrested a in his apartment in the Metropol Hotel was searched. There were seven of them, specialists in searches and arrests of people who did not dare to resist: Mityushin, Starovoitov, Rymchenko, Sergeev, Yaskin, Galkin, Gomozov. as witness attended porter hotels M. Meltzer.

During the search, the following items were seized: party card No. 1248428, passport, Mauser, Browning, cartridges for them, a gun, a hunting knife, personalized seal "Izvestiya TsIK", a notebook, letters, books "counter-revolutionary" writers 105 "things". From four rooms three sealed up, in one left wife and family son.

AT questionnaire arrested filled in that same day means: was born four august 1873 G. in Odessa. Professional - writer and professional revolutionary. All time worked at CEC USSR, now, due to disease, does not work, waiting destination, is engaged literary work. Father was small merchant. Education higher, lawyer, reporter, member VKP(b) With 1893 G. A family: wife - Sophia Yakovlevna, daughter Maria (sick) son, Vladimir, is an engineer-economist.

The interrogations of Steklov and all persons associated with him were conducted by the special representative of the 1st Department of the State Security Grigory Fedorovich Sharok. (born in 1900, in May In 1954, he was dismissed due to age into the KGB reserve with the right to wear a military uniform).

From protocol interrogation Steklov (2 April 1938 G.):

— You are under arrest as a member of an anti-Soviet group carrying out anti-Soviet activities. Testify about your disagreements With politics and activities VKP(b), about your connections and illegal activities.

— Disagreements With politics and activities VKP(b) I don't have and never had. I never expressed counter-revolutionary views and did not conduct illegal activities. Never neither to what anti-Soviet groups not adjoined

and hesitation from general lines VKP(b) at me not It was,
— You are not telling the truth... You want to mislead consequence. it to you not succeed do. You more With 1925 of the year, after your his withdrawals With work in editions
Izvestia harbored malice cultivated hatred to the leadership VKP(b)... We demand from you truthful indications .

— Never no malice against guides VKP(b) and governments at me not It was neither With 1925 of the year, neither later, and therefore I could not sow hatred against them ... In a separate In other cases, I might have doubts on certain issues. For example, about law against abortion, which, as I feared, was capable of causing the development of secret quackery and secret abortions ... I also had doubts about the excesses in the initial stage of the collectivization of agriculture, I feared that these excesses could damage the alliance between the proletariat and the peasantry. But the clarifications that followed shortly after, Com. Stalin outlived in me these doubts... relatives friends at me no.

Steklov asked the investigator to bring at least one of the facts his anti-Soviet statements. Sharok pulled out two sheets of paper from the table. On the first one was the text of the denunciation dated March 21, 1938. On the second — record of the interrogation of Mary Moiseevna Goldman, born in 1911, Komsomol member, student at the Dental Institute, wife of Steklov's son Vladimir.

Mary Goldman was interrogated on March 20, and the next day (maybe, on advice investigator) was written denunciation.
"— Do you know the political views of Steklov Yu. M.?
— Yu. M. Steklov is formally a communist, but in reality a double-dealer in VKP(b), hiding before last time their counterrevolutionary views...
— What specifically and on what policy issues of the CPSU (b) Steklov express anti-Soviet views?
— Steklov almost every new event of the CPSU (b) and the government met vicious criticism... He said: there real democracy, a at us in USSR her no... About the ongoing arrests of persons who figured at the past Trotskyist trials and Zinovievites, Steklov said that he did not believe in their guilt, that by doing so they wanted to get rid of the old real revolutionaries... He said, what at us not allow write the truth in newspapers... This situation in the USSR, according to Steklov, is the result of wrong guides..."

Goldman all their statements issued statement: "I I know Steklov Y.U. M. With 1931 of the year. Per all this time he showed myself how human alien Soviet power. it came to light in his permanent dissatisfaction with all activities parties and government. Our constitution he thought existing only on the paper, t. K. thought what each human fears at us talk open then, what thinks under fear to be filmed With work and arrested... I I think what this is human clearly anti-Soviet and negative configured."

By the time of the interrogation, Goldman was arrested and her husband, Steklov's son — Vladimir Yurievich. She was intimidated and obviously wrote on hint investigator.

Steklov all accusations rejected:

"— Categorically rejecting such accusations, I declare that, on the contrary, in surrounding me I always developed a love for the ideas of communism and Soviet power and aroused hatred only to world fascism the fight against which I considered and still consider it a priority. The accusation regarding my imaginary statements about our electoral system, I reject as categorically as clearly slanderous and belonging to not to me..."

In the investigation — Steklov confrontation protocol With Goldman from 4 April 1938 From he can see that Goldman confirmed what she said and wrote in the statement, Steklov same said what she is He speaks lie.

Many years later. April 23, 1956 in connection with the rehabilitation Steklova, convict KGB again invited to Mary Moiseevna Goldman, who lives with her daughter in Moscow. She is declared what remembers heard her in 1932- 1938 Steklov's anti-Soviet statements, as they lived together, in one apartment, but what full-time rates as such not It was.

— They brought him - Goldman said, "when I gave indications. But he was in flow two or three minutes. Me released. Who and how designed full-time bet, I don't known.

Investigator Sharok, realizing that Goldman's testimony alone was not enough for a "full-fledged" prosecution, began interrogate those, who was enter to Steklov.

April 2, 1938, brought as a witness Boris Grigorievich Kuznetsov (born 1903, member of the CPSU (b) With 1925 G , performing responsibilities direct Torah Institute stories science and technology AN USSR), on-

He said that he was familiar with Steklov's son, often visited him at his apartment.

"What can you say about political views and feelings Steklov? asked his Sharok.

Steklov clearly anti-soviet human... He mocked the Stalinist constitution and the electoral law ... Steklov condemned politics VKP(b) in areas science. He spoke of the fact that "they planted everywhere the ignoramuses who that interfere with work." About libraries and In the archives, Steklov said that at the present time serious scientific work could only be done in foreign libraries. There,- he explained, because books are not seized. Steklov denied the possibility of a revolution in the West. He said that a serving of castor oil was enough for Mussolini to cope with any revolutionary labor movement. However,- Steklov remarked, "Our methods of work there are sickening."

Kuznetsov was summoned on April 24, 1956 to clarify his testimony. At that time he worked as a senior researcher at the Institute of History, Natural Science and Technology Academy of Sciences of the USSR. Senior Lieutenant KGB Lunev, cooking materials for rehabilitation Steklova, asked if his testimony was correct. Kuznetsov confirmed that Steklov was indignant at the 1937 arrests and denied their necessity. Spoke, what Stalin in many things how supervisor, conceded Lenin."

The investigator showed Kuznetsov the original protocol of the testimony he signed on April 2, 1938. Kuznetsov noted: "The recorded statements of Yu. M. Steklov correspondent reality, but, how I now I think they do not give grounds to qualify Yu. M. Steklov as an anti-Soviet person and his views as counter-revolutionary views."

Sharok continued weave web.

2 April 1938 of the year he interrogated more one friend Steklov — Boris Pavlovich Barkhash, born in 1911, associate professor at Moscow State University, editor of the philosophical department of the journal Kniga i Proletarskaya Revolyutsiya. Barkash knew Steklov With 1928 of the year.

"What to you known about political views Glass? - followed question Sharoka.

"Steklov is a double-dealer and a man in the party who has completely decomposed morally and politically... In 1930, Steklov, in connections With 60 years old anniversary Ryazanov, Addressing his son, Vladimir Steklov, he said: "Remember my word. Today his awarded order, a all equals his eaten alive... It can't be otherwise. Stalin will not forgive him. Enough recall, how boiled Stalin when In 1926, Ryazanov, with his perfectly correct remarks, prevented Stalin from making a report at the 15th All-Union Party Conference. All the same, Ryazanov will be caught on something ... "

AT 1931 year, in connections With resolution Central Committee VKP(b) about the journal "Under the Banner of Marxism", in which the activities of Deborin and his "company" were assessed as Menshevik idealism, Steklov said that Deborin brought down With mind.

According to Barkash, Steklov owned the following following statements: "This is what the so-called discussion on philosophical topics of academician Deborin brought to. Stalin thinks that such methods of theoretical discussions, as a result of which people go crazy— contribute to the development of the theory of science in our country. Stalin must finally understand that in this way one can only disperse the scientific cadres and destroy any scientific work in our country ... Public critical thought has died out in our country. People are afraid to give an objective assessment of such an undoubted the biggest event how exit in light four volumes from supposed complete meetings works of Bakunin, published under my direction... It is completely incomprehensible what is happening now in our country. There was some fluff. All sorts of crooks-crooks occupy leadership positions. Then they are caught and imprisoned. Never before in the history of the party has this happened. We old revolutionaries have a different idea of the socialist society".

Barkash did not give a second explanation: at the end of 1941, how is listed in the document he, being on the front, disappeared without lead.

Pulling Steklov's various statements out of frightened witnesses, the investigator labeled them "anti-Soviet." Steklov did not recognize them as such or rejected them outright. But he declared the possession of the revolver at home illegal, indicating, however that it belonged to his deceased friend. What concern album CEC 1923 year with portraits of Trotsky, Zinoviev and Kamenev, Steklov said what album lay at him in library and he forgot about his existence.

On April 23, 1938, a special meeting of the NKVD of the USSR condemned Y.U. M. Steklov on the eight years prison conclusions. He was charged with anti-Soviet agitation. and illegal storage gunshot weapons. In and-new myself Steklov neither in how not admitted. His sent to Tambov prison. He wrote a cassation complaint, only on December 27, 1939, Steklov's archival and investigative file was sent for additional investigation, and the convict himself was transferred to the Oryol prison of the NKVD, a then, in April 1941 G., in Moscow in order of the investigative department of state security. By that time, master provocateurs from the NKVD had "concocted" against him another "thing". They acted according to the principle: "One thing is not enough for you, you are indignant, we will sew another one, but we will not release it, the NKVD is an organ, where not are wrong."

Instead of an investigation into the illegality of the conviction, Steklov was accused of continuing to engage in anti-Soviet propaganda in a prison cell. Witnesses — convicted cellmates of Steklov (M. Bekirov, N. Komarov, P. Galeev) stated that he campaigned against them Soviets and slandered the actions of the government. As far as one can judge, the "cellmates" were secret police, specially planted together with Steklov in order to provoke him and convey.

In any case, the stored in investigative deed request letters the head of the 2nd department, Fedor Petrovsky (after being dismissed due to age from the authorities, he worked as the head of the economic unit of the Ministry of Internal Affairs of the RSFSR). He offered to interrogate in the Krasnodar Department of the NKVD a sex worker nicknamed "Old", who was imprisoned with Steklov in the Oryol prison; in the Arkhangelsk Department — sexots Markina and Gorlova, in Odessa — Orlovsky's sex, and in the Orlovsky prison — a secret agent named "Gate". Was put a task take at them readings about Steklov.

Mustafa Bekirov, a Crimean Tatar (prior to his arrest, secretary of the Sudak District Party Committee) was interrogated on July 5, 1941 G. (walked war, but NKVD did his a business). He testified that he had met Steklov in a cell in the Oryol prison, and confirmed that Steklov was engaged in anti-Soviet propaganda, insulted the "leader of the peoples", sympathized with Trotsky and Bukharin, spoke about the advantages of the bourgeois the democracy.

Former political worker Komarov (July 1, 1941, Krasnodar) explained that he was in the same cell with Steklov and that the latter allegedly said: Bolsheviks brought Russia before provisions times Vasily Dark, that there is a cultural savagery of the country, arbitrariness and lack of rights. More one former cellmate, Galeev, approved expected that Steklov - "the enemy of the communists" and that he allegedly exclaimed: "Why to me need was this revolution!"

While the investigators were collecting this testimony, Steklov was tormented at the Lubyanka. This time it was Rafail Alexandrovich Goldman (later dismissed from bodies
"on facts discrediting the rank of an officer"). Exhausted Steklov wrote to Stalin on May 22, 1941: "Again, I don't know why, they put me in the inner prison of the NKVD, but on the this once appeal co me much worse than the one I complained to you about in 1938." He listed insults, swearing during interrogations, threats of physical violence. And continued: AND. AT., I I beg You save me from such a terrible treatment: after all, you know it well that all my life I have earned a different attitude towards myself. I don't have long to live — I am doomed to give up my spirit in a dungeon, in terrible conditions of confinement, and for what? I have been suffering for the 4th year already, my family has been destroyed... This cannot and should not be. Give me the opportunity to finish the work I have begun (about Bakunin [12], Chernyshevsky, Internationale, Marx and etc.), from which
6 volumes surrendered in seal and will be lost, I nothing others
except for purely scientific, desk work, I do not intend to do it. It's time for a long time it's time me let go.

A prisoner internal prisons NKVD (camera 33).
Y.U. M. Steklov, 68 years".

Steklov did not wait for an answer to the letter, although it is known that memory at Stalin was phenomenal.

During the interrogation on May 20, 1941, which lasted about 3 hours, Steklov stubbornly stated that "he did not carry out enemy anti-Soviet work." And on June 3, he again spoke in detail about himself, and only at the end of the interrogation did he realize for what purpose forced his this is do convict Goldman.

Steklov spoke about his pre-revolutionary arrests: the first time he was arrested in 1894 in Odessa by gendarmes. Accused of revolutionary activity. He was held in custody until July 1895 and was exiled to Vostochnaya Siberia on the ten years. Was in Yakutsk, in end 1899 Mr. fled abroad, lived in Geneva and Paris. Returned to Russia in november 1905 G., arrested in december 1905 in St. Petersburg, sat until May 1906, released. The third time he was arrested in February 1910 in St. Petersburg, he was accused of belonging to the RSDLP and the work of the Social Democratic faction of the 3rd State Duma. In the spring of 1910 was expelled per border.

AT 1908 G. was invited member Central Committee

RSDLP Bags-

Skim [13] to help the Social Democratic faction of the Duma in writing documents and speeches. He joined the Bolshevik Party in July 1917 (the seniority party from 1893 was established by the Central Executive Committee in 1921, since he actually worked all the time With Bolsheviks).

The investigator asked Steklov about Guchkov and Stakhovich, or rather, about whether "these monarchists" petitioned for his release. from under arrest in 1910 G. Steklov answered, that he knew AI Guchkov as a member of the State Duma, but did not have personal relations with him. Mikhail Alexandrovich Stakhovich knew since 1906, met him at the apartment of the historian Maxim Kovalevsky. He was a zemstvo figure, a representative of the liberal movement. Stakhovich really petitioned for Steklov to be released from arrest for the duration of his wife's birth. Whether Guchkov took part in this, he does not know. Here, probably, Steklov realized that the contempt "sews" him a connection with cadets or Octobrists and became noticeably be careful.

Since additional investigation is nothing new   gave   and, on   definition   convict   goldman,
"Steklov did not show anything about his counter-revolutionary activities," he was transferred to the Saratov prison. So Steklov got - albeit against my will, home of one of my favorite characters — Chernyshevsky. He died there, on September 15, 1941, in the hospital of the Saratov prison. Steklov's prison file was destroyed, only the history of his illness from August 21, 1941 in the 3rd building of the prison hospital was preserved. It shows that he was in the hospital from August 21 to September 8, 1941: two days later, on September 10, he was hospitalized for the second time. Doctor on duty Alexeev declared death from dysentery and extreme exhaustion of the patient. Death occurred at 4 am on September 15 from a heart failure. activities.

October 7, 1941 Lieutenant GB Goldman "for the death of the accused" a business Steklov stopped.

Soon from Steklov's wife — Sofya Yakovlevna addressed to Beria a statement with a request to reconsider her husband's case and at least posthumously rehabilitate him. On February 20, 1943, the secretariat of the special meeting of the NKVD in Sverdlovsk considered this statement and issued a verdict prepared by senior lieutenant of State Security Service Veretennikov: revision his cases, does not lead, ruled: complaint leave without satisfaction, about how through 1st specialist-department to inform the complainant at the address indicated by her in the complaint. Sofya Yakovlevna was informed of this decision on April 20 la 1943 G.

Again solicitation about rehabilitation Steklov turned him on son - Vladimir Yurievich. AT statement on the name General prosecutor countries R. BUT. Rudenko he wrote (5 OK- October 1955 G.): "AT ." February 1938 G. authorities NKVD USSR was arrested my father - Steklov Yuri Mikhailovich, CPSU member With 1893 of the year... By available at me information Steklov Y.U. M. died in prison hospital in Sarato- ve... Mother my, wife Steklova - Sofia Yakovlevna glass, was member CPSU With 1898 G. and passed away member parties in Tashkent, where was evacuated With group old Bolsheviks. I was arrested through several days after father my... 31 august 1955 G. was rehabilitated and restored in parties." 17 February 1956 G. USSR Prosecutor's Office excited a business about rehabilitation Y.U. M. Steklov. Investigator KGB interrogated more living witnesses, requested archives. 27 April 1956 G. took place interrogation Steklov's son — Vladimir Yurievich, representative director of the Moscow branch Institute "Orgenergostroy" [14]. He reported what relations his father and his former wives Goldman were hostile what explained testimony of the latter. What concern revolver, then he was donated Steklov his friend and nobody them not enjoyed.

Positive feedback about Steklov was received from a member parties With 1905 G. O. N. Mitskevich. Academician G. M. Krzhizhanovsky testified: "I know Steklov Yu.M. since 1917 as an active participant in the revolutionary movement, member communist parties With 1893 G. Being Yu. M. Steklov, the founder and editor of Izvestiya, did a great deal of party work to propagate the Leninist policy of our fell a victim enemies our parties."

In the file, certificates from the Central Party Archive are filed - about the revolutionary activities of Steklov; from the Odessa regional archive - about the date and place of his birth; from Leningradsky extract from the personal file of a university student. On March 23, 1956, the TsGAOR presented an interesting note: the French counterintelligence documents state: "Nakhamkis, aka Steklov, Jew, member Council With October 1917 G., member Bolshevik party since its founding. Together with Bronstein (Trotsky) and Sverdlov was the soul of the Jewish faction - the most energetic in the party. He is a close friend of Goldendakh- Ryazanov.

KGB investigator Lunev, having considered the available materials and not discovering accusatory conclusions on Steklov's case, proposed to intercede with the Prosecutor's Office countries about his rehabilitation. Judicial collegium for Criminal Cases of the Supreme Court of the USSR on June 13, 1956, considered the protest of the Prosecutor General in the case of Steklov and decided: decision of the special meeting under the NKVD of the USSR in relation to Steklov, cancel the case and proceed stop.

30 June 1981 G. AT. Y.U. Steklov requested Y.U. AT. Androkov return manuscripts father: trained them to the publication of Bakunin's work (4 out of 12 volumes were published), an unfinished work on the history of the International, etc. He was informed that since all the prison archives before 1957 had been destroyed, gone and edits his father.

* * *

[one] Figures USSR and revolutionary movements Russia / Encyclopedic dictionary Pomegranate.- M., 1989.— FROM. 704.
[2] Steklov Y.U. Favorites.— M., 1973.—S. 13.
[3] More about this cm.: Steklov AT. YU., Filonovich Y.U. TO. Yuri Mikhailovich Steklov. - M., 1976.
[four] Steklov Y.U. Favorites.—S. 109-110 .
[5] See: Dunaevsky B. A. Soviet historiography new stories Western countries. 1917-1941 g.— M., 1974.—P. 40.
[6] Steklov Y.U. M. Chernyshevsky and his political views // Marxist historian— 1928.—T. 8.—S. 129 131.
[7] See: Essays stories historical science in USSR. - M., 1966.- T. IV . - S. 355.
[eight] Valentinov N. Meetings With Lenin. - Vermont, 1953.— FROM. 113 119.
[9] Historian-Marxist.— 1928.— T. eight.- FROM. 140.
[ten] Steklov Y.U. Michael Alexandrovich Bakunin, his life and activity.—M., 1920.—Ch. 1.—S. 255.
[11] Dunaevsky B. A. Decree. so.— S. 128.
[12] Bakunin M. A. Collected soch and letters. 1828-1876.— M., 1934-1935, - T. 1-4 / Ed. and so on approx. Yu. M. Steklov.
[13] I.P. Meshkovsky (pseudonym of Iosif Petrovich Goldenberg (1873-1922). In 1909, one of the leaders of the Central Committee of the RSDLP for the work of the Duma faction.
[fourteen] V. Yu. Steklov was condemned by a special meeting of the NKVD on April 9 1938 for 8 years on charges of working as a Trotskyist organization in Glavenergo. He returned and was fully rehabilitated. Investigative file of Yu. M. Steklov No. 13406. There is also an additional volume No. 5586, where are rehabilitation materials.

GINGER PROFESSOR AT "SINGLE"

Nikolai Naumovich Elvov (1901-1937) was arrested on February 10, 1935. Investigator of the NKVD of Tatarstan Sergey Tsarevsky substantiated need arrest topics what that,
"Being professor public science in higher educational institutions cities Kazan, promoted among students ideas counter-revolutionary Trotskyism grouping for this goals around myself their like-minded people." AT the same day in apartment No. 9 on street Tolstoy, d. fourteen, where he lived then Elvo, was produced search. seized professor's documents, correspondence, manuscripts of articles, folders with various materials (programs seminars, theses lectures), books (many from them With donative inscriptions). AT questionnaire arrested meant what Elvo was born September 23, 1901 in Kyiv. Among the special signs are indicated: red hair, curly. Elvov pointed out that his father - a tailor, and he lives with his wife, Maria Semyonovna Bychkova, and son Sergei, five years old. And further about myself: a Bolshevik became in november 1918 G., With Togo time to 1921 — in the Red Army, fought, last military position — regimental commissar. Then he studied at the Communist University named after Ya. M. Sverdlov and the Institute of Red professorships on the historical department.

On February 11, 1935, the first interrogation of Elvov took place. It was also led by a former participant in the civil war, cysts Tsarevsky.

— The investigators know that you, as a Trotskyist, have been waging a counter-revolutionary double-dealing campaign over the past few years. work. What you you can to tell on this a reason ?

— I arrived in Kazan in April 1932, a few days later after my recovery member of the CPSU (b); I was expelled from the CPSU(b) in 1931 for Trotskyist propaganda in my chapters — history textbook of the CPSU (b) under the editorship of Comrade Yaroslavsky. Being reinstated in the party, on voucher Central Committee VKP(b) I and arrived on the scientific work in Kazan. Here I accepted leadership of the department of history USSR in Tatar pedagogical institute, in institute Marxism-Leninism was in charge section historical ri of Russia. In 1933 I also lectured on the history of the national economy at the Institute of Finance and Economics and on the courses Marxism at regional committee parties. Since the autumn of 1934, he began to lecture at Kazan University, as well as in many city institutions ... I admit myself guilty in volume, what I how Professor did not educate a lot of students in history ... on the exposure of myself as a Trotskyist ... I did not conduct Trotskyist work, but my behavior contributed this.

— The investigation knows that you involved alien element. Tell about this.

— In view of my fatigue, I ask you to postpone the analysis of this issue for the next time (the interrogation was completed at 24 hours).

On February 12, Elvov, at the insistence of the contempt, called to him the names of those with whom he prepared for publication a collection of documents on the history of Tataria. Of course, these names were known, but, as many of Tsarevsky's detainees later recalled, he forced them to sign pre-prepared texts of protocols. Therefore, this protocol The frequently used epithets "counter-revolutionary", "Trotskyist" were, most likely, one of those. Elvov said that he had a revolver, that he wanted to shoot himself, but considered it unworthy. February 18 Elvov firmly said what "not was conductor Trotskyist ideas."

— The investigation knows for sure that over the past few years you have been an organized counter-revolutionary Trotskyist campaign. work. Recognize whether you myself guilty?

— I do not plead guilty, since I did not conduct counter-revolutionary, Trotskyist work. (From the protocol of interrogation from fifteen Martha 1938 G.).

Elvov confirmed his acquaintance with the Kazan historian M. Korbut, who gave him two volumes of his book on the history of the university, and admitted that, having learned about his arrest, sheet With deed of gift inscription from volumes pulled out. He did not deny his connections with Moscow and Leningrad colleagues but noticed what nothing not know about them
counter-revolutionary work."

Apparently, Elvov knew that he would be arrested. Gone arrests many his acquaintances he how could be wary, but felt what bowl this his not passes. Shortly before his arrest, he spoke with Evgenia Ginzburg, who had recently returned from Moscow. She is reported to him about arrest G. FROM. Zaidel, major specialist on new stories about deprivation his doctor degree, executions students, about volume, what Moscow graduate students not sure, will see whether they on the next day their scientific leaders.

... Elvova friendly met in Kazan. I arrived he came to the city in 1932 after being exiled in Sverdlovsk and being reinstated in the CPSU(b), on a ticket from the Central Committee of the party. He was offered lived the post of dean of the Faculty of History, head of the Department of History of the USSR at the Tatar Pedagogical Institute. He was full of creative ideas, but he always remembered how his participation in the creation of the four-volume History of the All-Union Communist Party of Bolsheviks, published in 1926-1929, ended. under the general editorial Eat. Yaroslavsky. AT forewords by E. M. Yaroslavsky pointed out role Elvova in her creation. FROM. BUT. Piontkovsky wrote down in the diary how spring 1927 g. to him went Elvo and proposed write row chapters for the history of the party, edited by Yaroslavsky. Elvo There was an amusing guy, big, healthy, red-haired, with glasses, very intelligent, but more cunning,— he produced quite pleasant impression, was able in time fade away was pretty duplicitous. To write the history of the party of Yaroslavsky, Elvov collected people from all over DIY. At first he grabbed me with his teeth and hands, loaded on the me mountain articles".

Elvov acted in those years not only as the organizer of a large publications, he published several their works: in collaboration with N. Mayorsky - article "On the Question of the Character and Driving Forces of the October Revolution" (Proletarian Revolution.—1927.— No. eleven.- pp. 34-73) and the pamphlet "Leninism and an Assessment of the Character of the October Revolution" (M.-L., 1928); in 1929 together with P. Tashkarov — monograph "On one attempt to distort Marxism and Leninism ".

Yaroslavsky noted the importance of primary sources in writing the History of the All-Union Communist Party of Bolsheviks and the fact that "the compilers of this volume sought to give a particularly thorough picture of intra-party disagreements period 1917-1920s on the issue of Lenin's assessment of the driving forces, ... considered it their task to expose those "historians" who tried to introduce a business So, what in 1917 G. the Leninist party "ideologically rearmed" and that Lenin in 1905 and 1917 there were two strategic plans for the development of the bourgeois revolution into a socialist revolution " [1].

Elvov wrote about the activities of the party in 1905-1907, participated in the creation of its history during the revolutionary upheavals of 1917. What were the main conclusions of Elvov With co-authors (conclusions, deserving OK and conservative historians of the 70s [2])? Maiorsky and Elvov considered the position of the Bolsheviks in 1917 to be a natural and logical development of their position in 1905. They criticized the statements of G. E. Zinoviev and LB Kamenev about the "incompleteness" of the bourgeois-democratic revolution in Russia, about that the proletariat will not be able to defend power, that the country is not ready for a socialist revolution, since the condition for its victory may be only an international revolution. This last statement on thoughts authors, adhered to in 1917 and Mensheviks and Trotsky [3], vol. e. it was that what united opposition Stalin in 20s years.

The authors noted points of contact between Lenin and Trotsky (both were in favor of taking power), but emphasizing that there were more such coincidences between Trotsky, Kamenev and Zinoviev, because they did not recognize the socialist nature of the revolution. "That fundamental commonality of views, vols. Trotsky, Kamenev and Zinoviev, which existed in 1917, turned out to be historically more significant than the coincidence of real conclusions that existed between Lenin and Trotsky during this period. It was this fundamental commonality that was the deep reason that facilitated the creation of modern opposition bloc," they said authors [4].

Hardly need more evidence Togo, what before us is a politicized text typical of that time, which does little in terms of research, being simply a historiographical fact of the development of an unusually ideological historical science. It is enough to get acquainted with the "Lessons of October" by Trotsky, with his "Stalin- school of falsification" to make sure that there is another — and Good reasoned — points vision to the events described. Trotsky, long before Lenin, substantiated the idea of Only the possibilities, but also the inevitability of the victory of the socialist revolution in one country, moreover, in a country that is backward in socio-economic and political respects. Lenin's concept 1905 was different. Lenin believed that victory over tsarism would lead to a revolutionary-democratic dictatorship of the proletariat and peasantry, and only after the country had been cleansed of the remnants of the Middle Ages would it become possible to transfer the revolution to socialist lines. In March 1917, Lenin modified his point of view, substantiating the course towards a socialist revolution, in the course of which the questions of the bourgeois-democratic revolution would be decided casually and [casually].

In September-October 1917, as is known, Kamenev and Zinoviev spoke out against the uprising. opposite pole Occupation Lenin and Trotsky [6].

Trotsky came to a bloc with Kamenev and Zinoviev only in 1926, theoretically defending the proposition that it was impossible to build socialism in the USSR in the conditions of a capitalist encirclement, which in practice meant a struggle per power co Stalin. Brochure N. Mayorsky and N. Elvova was directed on the protection Stalin's course and was an attempt find the historical roots of the united opposition. FROM scientific point she does not stand up to scrutiny. Evidence in the form of quotes pulled from the works of Lenin, Kamenev, Zinoviev, Trotsky could neither confirm nor refute anything. Strictly speaking, the pamphlet was the opportunistic contribution of the authors to the inner-party struggle, evidence them commitment "general lines".

The book of P. Tashkarov and N. Elvov "On an Attempt to Distort Marxism and a large battle, by almost 200 printed pages of a review of the book by Ksenofontov "On the Question of the Ideological and Tactical Foundations of Bolshevism". The reviewers reproached Ksenofontov for the abuse of quotations and, most importantly, for the "revision of Leninism", which they saw in the break between Leninism and Marxism allowed by the author. Ksenofontov did not find in Marx and Engels the thesis about the possibility of the victory of the proletarian revolution in one country taken separately, therefore, in the opinion of the reviewer, he deserved comrades, accusations of a dogmatic approach to the views of the founders of scientific socialism, of Trotskyism and adherence to the "right" [7]. Tashkarov and Elvov, based on market conditions considerations often sinning against truth,
"proved" what, turns out, question about capabilities on-
The structure of socialism in one country was already decided by Marx, Engels and Lenin, something the opposition and Ksenofontov doubted...

The surviving protocols give an idea of what kind of information the NKVD wanted to get from Elvov. In the direction of the questions asked, the search is guessed All-Union terrorist organizations" — on the this time composed of historians. On the one hand, Elvov studied and worked in Moscow, know there many. FROM Another, in the early 1920s, historians eagerly quoted Trotsky and other political figures who were later repressed. Now this is them put in guilt — So "proved" them opposition commitment. Sympathetically quoted, responded positively — consequently, he was a member of the "counter-revolutionary organization", especially since the "Trotskyist" became synonymous "enemy people."

Elvov was asked about his meetings with Moscow and Leningrad historys and about those, who on accusations of "Trotskyism" was arrested in Kazan. Elvo confirmed (it would be ridiculous to deny) his acquaintance with the head of the university department Timofei Semenovich Ishchenko [8] and professor Michael Ksaverievich Corbut [9]. On the proposal to characterize the historian Efrem Medvedev [10] answered: "On the political side, I think that he is a young, rather seasoned, capable worker ... of counter-revolutionary, anti-Soviet conversations With him I don't led. AT January 1935 of the year Medvedev was in Leningrad, by return told Ischenko about arrests and expulsions
"Trotskyites", said that "and me (ie Elvov,— AL) can comprehend such same fate, topics more", what many in his time excluded from parties after letters Stalin in editorial "Proletarian" revolution".

At the end of April 1935, Elvov's changed behavior. On April 28, he declared that he was ready to "frankly confess" his "absolutely frank confessions" wants help parties "expose me and those, with whom I worked against the party." He "remembered" that he had become a Trotskyist as early as 1923, while studying at the Communist University. Sverdlov in Moscow, and explained this by a passion for the personality of Trotsky. "the biggest crime against the party and comrade. Stalin", which consisted in the fact that in 1929 he, in collaboration with P. Tashkarov, published a pamphlet "On an Attempt to Distort Marxism and Leninism". written from the point of view of the Trotskyist-Zinovivist positions along the general line." He said that Tashkarov had been with Stalin about this pamphlet, and also enlisted the support of the philosopher YE Stan and KA Popov, that Yaroslavsky had nothing to do with writing it. what did it consist of in his opinion, a departure from the "general line". May be, in, what's in the brochure nothing not talked about Stalin's contribution to the teachings of Marx, Engels, Lenin on the possibility of the victory of socialism in a separate country? After all, in 1929 the 50th anniversary of the leader was widely celebrated, and then the formula "Stalin - This is Lenin today. And then a book about Marxism-Leninism comes out, and the name of today's Lenin not mentioned at all...

In the protocol of interrogation of April 28, 1935, Elvov's detailed account of the situation at the Communist Academy and the Institute of Red Professors in the late 1920s - early 30s. [11]. The atmosphere must not have been the best. Politicism, the desire to "survive" or make a career on "loyalty" revealed far from the best moral qualities of the conflicting historians. The caustic and bilious Piontkovsky in his diary spokes of the "extraordinary customs" of that time: societies chilling out how about science. He does not feel much inclination towards theoretical questions, but works how ox and sit maybe hours on 14 a day... He wrote a review of Shestakov's lousy little book. The book is really worthless ... Shestakov found out, somehow grabbed the review and began to crack down on With Elvo. called out his to yourself and He speaks: "You are a guy young, a write about me dirty tricks, early, my brother." And then he calls Dubrovsky. From this Elvov studied and happened. He says: "Do you know Elvov?" He says: "I know, my student and learned from me. "But they didn't notice whether you per him immoral deeds?..." Well good that Dubrovsky knows Elvova, a another agreed would... in one moment I would have smeared the boy with mud. Even among the bourgeois professorships such skills not It was...".

At the beginning of 1931, Elvov was sent to Sverdlovsk. In the Central Committee he was told that this was caused not only by the fact that personnel were needed in the Urals, but also by the desire to somehow reduce the squabble between the groups in Moscow. According to his testimony, he managed revive work historys cities, wanted to hold a conference with the invitation of Mintz, Piontkovsky, Dubrovsky, but Stalin's letter, published in Proletarian Revolution, paralyzed all undertakings. Punitive measures were taken. March 2, 1932 Elvov by the decision of the Ural OK of the CPSU (b) was excluded from party for not gave 'deployed critics their mistakes... not opened and did not give an assessment of his anti-party work in the 4-volume history of the CPSU (b) edited by Yaroslavsky, which indicates his lack of sincerity and inability to in the future his work justify the confidence of the party" [12].

Elvov told how he worked in the Sverdlovsk school desk, communist university, editions newspapers
Ural communist. In Sverdlovsk, he became closer than others to the historian Semyon Izrailevich Kuznetso- vym [13]. Among Sverdlovsk acquaintances Elvo named also

Semyon Vladimirovich Ginger, Yakov Rafailovich Elkovich and Joseph Solomonovich Kogan [14].

Elvov admitted that during his meetings with Mintz, Dubrovsky and Piontkovsky sharp condemned letter Stalin in the "Proletarian Revolution", the pogrom speeches of Kaganovich and Mekhlis, and explained this by the fact that his condition and mood then they were extremely oppressed. When he was reinstated in the party and left for Kazan, he was greeted with harsh criticism for his participation in the work on a 5-volume book on the history of the CPSU(b). Like other authors of the multivolume, he was accused in Trotskyist smuggling." L. Mehlis stated that "... only the presence of rotten liberalism can explain, how shkolka Trotskyists history kov — Elvova, Keene, Mintz and others — uncontrollably smuggled anti-Party rubbish... The party and the branch of the Society of Marxist Historians in Kazan exposed attempts to imagine that Bolshevism in the Tatras Republic was formed on the basis of the organic development of various petty-bourgeois trends into the Bolshevik, that group The main struggle in the Tatar organization was a historically necessary stage and that the "leftists" were real Bolsheviks" [15].

16 February 1935 G. Baumansky district committee Kazan except-
Chill from the CPSU (b) Maria Semyonovna Bychkova, Elvov's wife per "loss class vigilance", non-information against her husband, "not exposing Elvov's double-dealing to the end." Returning from the camps and exile, October 2 1955 yes Bychkova wrote remembering about volume terrible time, as in 1930 she studied at the Moscow Institute of National Economy, came out married per Elvova, was student at him in the seminar. In 1932, together with her husband, she moved to Kazan, where she worked in the apparatus of Soviet control. "In 1935 Elvov was arrested. They started calling me as a witness in my husband's case... The first thing they offered me was when called in NKVD - write renunciation from husband and publish in printing... FROM first interrogation they said: if I refuse to expose my husband, they will take away the child, and a few days later my son was thrown out of the kindergarten. They kept me under interrogation for days and exhausted me with insomnia."

She was forced to vacate the apartment and go to relatives in Moscow. There they were again summoned to the NKVD. "In the office of Chief Molchanov, in the presence of many NKVD workers, an interrogation was held. Many questions were asked and the main one was — why am I not helping the NKVD in exposing Elvo.

On June 16, Bychkova was placed under house arrest in Moscow, and already 20th she is gave testimony, denouncing her husband. When asked about Elvov's acquaintances in Moscow, Bychkova named the scientific secretary of the editorial board of the history of the civil war in the USSR II Institute FROM. M. Dubrovsky, his wife of BB Grave, professor of Moscow State University SA Piontkovsky. Reported what attended at them meetings in 1930-1931 years, which spoke of the ignorance and vulgarization that flourished in historical science, the degradation of theoretical thought that a situation had arisen in which creative thought was replaced by hallelujah, and people were nominated gali per them zeal in praise guides The investigator also obtained evidence from Bychkova that the aforementioned historys critically responses about Stalin and Kaganovich.

Bychkova testified: "By arrival in Kazan Elvo met With editor Michael Korbut, vra- Chom Sergey Dikovitsky, agronomists Vintaykin and Shcheperin. He was skeptical about Stalin's rambling letter and ironically about his own "elaboration". Shortly before the advent in printing letters Stalin in magazine "Proletarian revolution" Mints sent Elvov a letter in which torom warning about the forthcoming publication of the letter Stalin and about volume, what Stalin negatively perceived 4-volume book on the history of the party. Mints' letter ended with the phrases: "Don't be shy!" After the publication of Stalin's letter, Elvov received the envelope With note from Dubrovsky and Grave, in which they expressed their sympathy to him". Thus, Bychkova confirmed much of what has already been said in their testimony her husband.

It was difficult for Elvov to adapt to the new situation in the country and in historical science. He tried to stand his ground, because of which, for example, his first lecture at the Pedagogical Institute (1932) ended in a scandal. Elvov characterized the ancient Kievan state as a slaveholding state. Experienced in political discussions and searching for enemies, the students saw this as a manifestation of "Trotskyism". Referring to Stalin's Questions of Leninism, they stated that the feudal formation dominated Kievan Rus. (And they immediately reported on what Elvov said in their hearts: "History will show who was right — Stalin or we"). AT 1933 year Elvo again said that in the teaching of history it will not allow falsification and that 1905 year he understands So, how outlined his in 4 volumes history of the CPSU (b). And this despite the ever more stringent criticism this work.

On the other hand, Elvov's colleagues emphasize his caution. Fatykh Kamalovich Saifi [16], the editor of the Yanalif magazine, being interrogated, testified that he knew Elvov on printing more before arrival his in Kazan, then I worked with him, but "I failed to notice in the behavior Elvov's research on the elements of counter-revolutionary Trotskyism... He was exclusively doggy, smart and careful. In 1934, I personally raised an anti-Party, anti-Soviet conversation about position peasantry, but he immediately strictly broke off me".

Under the leadership of Elvov, Saifi participated in compiling the collection "The History of Tataria in Documents and Materials". The first volume received a positive assessment in Moscow FROM. Piontkovsky and N. Rubinstein. Second - was not completed due to the arrests of the compilers. Saifi confirmed: "Personally, I did not notice any facts of his counter-revolutionary Trotskyist activity behind Elvov in the department ... Elvov practically led the department well ."

Gazi Salikhovich Gubaidullin [17] informed consequence that Elvova know With 1934 of the year, visited at him on the lectures, but did not notice in them either praise or criticism of Trotskyism. Gubaidullin could not refrain from remarking that his essay Elvov listen refused motivating topics what now, after killings Kirov, "will begin" consequence and repression, not before the report here".

Mukhtarama Akhmetovna Faridova [18], Elvov's graduate student, testified that she "was a fan of Elvov as a talented vogo professor, knew nothing about his counter-revolutionary activities. True, later the investigators forced Faridova to sign the protocols prepared by the investigator, to "confess" that in 1932-1934, while studying at graduate school, she was "a member of the counter-revolutionary Trotskyist organization in Kazan, which was headed by Elvo.

Zugra Bilyalovna Nadeeva [19], secretary of the historical department institute, on the interrogation 16 Martha 1935 G. showed:

"I know only Elvov's past mistakes, made by him in 4 volumes stories VKP(b) under editorial Yaroslavsky. How known Elvo these mistakes acknowledged in his time. Other facts dragging through Elvo Trotskyism in process of its scientific and pedagogical work I don't know." After exceptions from parties and newspaper Elvish insults understood, what has come his turn. He became destroy documents, manuscripts, forbidden books autographed by the authors. 6 February 1935 of the year killed personal correspondence, official information, organizational materials of 4 volumes stories VKP(b), Photo and even old plans and course programs. Later, the destruction of papers and books will confirm wife Elvova and housekeeper

In Kazan, Elvov was interrogated February 10 to On June 15, 1935, he was then transferred by special escort to Sokwu, because, as it turned out, his "counter-revolutionary activities" were connected with "a whole range of people" living there .

Elvov testified that he was invited to Kazan by Ikhak Rakhmatullin, manager department culture Tatar OK VKP(b). Piontkovsky, an old Kazan citizen, recommended to him Korbut, With which he and met on arrival in the city. Elvov gave a political description of the teachers of the Pedagogical Institute, dividing them into groups of chauvinists and nationalists, left and right, admitted that he was not always responsible for his work, but categorically denied "the presence of Trotskyist smuggling in his teaching."

Elvov considered his main business in Kazan to be the preparation of materials on the history of Tatarstan, which he prepared together with the staff of the Institute of History of the Communist Academy in Moscow. He defended in every possible way Nadeeva and E. Medvedev, who were "very devoted" to him and were not guilty of anything. "I ruined them with my conversations," lamented he.

especially detail has stopped Elvo on the environment in the editorial office of the Krasnaya Tatariya newspaper, where he had recently led the department of international information, and now on the pages newspapers has undergone shameless criticism.

Red Tataria", 2 February 1935 G. A report that a conference "On the counter-revolutionary Zinoviev group and its scum" was held at the Pedagogical Institute. In the assembly hall, which accommodated about 600 students and teachers, was played out very a farce typical of the time. The head of the department of culture of the city committee of the party, Shıkaev, "for discussion" invited one of the students to defend the position of GE Zinoviev so that others would expose him. as Zinoviev spoke student history faculty Rafikov, but

The "discussion" went on so sluggishly that Zinoviev-Rafikov's opponents were accused of insufficient activity. Among others, Elvov also spoke, and he won't applause, what not prevented city committee parties exclude Shikaeva

from VKP(b), a party committee Pedagogical Institute dissolve how "immature". ten February in Red Tataria" appeared article
"Patrons Elvova, in which leaders financial and economic Institute accused in volume, what just fired Elvova, a not exposed his how Trotskyist.

AT this same room — the note Trotskyist successor and his patrons", which stated: "As a result of the loss of class-revolutionary vigilance and the suppression of self-criticism, the Trotskyist successor Elvov could until the last time lead in Pedagogical Institute department".

Correspondence from Krasnaya Tatariya was abbreviated form reprinted in "Pravda" With comment.
On February 11, Krasnaya Tatariya published a resolution nie of the joint bureau of the Tatar regional committee and the Kazan city party committee. It recognized the lack of control over the activities of the "Trotskyist smuggler Elvov" as a mistake. All party organizations were asked to discuss the published articles, to condemn Elvov, that is, to expose "own ." Trotskyists." AT this same room

"unmasked" Professor university T. FROM. Ishchenko as a "double-dealer" and friend of Elvov. On February 12, the editorial of the newspaper called for showing "the disgusting appearance of Elvov, this Trotskyist last-born, double-dealer, grabber, impudent suppressor of self-criticism, disorganizer of educational work". Employees Elvova asked like this they could "not notice his anti-Soviet essence and subversive work". 2 May 1935 of the year, The answers to the questions of the investigator, Elvov summed up: "I am not a malicious counter-revolutionary, not an enemy...".

M. FROM. Bychkova, wife Elvova, on the interrogation 17 April 1935, she said: "Elvov's mood changed sharply after his return from the last train ki to Moscow and Leningrad in January. He was very irritable and did not answer any questions. On the day of arrival all repeated, what must see Ischenko, gone to him hours in 9 evenings (I arrived same he in 7 evenings) and returned hours to 11. AT this evening nothing to me Elvo not told. Only on the second day, when I came from work, Elvo told about volume, what he did in Moscow and Leningrad and about their moods. Been to Bertha Grave, consulted about release volumes on stories Tatars, but there I received an answer that even the last 10 sheets typed in printing houses, recommended take apart in due to the fact that the Central Committee decided not to publish his books. Elvov complained that Grave, who always greeted him with greetings, in, even home not invited. Then in Kazan was held a number of meetings to work out the events connected with the murder of Kirov. From these meetings Elvov came very dejected. After the conference at Pedagogical Institute 31 January and the performance of the student Rafikov, Elvov returned in a slightly better mood, reported that he had even spoken to him applauded. When same was published an article in Krasnaya Tatariya exposing Elvov, his mood deteriorated sharply, and he began to demand that my son and I leave immediately from Kazan. Elvo spoke to me, what he wants do away with With yourself and asked not condemn whether I him for it, since he does not see any prospects for his future. He burned papers, photographs and books. To him called from party collegiums 9 February, but he is there not went like that how from parties his expelled. O volume, what was done in the editorial office of the newspaper, Elvov always knew from Evgenia Ginz- burg, With which his introduced Corbut.

AT 1933 Elvova become criticize per speeches at the party of the city, where he stated that he belongs to the "peaceful Trotskyists, who did only literary mistakes (ie, until the end "not exposed"). At the beginning of 1935, he was turned away, abandoned, betrayed by those who had recently worked with him. Therefore, Elvov was not surprised - Xia, when docent departments Evgeny Grachev (more not knowing that soon too will be arrested) wrote on the him denunciation. AT German we walked talking about the impossibility work With "Trotskyist smuggler" and it was proposed to condemn him severely. No, it was not for nothing that Elvov once called Grachev "a political speculator and squabbler"...

On February 7, a meeting of the party committee of the Institute of Marxism-Leninism was held, in which Elvov was a member of the party nom accounting. Neither at whom not found good the words in his address. Neither at AND. Rakhmatullina, who invited his on the work in Kazan, neither at professors Ischenko, one from closest Elvova of people. Each vilified his, hoping that save myself. In vain. Soon betrayed and them. Now everyone unanimously accused Elvov of "hack work, worthless scientific works, double-dealing." turns out, he is in their lectures preached trotskyism, this is appeared in volume, what "in question about public formations he
"refuted Klyuchevsky, did not reveal the essence of Klyuchevsky's bourgeois views and did not give a Marxist-Leninist justification teachings about formations." Remained ambiguous how same was "Trotskyism"?

The decision to expel Elvov from the party was adopted unanimously. On February 10, a closed party meeting of the Institute this is solution approved, pointing out what Elvo excludes-

for "smuggling Trotskyist contraband in the teaching work, ignoring the role of Stalin in the development of Marxist-Leninist philosophy, smuggling and not exposing Menshevik idealism."

Marvelous, what party committee and meeting excluded his from the party, as if forgetting that he had already been expelled by the party commission under the Central Committee of the All-Union Communist Party of Bolsheviks. The decision of the party commission, replete with "cast-iron" formulations, was read to him by phone: "AT ." connections With note in "Pravda" from 5 February s. It was established that Elvov did not expose the anti-Soviet undertaking of Shikaev, Grigoriev and others, who prepared the student Rafikov, who repeated the counter-revolutionary slander of the Zinovievites-Trotskyists on the party. Elvov did not give a Bolshevik rebuff to this counter-revolutionary onslaught of double-dealers because he himself, only formally, in words he admitted his "literary" mistakes, but in fact, in his scientific and teaching work, he did not stop propaganda Trotskyism emasculating role parties from the history of the peoples of the USSR, tearing the role of the party from the history of the peoples of the country, covered up the ideologically alien and their wrecking work on the ideological front, and suppressed self-criticism.

Elvov, admitting his guilt only in clamping down on self-criticism and disrupting training sessions, gave evasive answers to all other accusations: "I was late", "I was far away", "I didn't hear", "I didn't 't know', 'I didn't read' than proved his insincerity and did not even mention in the questionnaire that he had been expelled from the party. Therefore, they decided: Elvova from the party exclude how double-dealer."

Elvov sat at home, burned papers, waited for arrest and decided whether whether to him live farther. He was afraid go to Ishchenko to do not let him down, sent Nadeev to him with a question - what to do? And received a cautiously evasive answer - apply to the regional committee ... On February 23, 1935, Ishchenko himself was expelled from the party with the same wording as Elvov - "Like a double-dealing Trotskyist." He will leave Kazan far away, get a job as a controller of the East Siberian office "Zagotzerno". But even there they will find him and bring him under escort in Kazan...

On May 29, 1935, a confrontation between Elvov and Ishchenko took place. Them was given question, right whether, what they hoped in Kazan it would be "easier to sit out" in connection with the "studies" that began after the assassination of Kirov. Both answered in the affirmative. Another confrontation took place on June 1st. Elvo and Ischenko confirmed friendly proximity, based on the similar political views and joint work in institute Marxism-Leninism.

Investigators asked Zyugra Nadeeva about acquaintances Elvo. She is named Ischenko, E. Medvedev, F. saifi, M. Korbut, Evgeny Ginzburg. Last

"I often turned to Elvov for advice on certain issues of newspaper work. Her Elvov attracted to compiling the first volume of the history of Tataria, to writing a history textbook for schools second steps. Elvov said that he had been to Ginzburg's apartment. At the beginning of 1933, Ginzburg was at Elvov's apartment, the purpose of visiting me not known." Not held out Nadeeva, gossiped:

"By rumors between Elvov and Ginzburg had an intimate relationship. Ginzburg said that she was greatly courted em as for the woman Elvov. And yet Nadeeva categorically denied the fact of any anti-Soviet and anti-party statements Elvo.

May 2, 1935 Elvov at the Kazan interrogation again returned to his Moscow-Leningrad ties. WHO- can, topics most he tried to stress my important in eyes local investigators. He told about meetings with Semyon Grigoryevich Tomsinsky, whom he had known since 1926 and who told him about the eviction from Leningrad t. n. 'unreliable element"; With Andrey Ilyich Malyshev, Deputy Director of the Leningrad branch of the Communist Academy. According to observations Elvova, among historys reigned atmosphere fear and confusion. Tomsinsky told him: "Look what is happening in the party - the guys are afraid to get together for a party. Pankratova — fears at myself, Vanag — at myself..." Only

MM Tsvibak, having learned about Elvov's interest in the history of Tataria, invited him to take part in the collective work on stories peoples USSR.

This mood plunged Elvov into a panic. He confessed that even in Leningrad he wanted to go to the NKVD himself and gave it to a friend my notebook book and notes to according to stories Tatars. But change my mind and left in Moscow, where he shared his experiences with Piontkovsky and Dubrovsky. They advised to be wary of the Mehlis (and the edited them "Pravda") sit out in Moscow. On the During interrogation, he repeatedly returned to the feeling of his doom after publishing a joint pamphlet with Tashkarov, believing that Stalin would not forgive him. And he repeated: "I am not a malicious counter-revolutionary ..."

twenty May 1935 G. on the interrogation went speech about AT. AND. Nevsky and his students P. AND. Anatoliev and P. P. Paradise, also to that time who were under investigation. Elvov admitted that he knew Nevsky, but rarely met with him, that historians who were critical of Pokrovsky and his were grouped around him. Nevsky gave a positive review of his work "The Party on the Eve of the Revolution 1905 in Russia and international arena, in which he did not find erroneous, Elvova, assessment of statements Rose Luxembourg about revolution 1905 of the year. At the same time, he referred to the words of Piontkovsky, who spoke about Nevsky's negative attitude towards Stalin's letter. in magazine "Proletarian" revolution".

In the four-volume history of the CPSU(b), the authors of the sections are not indicated, but from Elvov's interrogations it is clear that he wrote the chapters of the second volume on the socio-economic and political prerequisites for the revolution of 1905 and on the attitude to revolution leaders II International; in Volume IV - the theoretical part about outgrowth bourgeois-democratic revolution into a socialist one. Here Elvov opposed Trotskyism, idealized the views and Lenin's actions, however, at the beginning of 1929, at a meeting of the research group of the Lenin Institute, defending the provisions of a joint pamphlet with Majorsky, he called Trotsky a revolutionary [20]. Elvov's views largely coincided with those of Yaroslavsky, but as a professional historian who did not hold important political posts, he was more free in his statements. Now to him all this is remembered...

7 June 1935 of the year Elvova recommended stay on his connections with Petr Nikolaevich Ionov, head of the department of foreign literature of Goslitizdat; Grigory Samoilovich Fridlyand, Dean of the Faculty of History, Moscow University; Nikolai Nikolayevich Vanag, Deputy Director of the Institute of the History of the Peoples of the USSR of the USSR Academy of Sciences, Corresponding Member of the Academy of Sciences USSR Boris Mikhailovich Gessen. (All by that time they had been arrested, shot in 1937, later rehabilitated). Elvov's case was conducted by an investigator in Moscow Petrovsky. twenty June he interrogated Bychkov,
22 June — Elva.

Elvo was already broken.

— Investigation known what you on the pledge row years and up to their arrest were active counter-revolutionary work. Confirm whether you this is?

— Yes confirm. Indeed, for a number of years, right up to my arrest, I conducted an active counter-revolutionary work.

He signed protocol, in which "confessed" what since 1929 he was a member of the "counter-revolutionary" Moscow group of historians (SM Dubrovsky, SA Piontkovsky, BB Grave, II Mints, NL Rubinstein, AL Sidorov) [21]. At the same time, Elvov categorically denied the existence of any anti-party group in Sverdlovsk, where he worked for a short time. He admitted that he regularly corresponded with members of the Moscow group and met with them. Mintz called campaign unfolded after the letter Stalin in magazine "Proletarian" revolution", "whistle". AT similar expressions responses about her Dubrovsky and Grave. AT Kazan, acknowledged Elvo, he together With others
led fight With shortcomings local guides", although this fight was limited to talk. In 1932, Dubrovsky discussed expulsion from Zinoviev's party, the Ryutin case, while Dubrovsky expressed the opinion that Zinoviev and Kamenev were simply being dealt with and that Stalin was guilty in repression.

After signing the protocols of interrogations, where he confessed in everyone in how to him proposed confess, what, in fact, "pulled" the people closest to him, Elvov felt bad. On August 22, 1935, he applied to the head of the secret political department of the NKVD GA Molchanov, where he refused food, walks, books and the use of glasses. "All this for,- he explained, to get it over with quickly that vulgar life which I lead in the present time and which more already endure no way not can, and I don't see the need. On February 10, 1935, my life ended."

He wanted die. "Having spent without small seven months in solitary conclusion, having considered all and again change my mind, I came to the conviction that life my, undoubtedly, finished what prospects at me no... I subjected to extremely harsh regime (No goodbye, it is forbidden write — get letters, necessary things, although this is not prohibited by the rules prisons. Even pillows deprived, glasses and received the books literally teeth pulled out)... No life neither work, neither families to me not see. That, what drag out now, what lies ahead - I ca n't stand it anymore — it's over my forces. Life my finished and remaining strength i want attach on the then, to speed up this the end." Elvov announced, what starts hunger strike With 23 August. But through day, 24 august, I decided, what annuls their previous requirements and returns to ordinary prisoner's life

Soon he was acquainted with the indictment, signed by investigators V. Petrovsky, G. Lulov and endorsed by G. Molchanov. Elvov was accused of bei ng a member of an anti-Party group of historians, which spread lander on address comrad Stalin."

On October 15, 1935, a special meeting at the NKVD considered a business Kazanians. Elvo and his wife Bychkova
"for participation in the counter-revolutionary Trotskyist group" were exiled on the 5 years in G. Shenkursk; 3. P. Vintaykin - on the 5 years in Karakalpakstan; G. P. Shcheperin - on the 3 years in Kazakhstan; E. AND. Medvedev and 3. B. Nadeeva - deprived of the right to reside in sensitive cities for 3 years. Soon the sentences were reviewed: on May 27, 1936, Elvov was transferred from Shenkursk to the Gulag, to the Kolyma, to the Northern Camp. sent and Bychkov.

In 1937, "new circumstances" began to emerge. Tightening punitive politicians led to to that that in the camps and exiles they began to "catch" former "Trotskyists". Elvova again transported in Kazan. this test his psycho not withstood: 3 April 1937 G. he was placed in a Kazan psychiatric hospital and stayed there for several months.

AT last investigative deed Elvova single protocol interrogation. fifteen September 1937 G., sick and exhausted, he appeared before Military collegium Supreme Court of the USSR and again declared in last word, what guilty myself not recognizes terrorist work not led and did not cobble together any counter-revolutionary organization . The verdict was prepared in advance - capital punishment. AT night With fifteen on the 16 September 1937 G. Elvo was shot.

Gone years. Wife and son Elvova excited case of rehabilitation. Cases from twenty years ago were brought up, caused remaining in alive witnesses tried
"to voice" vote the dead.

Alexander Antonovich Dikovitsky, Kazan doctor:
"As an accusation, I was charged with participation in the Trotskyist group of Korbut and Elvov. In fact, no organizational activity in Kazan by this group of persons not was carried out."

Nikolai Nikolaevich Mayorsky, co-author of Elvov (together they in 1927 G. wrote brochure "Leninism and assessment of the nature of the October Revolution"), was a special correspondent for Pravda in Paris, was shot on August 13, 1937. what cooperated With Elvo and at writing
four Tomnik stories VKP(b). Neither in how his not accused.

AND, finally, contradictory Ishchenko's testimony (1936).

In his opinion, at the Communist University of Tatarstan, where they With Elvo worked we walked group struggle for the leadership of the institute, which was given a political coloring. "Before January 1935, I did not regard Elvov's views as Trotskyist... I did not regard conversations with him as counter-revolutionary." In January 1935, Ishchenko in the city committee made it clear that Elvov "cannot be trusted." Ischenko both everyone told Elvova, and they decided for a while friendly meetings interrupt...

surveying a business Elvova With rehabilitation Goals in 1958, the investigator wrote that the grounds for his conviction were the "confessions" of a number of people who knew him. The audit established "the inconsistency of the materials collected in relation to him". A copy of the testimony of the witness FM Mayorov was attached to the Elvov case, from which it is clear that he was not talking about Elvov, but about the director of the regional base for fur raw materials Lvov. However, in the protocol, the surname Lvov was corrected for the surname Elvov by adding the letter "E". The investigator of the KGB of Tatarstan, captain Taturkin, suggested that Elvov's case was dismissed for lack of corpus delicti. On March 18, 1958, the military collegium of the Supreme Court of the USSR agreed with this conclusion, supported by the prosecutor's office, adding the judgment of innocence Elvo.

* * *

[one] Story VKP(b).- M. -L., 1930.— T. IV.— FROM. 5, 6. Fifth volume "Historrii VKP(b) was written, was passed in printing house, but not g o n e o u t. - RTSKHIDNI . - F . 89.— Op. 7.- D. 69.- L. 10-11.

[2] cm.: The consignment and Great October. Historiographic feature article.- M. 1976.- S. 97, 106.

[3] Proletarian revolution.—1927.—No . 11.- C. 46, 49, 51, 53, 67.

[four] Proletarian revolution.—1927.— No. eleven.- FROM. 68, 69. Brochure N. May-Orsk and Elvova "Leninism and grade character October revo- lucia" (M.— L., 1928) repeated main conclusions them articles.

[5] Lenin AT. AND. Full coll. op . - T. 44.- S. 147.

[6] More cm.: Pantsov BUT. AT. L. D. Trotsky // Questions history.— 1990.— No. 5. - S. 71, 73.

[7] Tashkarov P., Elvo N. About one trying distortion Marxism and Leninism.-M.-L., 1929.- S. 17, 61, 114 140, 187.

[eight] Timothy Semenovich Ischenko (1903-1938), professor-philosopher, you-starter communist university them. Sverdlov in Moscow, Bolshevik in 1920-1935 gg. AT 1935 G.- manager department fi- losophy Kazansky university. Arrested twenty May 1936 G. on obvi- ing in Trotskyism. convicted on the 5 years camps. Died in imprisonment
one December 1938 G. Rehabilitated in 1956 G.

[9] Michael Ksaverievich Korbut (1899-1937), professor of history graduated Kazansky university, Bolshevik in 1919-1933 gg. Main labor— History Kazansky university in 2nd volumes (Kazan, 1930). Was arrested in February 1933 G. on accusation in Trotskyism exiled in

Kazakhstan. AT december 1936 G. returned in Kazan and again accused how "right". one august 1937 G. swear to execution. Rehabilitation rowan in July 1956 G. "per ." absence composition crimes."

[ten] Ephraim Ignatievich Medvedev (1903-1983) - professor of history, are- tovan 12 February 1935 of the year how student Elvo. Released from per- clue on disease through 3 With half month. Rehabilitated twenty October 1955 G. AT statement about rehabilitation Medvedev wrote (December 1954 G.): "eleven ." February 1935 of the year in Kazan on cause professors Elvova Nicholas Naumovich, at whom I was graduate student me called in NKVD Tatars, where convict Muzafarov unworthy methods managed force me sign harvested them in advance protocols interrogation... I in this is time was manager archives Tatar- skoy republics, assistant professor on department Leninism financial and economic mic institute... Per time 3 monthly isolation to me attributed labels: enemy, trotskyist, pest, as if I invited on the work in museum former Kazan governor and major mullah... After treatment nia in mental hospital me expelled from Kazan in Kuibyshev...»

AT signed Medvedev protocol denied awareness about any counter-revolutionary activities Elvova, but lead- dilis the words, as if would said them: "On the New area buried Lenin, a on the Old — Leninism"; Stalin loves effect, a Lenin was modest"; Vol'fovich ruined good worker Slepkova, such specialist, how he, now in Kazan No".

Moses Abramovich Volfovich (1888-1938), commissioner times civil war, party employee, With 1927 G.- vector Tatar- sky communist university. Editor many works on stories revolutionary movements in Tatars. Arrested and shot in 1938 G. Rehabilitated.

[eleven] By order Yaroslavsky Elvo, mints and Piontkovsky were theses to 25th anniversary first Russian revolution, in co-authorship with Dubrovsky and Grave - theses on the "People's will." AT IKP he together with Mintz AND. AND., Dubrovsky FROM. M., Grave B. B., Piontkovsky FROM. A. and others decided question about volume, who will become author stories VKP(b). On the situation in the ICP at that time, see also: Avtorkhanov A. Technology of power. - M., 1991.

[12] Having received encouragement letters from mints, Dubrovsky and Grave, Elvo filed statement in Central Committee parties With request about recovery in ranks of the CPSU (b).

[13] 31 July 1937 G. Kuznetsova condemn per then, what he With 1931 G. was Participant anti-Soviet organizations right, acting on the Hooray- le and was engaged wreck in areas popular education". He was shot 31 July 1937 G., rehabilitated in March 1956 G.

[fourteen] AND. FROM. Kogan, 1897 G. R., reporter, arrested 25 October 1936 G. on accusation in participation in counter-revolutionary Trotskyist-Zinoviev-terrorist organization." Sentensed to 10 years in camps. Rehabilitated in February 1958 G.

FROM. AT. gingerbread, 1896 G. R., reporter, arrested twenty January 1936 G. on identical accusation. shot 21 Martha 1937 G. Rehabilitation van in September 1957 G.

I. R. Elkovich, 1896 G. R., responsible editor Ural Soviet encyclopedias" and Sverdlovsk regional newspapers "Kolkhozny path". Was accused in commitment Trotskyism in accessories to the "counter-revolutionary Trotskyist organization, on the instructions of which spent anti-Soviet activity". Sentensed to fifteen years lage- ray. In time rehabilitation checks in 1956-1957 gg. it revealed, what although Elkovich "Trotskyist" not was, but was proven his guilty- ness "in provocative activities, how secret agent bodies

NKVD, in falsification and protocols of interrogation of arrested persons, in dacha are false x readings th on the whole ry d Party and Soviet workers, unfounded about repressed authorities and NKVD. Elkovich was one- important from Sverdlovsk familiar X Elvova, who name l his Participant- com anti- party th groups." AT 1936 G., being arrested, Elkovich became a chamber agent of the NKV D and together with an employee of the authorities Stromin 'constituted falsified e protocols interrogations and Yes- shaft fiction e testimony» on the 140 human, in volume including on the AT. TO. Blue - dick, B. Kuna, AND. B. Lapidus a and etc., per what received more 16 thousand rub.

[15] Mehlis L . W and liquidation fall behind I historical front//Pain - Shevik.— 1932.— No. 5-6.- C. 12.

[16] F. TO. saifi, editor and writer, 1888 G. R., arrested eighteen september l 1936 G., execution n 3 august 1937 G. Author many books and articles on stories Tatars. Material s and the documents on stories Tatar th ACC R With ancient times before reforms 1861 of the year" came out in Moscow in 1937 under general th edition of N. Rubinshtein, but no surname th compilers and editor.

[17] G. S. Gubaidullin (1887-1937) - historian, professor. In the Elv case and interrogated I kato witness.

[18] M. BUT. Faridova- Rakhmatullina, 1901 G. R., arrested a fifteen May 1937 d., convictions a 2 august 1937 G. on the ten years camp th With defeat in great- wah on the 5 years and confiscation th personal property. 16 december I 1955 G. was rehabilitated a on personal statement, in which informed, that during interrogations in 1937 she slandered herself "as a result of physical impact investigator".

[19] Z. B. Nadeeva, 1907 G. R., arrested a 12 February I 1935 of the year, released _ 22 Martha 1935 G. With subscription about travel restrictions from Kazan. Del about terminated _ about fifteen October I 1935 G.

[20] Proletarian I. revolution.- 1929.— № 5.- S. 182.

[21] Sergei Mitrofanovi h Dubrovsky, 1900 G. r., Bolshevik to With 1918 Prof., Dean of the Faculty of History and Leningrad about university, 25 december I 1936 G. convicted on the ten years prison concluding nia and 5 years defeat l in political rights. AT 1948-1949 gg. lived in Kazan, Work l in State Museum Tatars. On the preliminary investigation and court Dubrovsky th neither in how myself guilty not acknowledged. Show I am Elvov a against myself name l "ridiculous". Was rehabilitated n in February _ 1954 G.

Bert a Borisovna Grave, 1900 G. R., member parties Bolshevik in With 1920, professor - historian, head of the historical editorial office of Sotsekgiz. female a Dubrovsky. eight March a 1941 G. was a convicted a on the eight years la- hero. Guilty myself neither in how not acknowledged. Rehabilitated a in June 1954 G.

isaa to Israel h mints, born in 1896, Bolshevik to s 1917 historian- academician, laurea t Stalin and Lenin Prizes, Hero of Socialist Labor. To any _ judicial responsibility not involved. Died in 1990 G.

AFTERWORD

The 20th century holds the lead in mass repressions. Occurred they before Total in European countries with a totalitarian regime: Germany, the USSR, Italy, Spain — where there were dictatorial despotisms. Their history has shown the futility of totalitarianism, the impossibility build Millennial Reich" on the violence.

Nowadays it is hardly possible to understand the history of Russia, October 1917 G. outside European context without understanding the fact that any restrictions on dissent, the prohibition of democratic institutions, inevitably led to great terror, that the ideas of Lenin, Stalin, and their associates about socialism and methods for achieving it are characteristic of radical Marxists. The state of historical science was part of the Soviet system of that time. Stalinism is the essence, but also the particularity of such a regime, which had in different countries their national traditions and specifics.

Even a simple list of deformations of historical science under National Socialism in Germany [1] demonstrates something in common with the situation of historians in the USSR. Both there and here there were few professional historians in the parties that were going to power at first. Historians everywhere showed almost no resistance to the regimes; On the contrary, they were among the first to be subjected to repressions, deportations and exiles. In Germany, the racial principle was used for this, in the USSR - proletarian origin and revolutionary expediency. The gaps were being filled not so much by professionals as by ambitious regime advocates. They unified science, brought it into line with the ideological demands and prescriptions of the leaders. Few people managed in those years to confine themselves to the framework of special studies. and somehow be saved from encroachments authorities. As a result, historical science turned out to be morally responsible per what happened So how her representatives justified the existence and acts of inhuman regimes. Historians contributed to the legitimization of utopian ideas put into practice by people in power, asserted the legitimacy of the existence of such power.

The mass repressions of the 1930s only completed the formation of a totalitarian state. The crisis of Soviet historical science, the beginning of which many date back to the late 20s and early 30s. [2], arose much earlier she. The crisis was initiated by the creation of Marxist historical institutions and periodicals, the encouragement of ideologically trustworthy research for the authorities, the gradual ban dissent. 20—beginning 30s yrs.— it's only stage forcing process transformation editors in associates totalitarianism, when them professionalism began to be determined not by knowledge of the sources and methods of document analysis, but by knowledge of quotations from the works of the classics of Marxism-Leninism. The situation for those who really wanted to study history professionally became hopeless. This happened later as well. With the flourishing of totalitarian structures, authorities resorted in the second half of the 40s. to massive indoctrination and another wave repression (1948-1949 .) gg.). The same processes were observed in the 60-70s, when in reality began to show signs of the collapse of totalitarianism. It was then that the fight against dissidence became fierce, the expulsion and exclusion of historians began, their unpublished work has been the subject of harsh criticism. (an example of this — discussion of AA Zimin's research on the time of writing and authorship of The Tale of Igor's Campaign, the conclusions of which diverged With official version).

Undoubtedly, at Lenin and his followers It was right to his understanding stories. But such same right on the other understanding definitely must It was to be granted and topics who thought otherwise. This made not It was. it - source tragedy and crisis. Sermon unanimity, monopoly on the the truth supported punitive methods meant death science how such. Charge destruction, violent energy, directed on the creation new world order, brought their negative fruit and in areas of study stories. Cave hatred to otherwise opinion, passion to trampling opponent never not could be scientific proof rightness. it It was in the state where disagreement With dot vision power haves severe punishment. it It was in country, where reasoning about outgoing horror middle 30s were similar on the hero thoughts novel Arthur Koestler "Blinding dark" brigade commander Rubashov, prisoner in Soviet prison: The consignment - vicious shrine — is it possible to this is? Where and when to high goals we walked such base ways? If a they really right and the consignment create will stories, means, history itself - vicious! [3]. The brigade commander realized, when the trouble touched him personally, that the story could not be anti-human, and horrified

The totalitarian regime needed not comrades-in-arms, but executors. Tom, who not changed on likeness system, did not adapt to these changes,— There was little chance of survival. In many works of that time — even the most orthodox, print doom.

Today it is possible and necessary to talk and argue about ways of getting historical science out of the crisis. See them in new theoretical and methodological developments, solving source studies problems in breaking habitual stereotypes and established schemes [4]. But all this is not enough to overcome the existing situation. This requires a revision of the moral position of everyone, because without principle
"live not on lies" crisis not overcome. it proves and shows with his own eyes what happened. It calls for compassion and warns.

* * *

[1] Mommsen V. Historiography and sociology under National Socialism // Questions history.— 1990.— No. eleven.
[2] Barber J. Soviet Historia Crisis, 1928-1932.—L., 1981; Solovey VD Historical science and politics in the USSR 20-30s // Historical meaning NEP. - M., 1990.- S. 159; and etc.
[3] Neva.—1988.— No. 7.— _ FROM. 136.
[4] See: Gurevich A.Ya.O crisis modern historical science // Questions history.—1991.—No. 2-3.

Printed in Great Britain
by Amazon